T0065080

THE
ISIS
HOSTAGE

THE
ISIS
HOSTAGE

ONE MAN'S TRUE STORY
OF 13 MONTHS IN CAPTIVITY

PUK DAMSGÅRD

PEGASUS BOOKS
NEW YORK LONDON

THE ISIS HOSTAGE

Pegasus Books Ltd
148 West 37th Street, 13th Floor
New York, NY 10018

First Pegasus Books hardcover edition May 2017

ISBN: 978-1-68177-467-1

10 9 8 7 6 5 4 3 2 1

Printed in the United States of America
Distributed by W. W. Norton & Company, Inc.

Contents

Daniel Rye, October 2015

THE
ISIS
HOSTAGE

Foreword

The phone rang one afternoon at the end of May 2013. I had just returned home to Beirut after a two-week reporting trip to the Syrian city of Yabrud, which lies slightly north of Damascus. The trip had ended dramatically when the Syrian regime started sending fighter planes over the city. The bombs hit our neighbourhood and shattered the windows in the building where we lived. My photographer and I decided to leave Syria by crossing the border into Lebanon.

We were totally exhausted after working for days on end under the constant threat of danger. It wasn't just the bombings that made us feel nervous, but also the Syrian rebels who came from the many different groups in the area. We just didn't trust them. We knew that a French photographer was already being held captive a little further south. The mood in Yabrud had also changed considerably since I had been there a few months earlier and I was on my guard with everyone we met.

I was lying sprawled on the sofa, trying to recharge my batteries, when the call came. It was the accomplished war photographer Jan

Grarup on the other end. He asked me to keep our conversation strictly confidential. I sat up as he told me that the Danish freelance photographer Daniel Rye, who had been his assistant, had been kidnapped in northern Syria.

'Do you know anyone with contacts in the sharia courts?' he asked.

'No, I don't think so – no one springs to mind,' I replied.

According to the limited information available, a group of Islamic extremists were behind Daniel Rye's abduction and he would apparently have to stand trial before a sharia court. However, Jan had only a few details. I felt powerless because there was nothing I could do to help. My first thoughts went to Daniel Rye's parents. I had always worried that if anything like this should ever happen to me, my parents would be the ones to suffer the most, just sitting there waiting, with no idea where I was. It was too unbearable to contemplate.

The news of Daniel Rye's capture was just one of several events that emphasized the fact that my profession was under serious attack. Several of my foreign colleagues had been kidnapped in Syria. It was a much-discussed subject, because the prospect terrified us. In principle, we were all potential hostage victims and this meant it was becoming increasingly difficult for us to tell the important stories of the war and to report on the tragedy unfolding in Syria.

Over the following year an increasing number of foreigners were captured. A feeling of panic was spreading through the journalist corps in the Middle East and in the closed circles where we discussed the kidnappings. People we knew were being held hostage for indefinite periods of time. When I returned to Syria in September and November 2013 and in June 2014 it was with a great deal of trepidation.

The Islamist terror organization known as ISIS set the agenda for where we could go. Even if ISIS disappeared from an area that had been under their control, their tentacles reached deep into Syrian society and souls. The armed men I met in northern Syria in June 2014 had a wild and unpredictable look in their eyes. As it turned out, my friendly driver was a former ISIS fighter. 'But no more, Madame,' he reassured me.

I couldn't avoid the presence of ISIS in Baghdad, either. In spring 2014, ISIS attacked a stadium filled with several thousand people – men, women and children – who had come to a Shiite party election meeting that I was covering. When the first bomb exploded I completely lost my hearing and I hid behind a freezer in a makeshift street stall. When I saw bullets being fired wildly all around me I ran across the road, down which a suicide bomber drove his car shortly afterwards. It was a narrow escape and I felt the blast of the explosion against my back. More than forty people were killed that day. That spring the only positive news from the region was that several European hostages had been released after their ransoms had been paid, including Daniel Rye.

One evening in August 2014, while I was in a hotel room in Iraq, a video was uploaded on YouTube. It showed the murder of the American freelance journalist James Foley. He could be seen kneeling in an orange prison uniform in the Syrian Desert, at the hands of an ISIS executioner. An American colleague, whom I was supposed to meet for a beer later that evening, wrote to me that she was in total shock and we cancelled our plans. I couldn't sleep that night. It was so utterly tragic for James Foley and his family, and it was also a brutal attack on journalism. With these new developments, it was no longer enough to prepare yourself and your loved ones for the unavoidable fact that bullets and bombs could strike when you're covering a war.

I was now first and foremost a target; a potential and valuable political tool that could be used at will. The world was certainly no stranger to such tactics, but this was the first time, as a journalist, that the threat felt so intensely close, almost personal. Nevertheless, my greatest wish was to be able to travel to the ISIS stronghold in Raqqa and report on the Islamists and the life they had created for the civilians; I was keen to investigate them further and discover who they really were. Out of pure frustration at being so far away from the story, I seriously considered dressing in black from head to toe and travelling there with a trusted local.

Instead, I chose the next best thing. I decided to use my journalistic skills to write about what had happened to my colleagues and, through their stories, come a little closer to the core of ISIS. Daniel Rye had been a hostage along with James Foley, so I sent him a message via a mutual acquaintance, asking him if he would talk to me about his thirteen months of captivity at the hands of ISIS. He answered me on Facebook: 'Hi Puk. My name is Daniel Rye. You've probably heard of me. I suffered a slight occupational hazard last year. Luckily for me, it had a happy ending.' We met for the first time one Friday in early October 2014 at a basement restaurant in central Copenhagen. We agreed that Daniel's story needed to be told.

The ISIS Hostage is about surviving one of the most notorious kidnappings in recent times – a hostage drama carried out by Islamic extremists, against whom much of the West is at war, including Denmark, since October 2014.

Twenty-four hostages – five women and nineteen men – from thirteen different nations ended up in the same prison in Raqqa in northern Syria. It was controlled by the terror group known as ISIS – it later changed its name to Islamic State (IS) – which has conquered and administrates large areas of Iraq and Syria. Daniel Rye was one of those hostages and, at the time of writing, he was the last prisoner to leave captivity alive. Six of his fellow prisoners were murdered while in captivity.

This book is a journalistic narrative based on countless interviews and conversations with Daniel Rye and his family, and it follows the struggle to get Daniel released from the clutches of the world's most brutal terrorist organization. I also talked to a large number of other relevant sources: former fellow prisoners, jihadists and background contacts from around the world with extensive knowledge of the case and of the people who held Daniel Rye captive.

This story is also based on interviews with kidnapping expert and security consultant, Arthur. He led the search for both Daniel Rye and his American fellow prisoner James Foley, who ended his days in Syria. Arthur isn't his real name; in fact, he lives a very discreet existence, which is crucial for his work in negotiating hostage releases all over the world. It isn't in his nature to discuss his work, but he has nevertheless chosen to participate, because he believes that there is much to learn from this story. And, as he says, Daniel's experience also shows that 'where there's life, there's hope'.

This book describes the reality as experienced and remembered by Daniel Rye and the other contributors. It is told with respect for those who were murdered, those still in captivity and those who survived, as well as for their families.

Puk Damsgård
Cairo
September 2015

Happy Birthday, Jim

The plane had just taken off from Heathrow Airport and was high above the clouds when Daniel opened his wallet and took out a small piece of cardboard. He silently contemplated the white surface, studying the image of his own face sketched with thin pencil strokes. He wasn't wearing his glasses in the drawing and he had a beard, but otherwise you could tell it was him.

He showed the picture to his travel companion, Arthur, who was sitting next to him, his long legs stretched out under the seat in front.

'Actually, some of the stuff we did was quite enjoyable,' said Daniel, gripping the mini-portrait tightly between his fingers. 'We played our own homemade version of Risk and I did gymnastic exercises with the other hostages.'

The drawing was the only memento from his time held hostage by ISIS in Syria. It had been drawn by one of the other western prisoners, Pierre Torres, who had sewn it inside his sleeve and smuggled it out of captivity. Pierre was another of the lucky ones whose freedom had been successfully negotiated.

Once freed, Daniel feared the worst. The Islamic State started killing the remaining western hostages, which was the reason why, on 17 October 2014, he found himself flying over the Atlantic with Arthur on their way to New Hampshire. They were on their way to attend James Foley's memorial.

Daniel put the drawing back in his wallet and ordered a glass of wine to accompany the predictable 'chicken or beef' in-flight menu. After the meal he fell asleep, his head resting on the still folded and plastic-packaged blanket he was using as a pillow. His hair was sticking up from the static electricity and his mouth hung open. He woke up five hours later, just as they were preparing to land in Boston. Outside the airport terminal he lit a cigarette in the clear autumn air and inhaled the smoke deep into his lungs. He didn't usually smoke. In the meantime, Arthur went to pick up the keys for their rental car and they drove to their hotel on the outskirts of Boston.

The next morning they headed towards the Foley family's home town, Rochester, New Hampshire. The eighteenth of October 2014 dawned with sparse clouds in the sky. On this day James would have been forty-one years old.

In August 2014 the American freelance journalist had lost his life in the Syrian Desert. He was the first western hostage to have his throat slit by the British ISIS fighter known in the media as 'Jihadi John'.

Daniel had been held captive in Syria for thirteen months, spending eight of them in the company of James and other western hostages. Daniel had thought highly of James, who was always optimistic, even though he had been imprisoned since

November 2012. They had had plenty of time to get to know each other and Daniel had listened to James's anecdotes about his siblings and parents. Now he was on his way to meet them and to pay his final respects to a friendship that had started, and ended, in captivity.

The trees leaned forwards invitingly along Old Rochester Road, the narrow country road that wound its way through New England. Bright red maples stood out among the green pines, and shades of yellow, orange and brown clung to the branches like a final breath before winter fell. The scent of winter's impending arrival mingled with the smoke from Daniel's and Arthur's cigarettes. Daniel scrolled through the music on his iPhone and played the melancholy song 'Add Ends' by the Danish band When Saints Go Machine – a song he had listened to countless times since James had been murdered.

Nestling between the trees were tall, well-kept houses and there were pumpkins carved into cheerful faces with star-shaped eyes or else frozen in menacing screams. These jack-o'-lanterns kept a vigilant watch from the lawns and driveways. Even the local grocery store was overflowing with them, almost blocking the entrance.

When they turned into the Foley family's road, the orange changed to black. They passed a large house where a hooded skeleton guarded the door. The road curved among scattered houses and American flags that were stuck in the grass by the asphalt. The whole neighbourhood was in mourning for the tragedy that had befallen the family in the white house at the end of the road.

The large lawn at the front of the property was dense and damp, and light shone through the windows towards the driveway, where a couple of cars were parked. Daniel strode purposefully towards the front door, followed by Arthur. He knocked and entered when he heard voices. James's parents, Diane and John Foley, greeted them as soon as they stepped across the 'Welcome' mat. Diane gave Daniel a long, maternal hug, her thick, dark hair brushing against his face as she held him close. She squeezed his arm and led him around the crowded kitchen to meet the family. Above the door between the kitchen and the living room were painted the words: 'With God's blessing spread love and laughter in this house.' It smelled of coffee, perfume and toast.

'Meet Daniel.' Diane introduced him with a mixture of gratitude and pain in her voice.

After a year in captivity, Daniel had finally got the sense that he might be close to being released. James decided to send a message to his own family through Daniel, but he didn't dare write a letter. If it were found, it would jeopardize Daniel's release and might never reach his family. Instead, they sat next to each other in the cell and James dictated the words that Daniel repeated to himself over and over again until he could remember them in his sleep.

As soon as Daniel had been released and had arrived back in Denmark, he called Diane and repeated James's message, word for word, over the phone. It was the only and final greeting the family received from their son in captivity. Diane wrote James's words down to remember them.

For the memorial service she had printed out the words so that the guests and the rest of the world could read them too. The title was: 'A Letter from Jim'. It included a note to his grandmother:

Grammy, please take your medicine, take walks and keep dancing. I plan to take you out to Margarita's when I get home. Stay strong, because I'm going to need your help to reclaim my life.

'Thank you, Daniel,' said James's grandmother in the kitchen as she gave his hand a squeeze. The slight lady with the pearl earrings wiped her eyes and looked as if she was about to collapse under the weight of her sorrow.

To his younger sister Katie, the woman with the long, smooth hair, James had said this:

Katie, I'm so very proud of you. You're the strongest of us all! I think of you working so hard, helping people as a nurse. I am so glad we texted just before I was captured. I pray I can come to your wedding.

James's brothers Mark, John and Michael were also standing in the kitchen. They all wore dark suits and shared the same features as James: brown eyes under wide, dark eyebrows and a broad smile. Daniel felt as if he had known them for a long time, as James had talked about them at length, because he missed them so much. Daniel also knew that the brothers had been longing for good news about their brother. His message had given them a new burst of hope for a while:

I have had good days and bad days. We are so grateful when anyone is freed, but of course yearn for our own freedom. We try to encourage each other and share strength. We are being fed better now and daily. We have tea, occasionally coffee. I have regained most of my weight lost last year [. . .] I remember so many great family times that take me away from this prison [. . .] I feel you especially when I pray. I pray for you to stay strong and to believe. I really feel I can touch you, even in this darkness, when I pray.

James had finally found peace from his torment and now the family was trying to find its way back from the darkness. Mark and his wife Kasey were expecting their first child.

'His name will be James Foley,' Kasey said proudly of her unborn son as she stood in the kitchen in slippers, caressing her belly.

The service was set to begin at 10 a.m. Everyone emptied their coffee cups and put on their shoes and coats to go to the church. Kasey kept her slippers on when the family went out to the car. Diane insisted on sitting next to Daniel in the back seat; she took his hand and held it tight, while John drove in silence towards the church.

Our Lady of the Holy Rosary Church in Rochester was packed with family and friends. In front of the altar was a picture of James Wright Foley. He was smiling his charming, lopsided grin, which by all accounts had brought him great success with women. Yellow and red flowers encircled his face, the eyes giving a sense of the affectionate troublemaker he was.

There was no coffin to put in the grave. James's body had already been laid to rest somewhere in Syria. His family couldn't bring themselves to look at the last image the world had seen of him: a body in an orange prison uniform lying on its stomach in the desert with the arms by its sides. On top of the body, between the shoulder blades, was the head.

Most of the media had refrained from showing the ISIS propaganda video of James's murder. Daniel had watched it only to ensure that James was finally at peace. He had so many other images of James etched on to his brain and they flooded back to him as he sat in one of the front pews, staring straight ahead. His white shirt lit up like a moon against the dark jackets filling the church.

He thought back to one year earlier, 18 October 2013, when they had been together in captivity. Late in the evening James had casually remarked that it was his fortieth birthday. Daniel and the other prisoners had congratulated him and said they hoped his birthday would be better the following year.

Now Daniel was sitting in front of a photo of James, while Michael wept through his speech about a warm and loving big brother who had fought for a better world.

'James died for what he believed in,' he said.

Daniel could see James in Michael. He leaned forwards and put his elbows on his knees, his broad back shaking uncontrollably. It was the James he had known that Michael was describing to the guests; the James who always had time for others – even when they all knew that James might end up dying in captivity.

Daniel took off his glasses and sobbed towards the church floor, unable to repress a desperate wail, which came thundering out in convulsions from his stomach and along his spine. He let it all come flooding out for the first time since August, when Arthur had told him the news of James's death. He wiped away the tears with both hands, exposing the red scars around his wrists. They were imprinted into his skin like tattooed bracelets. Daniel put on his glasses again and looked towards the altar with flushed cheeks.

'Happy birthday, Jim,' concluded the priest, and the congregation said a prayer for all the refugees in the world and the Syrians who were living in a bloody warzone for the third year. They finished the service by singing 'I Am the Bread of Life'.

Outside the church, Daniel smoked another cigarette.

'A demon has just left my body,' he remarked to Arthur, before he screamed out loud to himself and to the autumn air: 'James, you asshole! I miss you! Why the hell did you have to go and die?'

The family drove out to the graveyard. A flat grey headstone lay in the grass, surrounded by red maple leaves and yellow flowers. Diane put her arm around her mother's shoulders as they stood in a semicircle and silently prayed. The clouds cleared and the sun's rays hit the burial plot. Daniel looked at James's headstone. It read: 'A man for others'.

'Look, here comes the sun. It turned out to be a bright day after all,' commented Diane.

After the ceremony James's family paid tribute to his life by holding a reception at the church. His former nanny remarked that he had died dressed in the bright orange colour of life, while the executioner wore the black robes of Satan. The priest, Reverend Paul, recalled one of the last evenings when he had eaten dinner with the family before James travelled to Syria.

'I said to James that his brothers and his sister were not thrilled about his decision to travel to Syria, back into the lion's den.

"Father," James answered. "I have to go back and tell the stories of the Syrian people. They're living under a dictator who tramples all over them as if they were grass.'" Reverend Paul added: 'Here, we have food on our table, but we have no idea what the Syrian people are going through. I know that James's mission came from the heart.'

Diane stood in the same spot for several hours, receiving condolences from the guests, who stood in a queue that wound around the entire room.

'God bless you all,' she whispered.

The next morning Daniel impulsively bought a sweater featuring New Hampshire's revolutionary war motto 'Live Free or Die'. Arthur and he also bought a couple of beers, some water and biscuits from an old lady's convenience store and drove out to the enormous forest surrounding Lake Winnipesaukee, where James had spent time as a child.

Daniel pulled the burgundy 'Live Free or Die' sweater over his head and wandered with Arthur along the humid forest paths for hours, getting lost between the bare trunks and russet leaves. Daniel took a deep breath. It was just as quiet as it had been sometimes in captivity – or back in the field near his childhood home in Hedegård. He knew what it felt like to long for death rather than life. Among the tree trunks, in the clinging mud that weighed down their shoes, he shouted, 'That's my motto from now on, Arthur: Live Free or Die!'

The Elite Gymnast from Hedegård

D aniel clapped his hands at the audience from the stage of the Ocean theme park in Hong Kong. It was 15 July 2011 and he was dressed in a seahorse costume on a light-blue stage decorated with painted coral. Below him, he could see people with umbrellas shading themselves from the sun. Techno rhythms were booming so loudly from the speakers that parents had to shout to their children, who sat in folding chairs eating ice cream.

He looked up to where he could just make out a platform against the sky, which was at a height of twenty-five metres. He had to climb up there, jump off – and land in a three-metre deep pool. It was the climax of the show.

He pulled off the costume that fitted his body like a wetsuit and threw it away from him. The audience was enthusiastically cheering the blond, fit, tanned twenty-two-year-old Dane in his black bathing trunks, who was now beginning to climb up to the platform. Every muscle in his body was tense. This was the moment for which he had been rehearsing and waiting.

After a few weeks of performing, he had become tired of being a bouncing seahorse turning somersaults on a trampoline. He would rather be the cool, bare-chested diver, who jumped off the tower in a high dive. Daniel was a perfectionist and, even though this was just a holiday job in a Hong Kong arena, he had insisted on learning how to dive.

When he reached the platform, there was barely room for his feet. He stood on the small square, leaning against the metal behind him and clapped to get the audience going. Then he turned around and jumped out in a backward somersault.

The landing had to be precise – legs first, side by side. If he hit the surface askew or his legs were too spread out at the moment of landing, then, because of the entry speed, water would be forced up his rear end. Afterwards, it would be like he was pissing out of his backside, which he felt would be inelegant when he should be taking the applause from the audience.

The dive took him out of his comfort zone. But Daniel was an elite gymnast who had competed internationally, so it was the simplest thing in the world for him to perform moves like an Arabian Whip Double or a Stretched Whip Flick Double or a Stretched Whip Double Hip with a perfect landing.

Daniel had been competing for years in European and world championships in power tumbling, a branch of gymnastics in which gymnasts perform eight different elements on a fibre track. The dive in Hong Kong added a new height element to his physical abilities. It was frightening at first, but he soon got used to it.

During the six weeks he was working in the theme park, his attention began to be drawn towards the Middle East. In his breaks he read about the revolutions in Syria and Libya in the local English-language newspaper, the *South China Morning Post*. He cut out pictures of demonstrations from Syria and hung them up in the shipping container where the artists rested between shows.

The Syrians were demanding reform and these demands were being met with live ammunition and police violence. When President Bashar al-Assad refused to listen and instead deployed the military and the police against peaceful demonstrators, the protesters demanded the removal of his regime.

The seeds of the war in Syria had been sown.

. * .

Daniel was born in Brøns, in south-west Jutland on 10 March 1989, the younger brother of Anita, who was seven years older. The family lived in a detached house where Daniel's mother Susanne also ran a hair salon. His father was a fisherman. Susanne was meticulous with her customer's hair, a trait which was also reflected in her insistence upon order and tidiness in the home. Daniel was just a year old when his father was diagnosed with brain cancer. One morning in early May 1992 he passed away on the sofa in the living room. His last wish was that Susanne would find a new man who could be a father to Daniel and Anita.

A few months later – and with that thought in mind – Susanne put her grief and obligations on hold for a night and went to a widows' ball in a nearby town, where she met Kjeld, a tall, handsome man. They were married exactly one year after their first meeting on 11 September 1993 – a date which became a day of happiness in Susanne's life. She and the children soon moved into Kjeld's red-brick house in the village of Hedegård, close to Billund in south-central Jutland. Their new home was twenty brisk steps from the yellow house where Kjeld's parents lived and where he himself had grown up. The couple had a daughter, whom they named Christina. Although Daniel had never known his biological father, he got a new one in Kjeld, who adopted him and Anita.

The family's single-storey house was surrounded by fields and woodland and had a lawn covered with molehills. There were horses and cows on the neighbouring land and just up the road was the local village hall. Behind Susanne and Kjeld's house was the big garage where Kjeld's lorry was parked and where they celebrated special birthdays. The couple added a bay window on to the house and turned the bedroom into a hairdressing salon, where Susanne cut her customers' hair during the day, while Kjeld made a living as a lorry driver.

Daniel passed his grandmother's yellow-brick house on his way to Hedegård Free School, where Kjeld had also been a pupil many years earlier. It was on a narrow asphalt road with no street lights. Motorists drove fast out in the country, so Susanne sewed reflectors on to Daniel's clothes. The neighbours smiled when he walked by and said that he looked like a Christmas tree. Susanne shushed them. If her son heard their jokes, he would rip off the reflectors.

As a youngster, Daniel loved to do somersaults and handstands. Susanne thought it was a healthy hobby and sent him to gymnastics in the neighbouring town of Give. From the floor of the hall, he soared through the air with extraordinary power and it was obvious to everyone that he had elite potential. When he got older, he dedicated himself to developing his gymnastic skills for two years at the Vesterlund sports boarding school, where he lived the disciplined life of an athlete and where, for the first time, he experienced a strange and unsettling sensation over a girl.

Her name was Signe and he loved her freckles, her reddish hair and her round, pale-blue eyes. She was the most talented girl in the school. She did the same jumps and somersaults as the boys, and Daniel noticed that she didn't doll herself up with make-up and nail polish like the other girls. While in school they were sweethearts, but the relationship petered out afterwards when Daniel became busy with his apprenticeship as a carpenter and training with the national gymnastic team.

It became commonplace for him to be laying a roof on a house with a pain in his back and having to make regular appointments with a chiropractor, until he eventually decided to drop his apprenticeship.

'I can always find time to become a carpenter. I can't always be on the national team,' was Daniel's answer to his mother when she admonished him about not finishing what he had begun.

Instead, he made unsolicited applications to all the gymnastics schools in Denmark for a position as an instructor. A school in Vejstrup in the province of Funen snapped him up. He taught gymnastics for a year, while also building stairs and mowing lawns, between participating in competitions. He took up photography, too, inspired by the photos his coach took of him as he soared and rotated through the air. There was something in those frozen nanoseconds that fascinated him. They captured the tension in the muscles or concentration in the eyes. So he borrowed Kjeld's SLR camera, which he took along in his bag when he went to compete in the World Championship in power tumbling in Canada in 2008. He photographed the gymnastics halls and hotel rooms; the bodies in their tight suits and the successes, sweat, somersaults and setbacks that shone out from the faces of the gymnasts. He photographed the gymnastics bubble in which he travelled around the world, and discovered that the camera was a tool he could use to explore people's lives.

He soon took ownership of Kjeld's camera, carrying it around with him to every competition. Later, he got in touch with his grandfather's friend, whose son was a photojournalist. Hans Christian Jacobsen invited him to Aarhus, where he patiently looked at Daniel's photographs of flowers and gymnastics. Afterwards, Hans Christian showed him his own photographs, which he had taken in some of the world's most troubled regions. Daniel stared at a photo of a boy who was jumping into a lake somewhere in Kabul – shadows, light, a boy in a ray of sunshine. Hans Christian's images sparked something in him and all Daniel could think about was getting out into the world and capturing it all with his camera. When he was twenty-one he bought his own camera, packed it in his rucksack and went off with his childhood friend Ebbe on his first trip outside the security of the gymnastics world. It was a journey that turned him upside down in a way that somersaults and back handsprings had never done.

Daniel sat several feet above the ground between the humps of a camel, looking at an expanse of sand in north-west India. The camel-driver was making the journey on foot in his long blue kurta, wearing a broad smile on his chubby face.

When they took a break during their five-day camel safari, Daniel couldn't take his eyes off the camel-driver. The man would fetch his leather pouch from the animal and take out a few potatoes, a little fruit, some rice and spices, which he would then cook in a pot over a small fire.

'He can make so much out of so little,' thought Daniel and he took photos of this simple, quiet life and of the camel-driver, who was at one with the sand and the four-legged animal.

At night they slept out in the open. The stars had never shone clearer. The wild dogs howled and, during that summer of 2010, the sky seemed unusually high.

In India's big cities the waste floated in the gutters and Daniel couldn't always get to where he wanted, because of the cows and goats that wandered around freely and shat everywhere. The tuk-tuks sped by close to him and the air was heavy – even on the beach where the boys played football. Daniel struggled with the contrasts, as well as the overwhelming feeling that he couldn't just escape into a gym. His travel guides were Lonely Planet and his friend Ebbe, who led him through a world of extreme wealth and extreme poverty.

Back in Denmark, Susanne could have won a world title in worrying as she followed Daniel and Ebbe's accounts of their travels on Facebook. One mentioned that twenty Indians had been involved in a mob-fight that they had watched on a beach.

'Mum, we're fine! Nothing happened to us, except that we're an experience richer,' they wrote, while uploading regular videos from their journey. In one, Susanne and Kjeld watched Daniel do handstands on a beach, while gaping Indians stared at the unbelievably flexible white man. With a red shirt slung across his bare back, he declared casually on the video: 'Three days ago, we arrived at Kovalam in Kerala, South India's answer to Goa. We've been playing beach football and having a really, really good time.'

What they couldn't see on the video were the changes inside Daniel. He had suddenly been torn away from his disciplined lifestyle. Now he was more often than not sleeping late, drinking beer at all times of the day and doing exactly as he pleased.

When he came home, he imagined he was back in Asia as he went through his photos and videos from the journey. He really wanted to learn the craft of photography properly, so he called Hans Christian, who suggested a photography course at the Grundtvig College in Hillerød, north of Copenhagen. Two days before the course began in January 2011, Daniel called the school.

'How much time do you allocate to the actual photography?' he asked. The answer was that they spent a lot of time on it.

'Many people have followed their dreams here,' was the message. Daniel no longer had any doubts.

The classroom door flew open. 'What's up, arseholes?' shouted a loud, teasing voice.

The experienced war photographer and photojournalist Jan Grarup plodded across the floor, wearing desert boots, a white shirt and tight jeans, his fingers heavy with rings. While Jan was lecturing, Daniel stared at his role model, who had won countless international photo awards and followed his own wild path. Jan showed photos from his reporting trips and answered every question with the same answer: 'It doesn't matter.'

Nothing mattered – which camera you used, how to compose your pictures, how to trim them and edit them.

'It doesn't matter. It's about taking your hearts and personality with you into whatever you're doing and photographing,' said Jan.

After the lecture, Daniel, in awe and with his heart pounding, went out on the terrace to find Jan. While they drank a cup of coffee, they discussed Daniel's ideas about undertaking long-term photo projects – for example, following some young people in their development through a whole year of boarding school.

Daniel discovered at the college how little he knew about what was happening in the world. He would absorb as much information as possible from people who shared their love of their chosen field when they came and gave lectures. In the beginning he was unsure of himself and hid behind his camera; the praise he had become used to for his somersaults and rotations was absent from his photography teachers. He would often sit in his room, staring at his work, which he thought completely lacked talent, until one day his teacher, the art photographer Tina Enghoff, praised him for his cheerfulness, energy – and talent. In particular, she thought that Daniel inspired confidence, which would be crucial for him as a photographer to be able to get close to the people he wanted to photograph. While attending the college, Daniel became more self-assured, developed his photography skills and learned to talk to people who had interests other than gymnastics.

After finishing his photography degree Daniel started a higher education course in Aarhus, but he kept missing classes. He was spending most of his time taking photographs for *The Gymnast* magazine and was also in training for the 2012 World Team tryouts. He was practising the jumps and rhythmic sequences that the jury would be looking for when he and about ninety other young men gathered, hoping to be included among the chosen few. After a weekend with series, track jumps and exercises on the trampoline, the selection committee invited Daniel in for a talk with the eight judges. He was among the remaining twenty young men chosen to compete for fourteen places. The decision was long in coming, but it appeared in his inbox one day while he stared indifferently at his computer during a class.

'Congratulations! You have been selected for the Danish Gymnastics and Athletics Association's ninth World Team.'

Fourteen young men and fourteen young women were selected. Daniel packed his bag and took time off from his courses in order to tour with the World Team. But a chance event would change everything.

At one training session, Daniel stood contemplating the long black and white track in front of him before starting his run. As he set off, he sensed he would have difficulty making the height he needed. He tensed up in his hips and buttocks to squeeze himself through the full rotation before landing. When he landed in 'The Grave', as the landing spot was called, his hips were tense, where normally they should be more relaxed. The only place his body could counter the imbalance was in his legs.

Daniel jumped out of the landing and grabbed his knee. His friends shouted from the other end of the hall.

'Oh, shit! We thought it was bad!'

'Yes, something went,' said Daniel, 'but I don't think it's anything to worry about.' He drove himself home to Aarhus, put ice on his knee and booked an appointment with a doctor.

'You've damaged a collateral ligament and a cruciate ligament,' the doctor said.

Daniel stared at him. 'Does that mean that I can't train and go on tour with the World Team?'

'Yes, I'm afraid it does.'

Daniel burst into tears on the sofa. Then he rang Susanne and cried down the phone.

It was his final farewell to elite gymnastics.

Daniel was turned down for a course in photojournalism at the Danish School of Media and Journalism in Aarhus, but he was accepted by the University of South Wales in the United Kingdom, which had an undergraduate course in documentary photography. However, it would cost 250,000 kroner (about £26,000) for four years, which he couldn't afford. Then he learned that Jan Grarup was looking for an assistant to help him with his photo archives – and to accompany him on a reporting trip to Somalia.

They wrote to each other over Messenger and Daniel sent some photos, including one of his high-dive in Hong Kong.

'Do you have your passport ready?' Jan asked.

Daniel sold his apple-green car to his parents and took the train to Copenhagen, where he alternately slept on friends' sofas and at Jan Grarup's place. Jan's small office was filled with thousands of stock files, which Daniel was allowed to see. Going through the photographic records from Jan's many years as a photographer in Africa, the Middle East and Asia was a journey of discovery into famine, disasters and conflicts, but the foreign faces came alive through his lens. Daniel gained insight into how to take photographs so that they captured a moment that stood out and told a story. He could feel Jan's soul in the photos and how he moved with his camera.

Daniel began to look forward to the trip to Somalia.

Daniel sped through the streets of Mogadishu on the back seat of a four-wheel-drive vehicle, followed by a pickup with eight guards. They towered over the bed of the truck in their camouflage shirts, tall and thin and carrying machine guns. Daniel was travelling without Jan, who had gone off on a job and hadn't allowed Daniel to join him. Through the car window, he saw skeletal houses that had collapsed due to bombs or were deserted and riddled by gunfire. Suddenly, in the middle of this spectral neighbourhood, he saw a football goal.

'Stop! Can we stop here?' he asked.

'You've got fifteen minutes, max twenty,' said the driver and Daniel jumped out with his camera over his shoulder. He knew that the Islamist militant al-Shabaab group would be able to sniff them out if they stayed too long in one place.

Children and elders in worn-out sandals were running around on the sand after a football, and when the kids saw Daniel, they ran over and passed him the ball, which he slammed into the goal. He squatted for a while with his camera in his lap to get them used to his presence. To the left of the makeshift football pitch, a bombed roof sloped down to the ground at a forty-five-degree angle and now served as a kind of viewing terrace from which people were watching the game. Daniel took photos, moving around between the players and loving the life-affirming fact that they were running about in their football jerseys amid such destruction. When his time was up, he returned to the car as agreed and they drove back to their guarded accommodation.

The photos from the football match in a bombed-out Mogadishu were part of a black-and-white series called 'Born in War', which he was documenting on this trip. It revealed what an incredible amount of hope he had seen in the war-torn city.

It didn't occur to him how dangerous it was to travel around Somalia until he was back home, processing his time there. The far more experienced Jan Grarup had been responsible for their security, so Daniel hadn't paid much attention. But it didn't deter him. He knew more than ever that he wanted to be a photojournalist.

. * .

Daniel had been travelling in the aftermath of a civil war in Somalia, but in the autumn of 2012 it was the Syrians who were at war with themselves. A popular revolution demanding reform had turned into a full-scale battle between armed rebels and a brutal regime. Daniel read articles and searched for images on the Internet that could give him greater insight into the conflict. He looked at photographs of bombed-out houses, lifeless babies covered in dust who had been dug out of ruins, camouflaged snipers lying in wait with Kalashnikovs, ambulances unloading the wounded at hospitals.

He couldn't find anything to compare with his football pictures from Somalia in the coverage of the Syrian conflict. The faces in the images merged into one another and he wondered what he should photograph to make Danes more aware of the war. How could he focus people's attention on a bloody conflict far away, where President Assad was sending bombers over Aleppo, the country's second largest city and industrial centre, in an attempt to put down the rebellion?

The sound of the bombers had become an everyday occurrence

for Syrians, just like the cluster bombs and Scud missiles that rained down on civilian areas. The rebels were fighting in different factions under the Free Syrian Army (FSA), but the opposition couldn't agree on a common goal and infighting had arisen between several of the rebel groups, who were also committing more war crimes in response to the hardening effect of their environment.

New groups were springing up each week – some of them with a more Islamist identity than had been seen in the war thus far. One of the largest and most powerful Islamist groups was Jabhat al-Nusra, which later turned out to be the Syrian branch of the terrorist organization, al-Qaeda. Jabhat al-Nusra was growing rapidly, with the goal of ousting the Assad regime and creating a more Islamist government. The group operated under the leadership of a Syrian war veteran, who, like hundreds of other jihadists, had crossed the border between Syria and Iraq with Assad's approval to fight the Americans in Iraq after the invasion in 2003. The self-proclaimed Emir of Jabhat al-Nusra, who went by the nom de guerre of Abu Mohammad al-Jolani, was a man the world knew very little about and who had for a long time kept the group from being directly associated with al-Qaeda. Instead, it had been created as a Syrian organization that looked after the interests of Syrians.

Jolani had been held at the US base Camp Bucca in the Basra province of southern Iraq. He had also been imprisoned for a while by the Assad regime and rumour had it that he had been crammed in with hundreds of other Islamists in Syria's notorious torture prison in Sednaya, near Damascus.

At the beginning of the revolution in May and June 2011, President Assad granted amnesty to numerous political prisoners

THE ISIS HOSTAGE   31

from Sednaya – most of them with a pronounced Islamist profile. The president was aware that the prisoners were likely to join the rebellion once they were released and would Islamicize it. This would benefit the Assad regime by supporting its narrative that the revolutionaries were 'terrorists', dangerous to Syria and the region as a whole. The plan worked as intended and the threat from the Islamists became a self-fulfilling prophecy, not least because the Assad regime was primarily attacking the moderate factions. As had been seen so often before in the Middle East, corrupt totalitarian regimes and militants kept each other busy and used each other in an almost symbiotic relationship.

Some of the prisoners released from Sednaya joined Jabhat al-Nusra, and in the autumn of 2012 fighters from the weaker and more secular factions of the Free Syrian Army also began to switch to the more successful Jabhat al-Nusra, where they had access to better weapons and stood in a stronger position alongside more fearless, experienced soldiers. In December 2012 Jabhat al-Nusra was added to the US list of terrorist organizations, because of the movement's links to al-Qaeda in Iraq, but that didn't stop its momentum in the Syrian Civil War.

In March 2013 Jabhat al-Nusra and another Islamist movement, Ahrar al-Sham, announced an offensive called 'The Raid of the Almighty' against the city of Raqqa in north-east Syria. Raqqa was the first provincial capital to fall quickly to the rebels. The black Jabhat al-Nusra flags flew over the city and the rebels captured the government's administrative headquarters, where they recorded a video of the captive governor which was broadcast on the opposition-friendly channel Orient Television. The Assad regime had lost its grip on Raqqa to groups with an Islamist profile.

Meanwhile, the civilians were caught in the middle. In Aleppo wide pieces of fabric were hung across streets and alleyways to block the snipers' view into people's apartments. Schools were either closed or destroyed and it had become difficult to find food. The lines of fire, the battle fronts, and the regime and rebel checkpoints constantly moved around residential neighbourhoods. Those who could packed a couple of blankets, some clothes and fled.

While the civilians were fleeing, several thousand foreigners from Arab and western countries came to join the fight in Syria.

One of them was the Belgian Jejoen Bontinck.

. * .

Jejoen's friends had already gone to Syria. They had been recruited through the network Sharia4Belgium, which regularly contacted Jejoen to persuade him to take part in the war. He had just turned eighteen and had no girlfriend, no job and wasn't in school, so there was nothing to prevent him from seeking adventure. In February 2013 he packed his father's sleeping bag and told him he was going to Amsterdam with some friends.

It took less than a week for the young Belgian-Nigerian man to arrange the trip from Belgium through Turkey to the Syrian governorate of Idlib. Friends from Sharia4Belgium who were already in Syria described the route for him. Like many other fighters in Syria, he travelled through the official border crossing at Bab al-Hawa and, on 22 February, after a short drive, he arrived at a large villa in the Kafr Hamra neighbourhood, a well-to-do suburb of Aleppo, just north of the city. He didn't know which faction he was actually joining, but he had been reunited with his friends.

The water in the villa's pool was dark green and shallow, while the lawn around it looked like a park where the flowers and shrubs hadn't been attended to for a long time. Jejoen was far from being the only foreigner. The grounds were huge and teeming with Dutch, Belgian and French men. When he first arrived, he worked out that there were at least sixty of them and eventually some had to be moved to another villa, because there wasn't enough room.

Jejoen was welcomed by a man who bore the nom de guerre Abu Athir. Several of Jejoen's friends just called him 'sheikh', as he was the leader of the Mujahideen Shura Council faction. Abu Athir had been hit in the leg by shrapnel and hobbled about the villa on crutches, surrounded by guards. He never carried a weapon, but left it to the European fighters to guard him as he drove around the area, either in a Jeep or a Mercedes.

There was a hierarchy in the organization and the new recruits had to work their way up and win Abu Athir's trust before being sent to fight on the front lines. Abu Athir and his men had developed an elaborate vetting process, so recruits went to the front only when they had been tested and were clearly not working for foreign intelligence services. Newcomers were initially given the task of guarding either the villa in Kafr Hamra or Abu Athir himself when he was in meetings or sleeping.

The fighters whom Jejoen met were roughly the same age as him. Some had left their jobs or studies to fight in Syria; others were like him, with nothing to lose. When they arrived, they responded only to the warrior names they had chosen for themselves. Some of the foreign fighters already spoke Arabic and many of them established themselves in Syria by marrying

locally or bringing their wives into the country. They wanted to
live their life in the coming Islamic state.

Jejoen stayed at Abu Athir's villa only for a short time before
being sent to one of the Syrian regime's old military bases half
an hour's drive away. Abu Athir's men had seized control of the
base and now used it as a training camp for new recruits.

There were more than fifty people at the base, most of them
Europeans from France, Holland, Belgium and Germany. They
received military training – physical exercises, target practice,
strategic warfare and Islamic teachings. Jejoen thought the
training was very professional, which wasn't a coincidence.
His trainer told him that he had previously been an officer in
the Egyptian army. Now and then, Abu Athir came by in his
Mercedes to watch the recruits at work. Jejoen received not
only food and shelter, but also access to a special brotherhood,
something he had never experienced before. He ate, slept and
trained with other men who had come to join the war. It was
easy to feel he belonged.

Some months later, Jejoen's path in Syria would cross with
those of Daniel and James Foley. It all began with a landmark
event that took place on 8 April 2013 and quickly changed Syria
and the organization led by Abu Athir.

On that day, a long audio recording of 21 minutes and 30 seconds
was posted on jihadist Internet forums. On the recording could be
heard the voice of Abu Bakr al-Baghdadi, the leader for several
years of al-Qaeda in Iraq (ISI). He confirmed what many observers
had suspected: that ISI was operating in Syria through the Jabhat
al-Nusra faction.

'It is now time to declare before the people of the Levant and the world that the al-Nusra Front is an extension of Islamic State in Iraq and a part of us,' Baghdadi said. He continued, 'We worked out the plans for them and set the framework and supported them financially every month and gave them men who know the theatre of war, from immigrants to locals.'

Baghdadi then announced that his organization would now be renamed the Islamic State in Iraq and the Levant. In Arabic 'al-Sham' means 'the Levant', so from that moment on both acronyms ISIL and ISIS were used. Baghdadi stated that ISI and Jabhat al-Nusra were now unified under the new name ISIS, which reflected significantly greater cross-border ambitions for an undivided Islamic caliphate in Iraq and Syria.

At that moment, the world didn't know what consequences the audio recording would have for the region. Baghdadi wasn't yet a well-known name in American and European living rooms. There was only limited information about him and a few photographs.

Behind the nom de guerre Abu Bakr al-Baghdadi hid Ibrahim Awad Ibrahim al-Badri. He was apparently born near the Iraqi city of Samarra in 1971 and was awarded a master's degree and a doctorate in Islamic studies by the Islamic University in Adhamiya, a suburb of Baghdad. People who knew Baghdadi in his childhood described him in several media sources as a quiet type who liked football. At the turn of the millennium, he had an education, a wife and a son.

In March 2003 US and UK forces invaded Iraq. Six months later Baghdadi had formed his own Islamist movement called Jaysh Ahl al-Sunnah wa al-Jamaah, which, loosely translated, means 'Army of People of the Sunni Muslim Community'. On 31

January 2004 Baghdadi was arrested by US military intelligence while visiting a friend in the city of Fallujah in the so-called Sunni Triangle north-west of Baghdad, where a rebellion had broken out after the ousting of Sunni dictator Saddam Hussein.

Baghdadi was imprisoned until December 2004 in Camp Bucca, the American prison near the border with Kuwait, where he developed relationships and friendships with other inmates. Jolani, the leader of Jabhat al-Nusra, was in the prison at the same time, but the two men didn't meet. Baghdadi was released after almost a year because the Americans regarded him as a low-level prisoner who did not pose a significant threat to US forces in Iraq.

In 2007 he joined al-Qaeda's Shura Council and in May 2010 Baghdadi was chosen to be the head of al-Qaeda in Iraq (ISI). Under his leadership, ISI conducted a wide range of well-planned and spectacular suicide attacks in Iraq. In March and April 2011 alone, the group accepted responsibility for twenty-three attacks south of Baghdad.

Baghdadi's audio recording of 8 April 2013 was the beginning of an ideological and political power struggle between Jolani from Jabhat al-Nusra, who didn't recognize the merger with ISI, and Baghdadi – a struggle that would lead to ISIS breaking with al-Qaeda.

From that day on, Arab and western jihadists had to choose between two variants of extreme Islamism. Many of the rebel leaders chose Baghdadi's ISIS and thereby took many foreign fighters over to ISIS, among them the Belgian jihadist Jejoen, whose group, the Mujahideen Shura Council led by Abu Athir, swore fidelity to ISIS.

This declaration was the beginning of ISIS's aggressive expansion into the Syrian Civil War.

. * .

Daniel began his preparations for a reporting trip to Syria in the midst of these political manoeuvrings between Islamist factions. He wanted to portray the Syrians who could not or would not flee, to find out how they were living in a state of emergency.

At the same time, he began seeing his school sweetheart Signe again. They had kept in touch for a long time after splitting up and wished each other happy birthday every year. One night in October they were out drinking beer at a bar in Copenhagen until 4 a.m. and, after several months of orbiting each other, they got back together. Daniel was happy to once again be with the woman with the most beautiful eyes in the world.

In early April 2013 he travelled to Gaziantep in southern Turkey to investigate the situation. He came into contact with a so-called 'fixer', a person who knows the local area and on whom journalists rely. The fixer, Mahmoud, drove him along the border to the official crossing in the town of Kilis, which led to the Syrian town of Azaz.

'You can also go to Syria now. We can just enter,' said Mahmoud.

'No, thanks – I'm only here to get a feel for the atmosphere,' said Daniel.

He spoke with Syrian refugees to get an idea of the situation in their homeland. He sought out journalists and NGO workers who described how the war had been moving in new directions. And when he returned to Denmark, he called a man named Arthur, who would later turn out to have a great impact on his life.

. * .

The boats were sloshing around in the water along the quayside in Copenhagen's Nordhavn neighbourhood. Daniel was walking beside a tall, pipe-smoking man and his black dog, which ran around them, off the leash, sniffing here and there. Daniel had called Arthur because he had heard that he was a walking encyclopedia of practical and safety-related advice for journalists travelling in Syria. Arthur had immediately invited him out for coffee.

It was 24 April 2013 and Arthur happened to be home in Denmark on a stopover between his many trips to Turkey and Lebanon. As the owner of a consulting firm specializing in security, he had many years of practical experience as a negotiator and investigator in kidnapping cases around the world – from Nigeria and Somalia to Syria, Poland and Egypt. When he met Daniel, he was working on a remarkable kidnapping case in Syria, which he couldn't talk about openly.

Daniel later learned that in late November 2012 Arthur had received a call from an acquaintance in the United States who was working as a hostage negotiator. He told him that the American freelance journalist James Foley had disappeared in Syria on 22 November. Arthur was assigned to the case and immediately flew to Turkey, where James's friends and acquaintances had already started searching for him. Arthur's first task was to separate rumour from fact, which turned out not to be so straightforward. No one had any real information about who had taken James. Although Arthur knew from James's driver and fixer exactly where and how James had been kidnapped, no one recognized the perpetrators. It was like trying to find a needle in a haystack of contradictory information that Arthur had collected from his network of local informants. Some reported that Foley had been seen in Aleppo; others that he was in Saraqeb.

Reports also came in that someone had seen his body. After long deliberations, James's family and one of the newspapers he worked for, the *Global Post*, launched a public campaign in January 2013, entitled 'Free James Foley', but it was a double-edged sword.

On the one hand, the campaign focused on James's personality and therefore spoke to the kidnappers' compassion. It also helped to spread the news that someone was looking for him. On the other hand, no one knew who had taken James, and Arthur feared that a sustained media campaign could backfire, because it would focus attention on a case that the kidnappers might think should have been 'run under the radar'.

'We risk damaging the negotiating environment,' Arthur pointed out to the family and the *Global Post*. In fact, the campaign only led to more misleading information. However, in the spring of 2013 the hunt for James turned south towards the Syrian capital of Damascus. The investigation changed course, spurred on by at least two other kidnapping cases in which the hostage had ended up in the hands of Assad's informal militias, the Shabiha. James had been taken within a radius of about six miles from a place where it was known the Shabiha were operating, so, in the FBI's opinion, Arthur had to consider that scenario as a possibility.

It was a matter of determining who had the means and the motivation to hold someone secretly captive for months on end without making any demands. The Assad regime seemed like an obvious choice, but the question was whether the insurgency also had the capability to make people disappear.

It was with the James Foley affair and the critical situation in Syria in mind that Arthur was now walking along the waterfront, giving the young photographer advice.

'It isn't the best place in the world to go right now,' said Arthur, as they strolled along the harbour and looked out over the water.

Daniel looked up at the tall man, who, seriously but also with a twinkle in his eye, gave him his four-hour 'stump speech' of the most important things to remember if he went to Syria. As a starting point, Arthur advised against making the trip, because the risk of kidnapping had grown since the end of 2012. The mood towards journalists had changed, especially among some of the Islamist rebel groups. Arthur told Daniel that he should beware of Islamists from Jabhat al-Nusra. They were operating in northern Syria and were behind the kidnappings of several journalists.

'Most cases, however, were resolved fairly easily in a few days or months,' said Arthur, who mentioned the kidnapping of James as the most dramatic and still unresolved.

Daniel listened intently and wrote down all the information Arthur gave him.

'I have all the prerequisites for being an idiot,' said Daniel, who had never been to the Middle East. 'My greatest fear is that I'll end up on the front page of the tabloids as the idiot who hadn't thought about the risks involved.'

Arthur went through a series of basic safety precautions. First, Daniel had to make sure not to be seen by too many people or walk around with people he didn't know.

'It's a jungle where you don't know who you can trust,' he continued.

In addition, Daniel should take out insurance, give his family written information about his trip and constantly send messages home about where he was. Arthur thought to himself that it was the last two measures that James hadn't taken into account, which had made it difficult to locate him.

If Daniel were kidnapped, the golden piece of advice was: never tell a lie, create a routine for yourself and play the game. Arthur recommended that Daniel take only a brief trip to Syria and not to stay too long in one place.

'Stay close to the border, so you can cross back again before it closes around five p.m. Don't stay there overnight,' said Arthur finally.

When they parted, Daniel felt well equipped, even though he was taking a risk by travelling into a war zone, especially for the first time.

He compared going on this trip with learning a new gymnastics routine. The chances of landing on his head and breaking his neck was highest the first few times, when he was still a beginner. He vowed to himself that he would follow Arthur's advice. He would take care not to travel too far into Syria and make it just a short trip to get a feel for the atmosphere.

But in Syria all the rules, statistics and know-how dissolved and there was one unknown that no one could avoid: no matter how experienced and prepared a journalist is, they can end up in the wrong place at the wrong time. Syria was no longer the place to take a risk or try one's luck. The kidnapping of James Foley was proof of that.

. * .

Daniel bought a ticket to Turkey, departing on 14 May 2013. He spent the weekend before at home with his parents, where he packed a bulletproof vest and a first-aid kit borrowed from Arthur.

Susanne and Kjeld were well aware that there was a war in Syria, but they had given up trying to follow what was happening. Susanne was focused on her new job as an assistant in a clothing shop at the Legoland amusement park and Kjeld transported grain around Denmark.

Susanne was in the kitchen while Daniel was packing. 'What are you going to do down there?' she asked.

'So many people are being killed or fleeing,' said Daniel. 'I want to photograph the people who are staying and trying to create a daily life in the midst of war.'

They talked through his trip in detail. Daniel would be travelling to the border town of Azaz, a few miles inside Syria. He would stay there for a couple of days so he could get out quickly if the war came closer.

The situation in Azaz at the time was more peaceful than elsewhere. Rebels from the Free Syrian Army had taken control of the town and the border post after heavy fighting with regime forces in August 2012. This had opened up new paths into Syria for jihadists and journalists. Since then, the rebellion had changed and had become more Islamist; new factions and power struggles had arisen. The Assad regime did bomb Azaz now and then, but Daniel wouldn't be going directly to the front line.

'It's the equivalent of going to Tønder, while the war is being waged in Copenhagen,' explained Daniel soothingly, referring to a town 200 miles from the capital.

Susanne decided that, for once, she wasn't going to worry. In addition, Daniel had left a document for her in which all the information about his trip was described in detail. It lay on the kitchen table, written a little messily with a blue ballpoint:

Fly to Gaziantep on Tuesday the 14th, 14:20. Spend the night at a hotel in Kilis. On Wednesday morning I cross the Syrian border at the Kilis border post. Being picked up by Mahmoud (Skype name), the fixer. We drive to Azaz and stay there for three days. On the 18th I'll be driven back to the border, take a taxi to the airport and fly home to Denmark at 22:50.

The time of the flight from Turkey was crossed out and changed to 19.55.

Arthur's telephone number was also on the note; they should call him if Daniel didn't get in touch.

Susanne drove Daniel to Give Station. She had to be at work at Legoland at 11.30 and was wearing her work clothes – red shirt and blue trousers, Lego's cheerful colours. She waved goodbye from the driver's seat and didn't get out of the car to give him her standard warnings and advice like she usually did. Normally, she would stand there at the station sobbing and Daniel would laugh. It was also the first time she didn't give him a farewell hug.

'See you in a week's time,' said Daniel and jumped on the train to Copenhagen to visit his girlfriend.

He told Signe about the list of numbers his parents had and said that Kjeld was his main contact. He would try to give her updates while he was out there. She told him to take care of himself.

'I don't think I can cope with finding a new boyfriend,' she laughed.

On the morning of Tuesday, 14 May they kissed goodbye and Daniel drove to the college room he had sublet when it had become too complicated to keep sleeping on different friends' sofas. He vacuumed, so that the person he had sublet from could come home to a clean room.

Then he drove to Copenhagen Airport.

Syria Round Trip

On a curb near the central roundabout in Raqqa three men sat in a row, blindfolded. An ISIS-fighter was looking at them, while speaking into a megaphone from a white police pickup. An armed man stood on the bed of the truck. Masked fighters were walking around the square with black ISIS flags, while civilians gathered in front of a kiosk with Coca-Cola signs to see what was going on. Some people were filming with their mobiles.

Attention was being paid to the three men in the middle, who, according to the speaker, belonged to the Alawite sect, like President Assad. When he finished speaking, the three men were shot in the back of the neck with a pistol, dying instantly. Several shots were fired, making the lifeless bodies on the asphalt jump with each bullet, until the fighters turned their weapons towards the sky and shot at random, shouting '*Allahu akbar!* God is the greatest!'

The footage from the eyewitnesses' mobile phones was posted online on Wednesday, 15 May 2013 and demonstrated for the first time the methods used by ISIS in Raqqa, where they now had so much power that they could shoot people without trial in the middle of an open square.

That same day, Daniel tried to enter Syria.

When he landed in Gaziantep on the previous evening, he drove towards the border town of Kilis as planned and found a hotel to stay in overnight. The next morning he took a taxi to the border where he had arranged to meet his fixer, Mahmoud.

But the plans for the trip were beginning to fall apart. Mahmoud didn't answer his phone. Daniel tried to find him at the border crossing among a mass of refugees who were wandering around with blankets, pots and children in their arms. The staff at the Syrian Media Centre at the border post refused to let him go on, unless he could produce a letter confirming he was a photographer.

When he couldn't find his fixer, Daniel drove back to Kilis and had to wait until late in the day before Mahmoud rang him.

'I can't go to Syria with you as agreed, but call my friend Ahmed. He'll come with a colleague, so you can talk it all through,' was his rather vague message.

In the meantime, Daniel got the necessary letter from a French photo agency and edited a travel video in his hotel room. The film began above the clouds during the flight to Turkey. He called his video diary 'Syria Round Trip' and he sent it home to Signe.

'My name is Daniel Rye,' he told the camera. 'I'm twenty-four years old and right now I'm on a layover in Istanbul eating chips. I'm on my way with my camera to Syria to document the lives of the people who live surrounded by war.'

He had also filmed the drive towards the border. Wearing sunglasses, he said, 'Now I'm standing at the border crossing between Turkey and Syria, near Kilis. I was very nervous about whether it was at all possible, but now all the pieces have fallen into place. Let's go.'

But the pieces hadn't quite fallen into place and he filmed the last scene while lying in bed.

'Yes, well . . . now I'm lying here in a hotel room in Kilis. Now we have to see if I can succeed tomorrow. Otherwise, it's a load of crap. It's just a load of *craaap*.'

The round table at the outdoor café wobbled on the uneven asphalt of the terrace. Daniel ordered a cup of thick Turkish coffee and lit a cigarette, while restlessly looking through his sunglasses at the cars that drove past in the narrow street, swirling up the dust. It was Thursday morning, 16 May, and the new fixer, Ahmed, arrived at the café on time, along with a woman named Aya. They presented themselves to Daniel and sat down in the rickety metal chairs.

Ahmed had long, greasy, black hair, spoke energetically about how possible the whole trip was and invited Daniel to his wedding in a few months.

'I can arrange the trip. I've done it many times before, and I'm good at it,' announced Ahmed, in a way that Daniel thought was a little too cocky.

He preferred Aya, who looked like she was around his own age. She spent most of the time listening with a serious expression on her face. Her eyes were heavily made up with pencilled eyebrows, and a white scarf covered her hair. She was wearing tight, black trousers that followed the soft curves of her hips and a long black cardigan, which hung over them. Her bare feet were tucked into a pair of flat and rather impractical sandals by comparison with Daniel's leather boots. She said she was a nurse and had lived in Aleppo, but she had fled from the war after she had narrowly escaped being put in a regime prison.

Daniel thought to himself that, as a nurse, she must be good at first aid, and that women were by nature probably a little more careful than men.

'I can take you to Aleppo,' she suggested to Daniel and told him that she had been part of the revolution against Assad from the beginning and had gone to Aleppo with journalists several times.

'No, I'm not interested in the war as such,' said Daniel. 'I'd really like to meet the people who are surviving. My plan is to go to Azaz.' Aya spoke good English and that made him feel secure.

'We can easily meet people in Azaz who are trying to survive,' she said. They agreed that Aya would take Daniel from Turkey to the Syrian border town.

He went back to his hotel, charged the batteries for his camera and checked out of his room, after which they drove towards the border.

Just before they reached the border crossing, Aya asked him to get out of the car. She wanted to drive on alone and cross the border illegally somewhere nearby, while he was standing in the interminable queue of Syrians.

When the Turks had put an exit stamp on his passport, he walked the half-mile or so along the asphalt between the Turkish and Syrian border posts. He had his square, leather bag on his back with all the essentials: sleeping bag, first-aid

THE ISIS HOSTAGE 49

kit, camera and computer. The bullet-proof vest and helmet were in a separate bag.

At the Syrian border post, rebels dressed in camouflage and multi-pocket vests and carrying loaded Kalashnikovs walked around among the refugees living in a makeshift camp nearby. The border-control post amounted to a small shed, where Daniel showed his photographer documentation and was given permission to enter Syria. Aya was waiting for him near the shed, as agreed, but she wasn't alone. Beside her stood a balding, elderly man dressed in a grey shirt and trousers.

'Who's he?' asked Daniel.

'He's from the Free Syrian Army and he's going to drive us to Azaz,' said Aya.

They got into the old man's car. Daniel was sitting in the front passenger seat, next to an assault rifle, which he noticed had the stock downwards and the barrel pointing at Aya sitting in the back.

'Can't he point the gun somewhere else?' asked Daniel uneasily, but Aya didn't translate what he said and the barrel remained pointing straight at her.

Arabic music flowed out of the car speakers as they drove past goatherds and through small villages. Daniel took a picture of the white-and-brown goats crossing the road in front of them. Then he looked up at the sky. The sun was still shining, but dark-blue thunder clouds were on the horizon across the golden fields dotted with whitewashed houses.

They must have made a detour on the way to Azaz, because they suddenly drove into a farm, where they were served a metal bowl filled with food, which they ate while sat on the floor in the living room.

'It's great to get something to eat, but that wasn't our agreement,' Daniel said to Aya while they ate. 'I'd like to go straight from point A to point B.'

He was remembering Arthur's advice to avoid being seen by too many people and not to drive around the area at random.

'Yes, I know, but the driver insisted that we had to have something to eat,' she replied patiently and referred to Syrian hospitality, which was often at odds with security advice.

Outside, one of the residents of the house was climbing a plum tree. Daniel took photos of the man sitting on a branch, shaking the bitter green plums on to the ground; the man gave them a bagful for the trip to Azaz.

When they reached the outskirts of town, they stopped beside two brothers who stood with their doves at the roadside. Their father used to sell vegetables, they said, but now there was more money to be made selling bricks and cement to rebuild bombed houses, should anyone dare to bet on a future in Azaz.

'Why do you have the doves?' asked Daniel.

Aya translated.

'Because birds are free,' said the boys.

Daniel wrote it down in his notebook and took some photographs of a flock of white birds against the heavy, ominous sky.

Shortly afterwards, he photographed the town's ruined mosque. A boy in a Kung Fu Panda T-shirt and his older brother in military trousers were playing in some burned-out military vehicles. Others were busy removing valuable copper wiring from an armoured vehicle.

A hairdresser's was still open, so Daniel and Aya went in and had a nice chat. After fifteen minutes, they said goodbye to the friendly barber. But as they stepped out on to the street, a vehicle suddenly came along at high speed and stopped abruptly in front of them. Daniel took note of the passengers: a group of masked men with Kalashnikovs.

'Get in the car,' ordered Aya hurriedly and signalled to him that she would talk to them.

Daniel got in the back seat, while listening to Aya, who was explaining in Arabic. The men asked several questions and seemed so unfriendly and intimidating that Daniel looked down at his feet. Aya could hear that one of the men, the only man not masked, spoke with a Tunisian accent. They asked who she and the blond man were and she explained that they were in Azaz to do stories about the war.

'What's going on?' asked Daniel, when the masked men had finally driven off again.

'They just wanted to know what we're doing,' said Aya.

'It seemed very intense.'

'Don't worry about it. That's just how Arabs are,' said Aya, who didn't seem frightened by the episode.

Daniel was shaken – and so was the driver, apparently, because he didn't want to continue working with them. Aya called Ayman, a friend who lived in Azaz, and soon afterwards he picked them up and drove them to a bombed-out neighbourhood in the city.

The children were playing in the rubble as the sun was setting. A living room was half blown away. Portraits were still hanging on the wall, and green climbing plants clinging to the shattered outer wall brightened up the scene.

When the sun had gone down and there was no longer enough light for Daniel to take photographs, they bought chicken and

Pepsi from the local kebab man and drove home to Ayman's empty apartment. His wife and two daughters had fled to Turkey, like so many others from the city who weren't able to maintain a normal life for fear of the fighting and the sporadic bombing from the regime. Ayman also spent most of his time in Turkey, but used the apartment now and then when he was working in Azaz.

There was a sudden power cut and Ayman lit candles in the living room. The artificial flower decorations on the shelves cast shadows against the ceiling, while they sat around the coffee table and ate.

After eating, Daniel, Aya and Ayman climbed up on the roof, from where they could glimpse small flashes of light in the distance. Daniel was told that it came from the fighting that was going on at the air base a few miles outside the city. Up there on the roof, in the darkness, he took a picture of his own shadow on a wall; it was the last photograph he would take in Syria.

Afterwards he drank a cup of tea, while he transferred the day's images to his hard drive and sent texts home to his father and to Signe, as he had promised. He said that the day had gone well, that he had already taken a lot of photos and that the people were nice.

'I love you,' he wrote.

The three of them blew out the candles and Daniel crawled into his sleeping bag on a sofa in the living room. The day's experiences whirled around in his head, especially the masked men. Who were they? He feared for a moment that they would come round at night, and wondered if he should have tried to get out of Syria after he had been seen. But he calmed himself down.

He was being too paranoid. Aya had spoken to them and, if the men had wanted to kidnap him, they would have done it then.

He eventually fell asleep.

. * .

Kjeld and Susanne were at home in their red-brick house on the Thursday evening when a text message appeared on Kjeld's mobile. It was the first time ever that Daniel had written 'I love you'. Signe wrote to them at the same time to say she had received a message that the day in Syria had gone well.

'We're sitting in the candlelight drinking tea. It's just as quiet as Hedegård,' read Daniel's message.

If that was true, it must have been really quiet, because the only thing that could be heard outside the windows in Hedegård was the whistling of the wind.

. * .

Daniel leapt out of his sleeping bag early on Friday morning. He wanted to go outside and take photographs in the soft morning light. Before he went off with Ayman and Aya, he packed a bag with the essentials: camera, passport, wallet and mobile. He left his leather backpack with the sleeping bag, computer and hard drive in the apartment. As there was no fighting in the area, he also left his bulletproof vest and the first-aid kit.

They drove to the city centre, where they met a large family who were fleeing, squeezed into a two-seater pickup. Blankets and mattresses were bulging on the bed of the truck.

'May I photograph them?' asked Daniel, but the family didn't want to be photographed and drove off quickly.

An elderly gentleman walked across the road towards them. 'You aren't allowed to film here,' he said.

The old man told them that they had to have permission to photograph from the local authorities. Daniel looked enquiringly at Aya.

'Who are the local authorities?'

'They're all right. I know them,' said Aya and she told him that the rebels controlled the area.

She knew where the authorities were and they decided to go there. They cut across a square and stopped in front of a sand-coloured building surrounded by a high wall. Before the rebels had taken control of Azaz, the building had housed the Assad regime's local council office. They knocked on the black metal gate.

The first thing Daniel saw when the door opened was a boy. At least, his height corresponded to a boy about twelve or thirteen years old, but he couldn't see his face because a black hood was pulled down over it; he was carrying a gun.

'What are you doing here?' asked the youngster.

'We just need a permit from your superiors,' said Aya.

They were told to wait in the yard and the boy disappeared into the building. While they were waiting, Daniel took note of the long, unmown grass and wild bushes in the garden. A grey-haired, elderly man in camouflage clothing soon came out into the yard and spoke to Aya in Arabic. His eyes were angry and the rest of his face was devoid of expression.

The boy with the black hood came out again. 'I need to borrow your camera,' he said.

Daniel didn't dare disobey, and he reminded himself that he had downloaded his photos from the day before on to the computer and hard drive, which were in Ayman's apartment.

Meanwhile, the grey-haired man continued talking to Aya in a tone that was getting faster and louder. Aya was looking down at the tiles in the yard, which made Daniel nervous.

She said she knows them and now she's staring at the ground. What the hell's going on? And it also happened yesterday . . . I certainly won't use Aya again, she hasn't got a grip on things, he thought to himself, and he couldn't help looking at the gun in the grey-haired man's belt.

Suddenly he began pointing at Daniel, while spewing Arabic at Aya.

This is about me, thought Daniel, and his vision momentarily went black, as if he had been standing too long.

Cold sweat was trickling out under his blue shirt as the grey-haired man motioned for them to go inside. At the entrance, Daniel took off his boots and put them next to a lot of other shoes on a carpet that was laid out over the stone floor.

They were shown into a small, shadowy room with sofas along the wall and a wooden table in the middle. Daniel sat down furthest away from the door next to Aya, while Ayman sat in a corner.

The rebels asked for Daniel's papers and disappeared with them into an adjoining room, while the old man began questioning him through Aya, who translated. There was also another man on the sofa, who had comically put his glasses on over his black face mask.

'I'm a photographer from Denmark,' said Daniel. 'I've come to do a story on how the war is affecting civilian Syrians.'

Ayman was silent and deathly pale, and Daniel had only one thought in his head: *If we get out of here, we go back across the border straight away.*

A tall, heavily built man entered the room and confronted Aya. He had a scarf wrapped around his face, so Daniel could see only a pair of eyes made up with black eyeliner.

Aya stared stiffly at the floor.

'They say they don't believe you, Daniel. They say we're spies.'

'But I am who I say I am. I'm a photographer from Denmark, here to portray the war,' he repeated.

'He says they know that sensors are put on cars so drones can come and destroy the town,' translated Aya.

Daniel remained silent and looked away as masked men in tunics and with Kalashnikovs over their shoulders came and went in the living room.

'Sit properly,' was the order when Daniel crossed one leg over the other.

Instead, he had to sit with his knees together side by side, while he was presented with new allegations.

'We've checked your camera. You've taken many pictures of the places where the fighters live. You're going around gathering information in the area. Who are you?'

Daniel reiterated who he was.

The grey-haired man then asked Aya to write a long letter by hand. Afterwards, Aya translated to Daniel that they could go back to Turkey when he had signed the letter. A friendly person served him with a cup of tea. For a moment, Daniel had a feeling that they just wanted him out of Azaz. The men chatted casually and laughed as he signed the letter.

'They say that you have to stand up now,' said Aya.

Daniel had managed to drink only half of the tea and his fixer seemed nervous.

'They say that you have to turn around and put your hands behind your back. It's just normal procedure,' she reassured him.

Daniel's head was spinning when he got up and he didn't have time to respond before his hands were twisted behind his back and handcuffed. Some foreign fingers approached his face, removed his glasses and blindfolded him. There was silence in the room while his wallet, mobile and passport were removed from his pockets. He didn't resist. Not even when he was led away from Aya and Ayman in the living room and down into a basement, where he was pushed down on to a mattress.

He lay on his side with his arms behind his back as he heard the door being slammed shut and locked. The handcuffs burned his wrists; the blindfold felt tight. He was so afraid that all his thoughts and feelings disappeared.

. * .

On Friday morning Kjeld and Susanne got up early and Kjeld drove to work. Susanne was going to the hairdresser at 11 a.m. to have her hair done and then on to work in Legoland. Daniel's younger sister Christina went to her high school.

That evening Kjeld and Susanne were packing to visit some good friends who had a summer cottage on the island of Fanø.

'I can't understand why I haven't heard from Daniel all day!' said Kjeld.

'Maybe he's forgotten to write,' said Susanne.

Signe was also wondering about the silence. She contacted Kjeld to ask if he had heard anything. Kjeld's 'no' meant there had been no sign of life from Daniel since Thursday evening. At 10.37 p.m. on Friday Signe sent an email to her boyfriend.

'Would you reply to my mail? I'd really like to hear from you xx.'

When Kjeld and Susanne sailed to Fanø on Saturday morning, they still hadn't heard anything from Daniel. Kjeld also sent him a message.

Susanne felt a creeping uneasiness, but pushed it away by telling herself she was always getting worried for no reason.

While they took a long walk on the beach and ate lunch, Kjeld was constantly checking his mobile. Susanne tried to convince herself that Daniel was just getting lazy about writing; at any rate, he was out of Syria and on his way home.

But these evasive explanations didn't help. A knot was forming in her stomach. They tried in vain to call Daniel's mobile and they called Signe, who hadn't heard anything from him either. Nevertheless, she would still go to Copenhagen Airport to pick him up at 10 p.m., as agreed.

During dinner on Fanø, Susanne noticed that Kjeld wasn't drinking any red wine. She looked at him enquiringly. He leaned over towards her ear and whispered, 'I think we'll have to go home this evening.'

It was the final of the Eurovision Song Contest and Susanne and Kjeld and their friends watched with 150 million other viewers as a barefooted Danish girl, Emmelie de Forest, sang herself into the hearts of Europeans to win with 'Only Teardrops'.

Kjeld had difficulty concentrating and, just after 10 p.m., Signe rang. Daniel hadn't been on the plane. But was it the one he should have been on? There was confusion about the arrival time. The note Daniel had written was at home on the table in Hedegård. Kjeld remembered that Daniel had crossed out the flight time and written a new one, but no one could now say with certainty when he was supposed to arrive.

'We have to go home,' said Kjeld.

The last ferry sailed from Fanø at 11.30 p.m. They just made it.

When they got home, Kjeld immediately found Daniel's note. He should have landed by now. Kjeld went into his office and at 1 a.m. he called Arthur's number.

. * .

Daniel didn't know how much time had passed before he heard footsteps on the stairs and a man ordered him to sit up and cross his legs. A hand pushed the blindfold down around his neck and Daniel could just make out the contours of a man sitting on a stool, holding something that looked like his notebook.

The man's movements were calm. He asked questions in broken English about Daniel's notebook and the names and experiences written in it. As Daniel was practically blind without his glasses, the man had to hold the notebook up to his eyes, while he read the notes out loud in Danish.

Daniel told him he was a gymnast and reminded himself that he shouldn't talk about religion but about family, which the kidnapper might be able to relate to. To illustrate that he was telling the truth, he got up from the mattress and did the splits with his hands cuffed.

'Stop that,' the man said. 'If the others see that I'm sitting like this with you right now, I'll be in trouble.'

Daniel was overflowing with questions he didn't dare ask, frightened of provoking his kidnappers.

'I really hope that the others believe your story as much as

I do. Whatever happens, they won't kill you,' the man stated, before blindfolding Daniel again and disappearing from the basement.

Soon there was noise on the stairs, as if several people were coming down into the basement room. Daniel heard the tramp of boots – and the sound of a stun gun that buzzed close to him. Suddenly there was a huge blast as a shot was fired into the ceiling. His ears were ringing.

'You, CIA!' a voice shouted.

Daniel didn't answer; his thoughts were whirling in his head.

'We shoot you! We cut your head off!'

Fuck, fuck, fuck, fuck, fuck, fuck, fuck. Will this take three days . . . or three weeks? he wondered.

Daniel felt several pairs of hands on his body, carrying him up the stairs, and then they beat him over the head with what felt like the barrel of a rifle, before he was loaded into a van. At first he thought he was alone in the back of the car, but after they had driven a little way, he heard Ayman's tearful voice. He was either shouting or praying to Allah.

The smell of diesel fuel entered Daniel's nose and he tensed his muscles to keep his balance against the swinging of the vehicle. He felt defenceless with his hands cuffed behind his back.

They were going to die. He could hear that in Ayman's prayers. He imagined drowsily how they would soon stop the car and shoot him and Ayman, a bullet in the back of the head for each of them. He became strangely peaceful at the thought. Sounds and smells and dreams disappeared instantly. All that was left was the memory of his life.

*I have experienced a lot in my short life. I'm grateful for that. Maybe I've
constantly been pushing at the boundaries. Now I've felt the real world.
Some things have consequences and that is what is happening now. I
will go to my father; maybe I'll meet him now. And Nan and Günther
the cat. Signe, we found each other again. Mum and Dad, you have
been the most wonderful parents . . . and Grandma and Grandpa . . .*

The car stopped, pulling Daniel abruptly out of his thoughts. He
was dragged from the car and thrown into a cold basement room
with a tiled floor that seemed like a bathroom.

He fell asleep on the hard floor in the foetal position, with
handcuffs and blindfold still in place, and woke up only when cold
water was thrown over his head. Other prisoners were brought
into the room, but Daniel didn't dare to speak to them or Ayman.
Perhaps they were spies and his driver's accomplices, he thought.

During the night, his body shook with cold. During the day, what
sounded like young men came and made frivolous interrogations.

'Do you have a girlfriend?' asked one of them.

'Yes, Signe,' said Daniel from his position on the floor. The
young men laughed triumphantly.

'You should just know that when people like you disappear,
the girls leave you. She's probably screwing someone else already.
That's what they do in the country you come from.'

After two days the blindfold was removed and Daniel and
Ayman were handcuffed together, Daniel's left hand with Ayman's
right. The kidnappers weren't taking any chances, pulling a set
of shackles through the bars of a small basement window and
putting them on their hostages' feet.

Daniel and Ayman sat down together and cried.

. * .

Arthur was in Ukraine and still awake when his mobile rang at 2 a.m. on Sunday, 19 May. He didn't recognize the number on the display.

'Hello, my name's Kjeld Rye and I'm Daniel Rye's father. Excuse me for calling so late.'

Kjeld explained that his son hadn't come home from Syria on Saturday evening as planned.

'Why do you think something has happened to Daniel?' asked Arthur.

'Because we haven't had any text messages, as we agreed,' said Kjeld.

Arthur knew there could be many reasons why Daniel hadn't kept in touch. The telephone network was often down in Syria; the borders opened and closed without notice; Daniel could have been slightly injured and be lying in a hospital. But the matter had to be investigated, so Arthur asked Kjeld to send him all the information he had been given by Daniel.

A few hours later Arthur was contacted by Signe, who had left the airport, out of her mind with worry. She wrote:

I've just talked to Daniel's fixer. Daniel has been arrested by the Jabhat al-Nusra faction just outside Azaz while taking photographs. He has been in their custody since 10 o'clock Friday morning. His fixer says they are negotiating and that Daniel will most probably be out again in a few days. He says that they aren't violent, but very angry. Daniel's parents can't speak English, so right now I'm the one who has contact with the fixer. You are welcome to call me when you read this. And maybe call his parents, so they can be reassured.

First of all Arthur had to try to map out Daniel's route into Syria and make contact with the people he had been with or spoken to on the trip. Signe's exchange with the fixer Ahmed was a good start, although Arthur always approached sources critically.

Arthur had learned from the James Foley case how important it is to control information, so there were not more rumours than facts in circulation. If too many people became aware of Daniel's situation, it would make collecting intelligence on him more difficult. It couldn't be ruled out, either, that some of the people with whom Daniel had had contact were behind the kidnapping. So there was an important question buzzing in Arthur's head: who was Ahmed?

In their chat, Ahmed had written to Signe:

'Don't worry, we'll get him out. We'll wait two more days and then they will no doubt find out, after looking at his camera, that there's nothing to it – that there are only interviews with families in the area.'

'OK,' Signe had answered. 'I understand. But is there money involved?'

'No, it isn't about money,' said Ahmed. 'It's about whether there is anything suspicious about him. And besides, it could well be that they contact you or his parents, because he mentioned your name. He apparently told them that he wanted to leave the country and go back to his girlfriend.' Ahmed had added that Signe – in case she was contacted – should say that she was going to marry Daniel in July. It would make things 'easier'.

Arthur's inner alarm bells rang whenever someone said 'Don't worry, we'll fix it', because it was usually hot air. He had to get hold of Ahmed as soon as possible, so he didn't get involved any further. It could be that Ahmed was wrong, was being misinformed or was even part of the game.

Arthur knew that anything was possible in Syria – like, for example, making James Foley disappear without a trace for seven months.

The same thing mustn't happen to Daniel.

. * .

That night Kjeld spent several hours in his office, speaking alternately with Arthur and Signe. He wrote half-sentences and fragments of telephone conversations down on the note Daniel had left. 'Jabnat almusra, Azaz,' he wrote and framed it in a square, but corrected it later to 'Jabhat al-Nusra', which was written beside 'three options' and 'closed border Syria'.

'I'm afraid it's not good,' he remarked quietly to Susanne.

She cried, at a loss for words.

Just past 3 a.m. Christina came home from a friend's eighteenth birthday party at Hedegård Community Hall.

'Why aren't you on Fanø – and why are you up?' she asked, surprised.

Susanne told a white lie to spare her. She was about to take her high-school exams and they didn't want to upset her.

'So many people came over that we decided we would rather sleep at home,' Susanne replied.

'My God, you really have become old and boring,' said Christina and went to bed.

A mountain of practical tasks were clamouring for attention and Arthur gave Daniel's parents instructions as to what they should do. At 10 a.m. on Sunday morning Kjeld rang the family's banker in Give and asked him for a printout of a statement for Daniel's account, so that the family could see if he had paid his insurance and which company was insuring him. In addition, Kjeld requested that he call them if any money was drawn on the account. Arthur had experience of other cases in Syria in which the kidnappers had used credit cards to withdraw money or make purchases online.

Daniel had done what he was supposed to do and insured himself with an independent international insurance company. The sum insured was 5 million kroner (about £520,000), which would cover any expenses in connection with a kidnapping and the costs for a security consultant like Arthur to carry out an investigation.

Kjeld also rang the police. Arthur had already informed the Danish Security and Intelligence Service (PET) about the matter. PET had to ensure that the police treated Kjeld's report with discretion at every level. This was crucial, since the daily police report could be leaked and used as a resource for journalists. The authorities didn't want news of the missing Dane to come out.

Arthur also informed the Danish government about Daniel's disappearance. He contacted the Danish Embassy in Beirut and the Citizens Advice Bureau at the Foreign Ministry in Copenhagen, which assists and advises Danes who get into difficulties or have accidents while travelling abroad.

Arthur had emphasized to Daniel's parents how vital it was that only the relevant authorities knew anything. Any media attention could hurt Daniel's situation and, since it was still unclear what had happened and who had taken him, they had to keep it a secret.

Susanne and Kjeld told Christina, who was in the middle of her exams, that Daniel hadn't come home yet because 'the borders had been closed in Syria'.

On the other hand, they told Daniel's older sister, Anita, the truth. She knew that Daniel was going to Syria, but in the months leading up to his departure she hadn't had much contact with him. She lived with her partner in Odense and she was used to Daniel travelling a lot.

Three days after Daniel's disappearance, Kjeld and Susanne drove to Signe's apartment in Copenhagen, where they met Arthur, who was now back from Ukraine. They lied to Christina again, telling her that Kjeld had a meeting with the agricultural firm DLG and that in the meantime Susanne was going to do some shopping.

At the meeting, Arthur updated them on the situation in Syria.

'It can take anywhere from a few days to . . . well, much longer,' said Arthur and he told them briefly about the James Foley case and others.

He asked the family to keep an eye on Daniel's Facebook profile.

'Leave all channels of communication open,' said Arthur. 'The kidnappers must be able to check who Daniel is. If they encounter a black hole, they'll become suspicious.'

In addition, he sought information about Daniel, so that he could get an investigation going and so that he could get 'proof of life' on Daniel if the kidnappers made contact. A proof of life could come from Arthur asking the kidnappers a series of questions that only the captive could answer or from a photograph of the person they had kidnapped.

Kjeld, Susanne and Signe wrote a list of information: about a scar on Daniel's lip, which he got when a spade hit him in the face as a boy; that he had worked on a pig farm while he was at the Free School; that he drank coffee without milk; that he had celebrated his twenty-fourth birthday with Signe at Flyvergrillen at Copenhagen Airport; that there was a black-and-white horse poster hanging over Signe's bed; and that they were going to Morocco for a month in July.

Kjeld and Susanne went back home to Hedegård in a composed and hopeful mood, while Arthur boarded a plane to Antakya in Turkey to meet his contacts.

. * .

Daniel woke up early because Ayman had to perform his morning prayers. They were chained together, so a routine had begun whereby they swept away the dust on the floor with their hands, folded the blankets they had been given and sat upon them to pray. Daniel prayed with Ayman five times a day and it felt reassuring. In those minutes of prayer Daniel shut out the world and explored Ayman's faith. They were given bulgur wheat, bread and olives twice a day, and they shared a one-and-a-half litre bottle, which they filled with water when they were occasionally allowed to go to the toilet.

When Ayman told Daniel about his wife and two daughters, who were now living in Turkey, he began to cry. Daniel cried too when he talked about Signe and his family.

'When we're set free one day, you must come to Denmark to visit Legoland with your daughters,' suggested Daniel.

Ayman taught him a few useful words in Arabic, so he could ask for water and to be allowed to go to the toilet. Sometimes new guards arrived and asked them who they were. Then they left again.

Time became endless. Daniel began pulling threads out of his blanket, which he then shaped into letters and a car on the floor. Ayman read the Koran, which he had asked for and received.

One morning they awoke to find their linked hands, which were exposed while they slept, red with mosquito bites. They launched a hunt for the pests and Daniel felt a twinge of conscience about killing them.

They had been sitting in the same room for a week when, early one morning, a prison guard released Ayman and led him away. Daniel waited for Ayman to come back, but he never saw him again. He was convinced that Ayman had been set free and he now sat alone in the cell, waiting for it to be his turn.

But no one came and fetched him. Not even when he had to go to the toilet. He pounded on the door; he shouted and pounded again.

He didn't know whether he could hold out, because he had no idea how long it would be before they let him go to the toilet. He looked around the room. In one corner there was a plate of bread crumbs, a cup and a half-full water bottle. His insides were about to burst. He filled the cup with water, so the bottle was almost empty. Then he pulled down his trousers, put the remains of the bread under his behind – and shat on the bread. Afterwards, he stuffed the bread and faeces into the nearly empty water bottle. Some of it stuck to the side, some of it stuck to his

THE ISIS HOSTAGE 69

fingers; it stank and he was embarrassed, even though he was alone. He screwed the lid on the bottle, placed it in the corner and used the water in the cup to wash his hands and the floor. He felt relieved, but hardly dared to think about the bottle of shit in the corner.

Many hours later, when the guard finally stood in the doorway, he became angry.

'Don't you know that it's *haram* to shit on your bread? How could you do that?' he shouted.

Daniel explained that he had knocked on the door and had called out.

'You have to tell us when you need the toilet,' said the guard.

He was given a bath and clean clothes, while his own were washed. There was hot water and soap and Daniel wondered if they were getting ready to release him like Ayman.

The next day he was given a pen and some sheets of paper. He passed the time by writing a story that took place one thousand years from now, in 3013, which featured a family who lived in a basement during a world war. It was a story about living where there was never any light and still being able to create something.

He had been imprisoned for ten days when the door opened suddenly one evening. Masked men with weapons burst in. They were rough as they held his head and blindfolded him.

'We will shoot you, *kufr*, infidel!' they shouted as they dragged him up the stairs and out to a car. He felt alone without Ayman and had no idea where they were moving him. Were they taking their infidel further into Syria or to the gallows?

What did they want with him?

A Noose around the Neck

Arthur sat in a cafe in the Turkish border town of Kilis. In front of him was a cup of strong Turkish coffee with thick sediment at the bottom. He hadn't slept for the last twenty-four hours, but was keeping himself awake with caffeine and cigarettes. The Syrian combatants were night owls; they went to bed at dawn and usually didn't get up until noon, which was why Arthur spent every minute questioning anyone who might somehow be involved in the complicated network surrounding Daniel, as well as tracking down locals who could travel into Syria to look for him.

Across from Arthur sat a carefully made-up young woman with a tight scarf wrapped around her head. Aya was distraught that she hadn't been able to get Daniel out of Syria with her. She had been hired to help Daniel, but had failed. Arthur scribbled down scattered notes as she relayed her version of what had happened on the day they were captured.

'When we were sitting on the sofa, I actually felt quite safe, until the Iraqi turned up,' she told him. 'He accused us of being spies. I was so scared that I didn't translate everything for Daniel.

She had recognized one of the men: the unmasked Tunisian. He was one of the men who had stopped them the previous day. He had appeared in the doorway when Daniel was handcuffed and dragged to the basement.

'The Tunisian told me I deserved to die,' she said, but she was released some hours later. Luck had been smiling upon her, Aya thought.

'One of the men who was a foreigner later helped me get away,' she continued. 'He showed me his French driver's licence and I think he released me without asking his boss.' Aya was certain that Daniel's kidnappers were Islamists. She had thought for sure that she would be taken captive too.

Arthur was particularly interested to hear that several foreign fighters were part of the group that had taken Daniel. He was also relieved that Daniel had been taken at the former regime headquarters. This would allow him to find out who had been in command in the house in Azaz that day. In the previous months at least five foreign journalists had been kidnapped by Islamists from Jabhat al-Nusra, but after a few days in captivity most of them had been released with no ransom demands. Daniel had already been held hostage for ten days.

Even though the fixer, Ahmed, had written to Signe on the first night that Daniel had been taken by Jabhat al-Nusra, new information suggested a different scenario. When Arthur spoke with the Jabhat al-Nusra contacts he had acquired while working on James Foley's case, he was informed that Daniel was being held by a group that was beyond their influence. And, unfortunately, in the time it took for the information to reach him, the situation may have already changed. But several people in Arthur's network independently reported to him that the captors were from Dawlah al-Islamiyah, otherwise known as ISIS. Since there were few precedents, nobody had the prior knowledge or experience to gauge what ISIS would do with western hostages. The informants said that the al-Nusra Front or other rebel groups might be open to negotiations, should they be the ones behind Daniel's kidnapping, but ISIS was a different story. ISIS members rarely spoke to non-members, such as Arthur's informants.

According to the information available, Daniel had been kidnapped for taking photos without permission and had committed a crime according to sharia law's prohibition against pornography. Arthur couldn't know that Daniel's photos consisted of plum trees and doves flocking around two brothers.

Still, he couldn't get any information on Daniel's exact location. Arthur's contacts were working on the assumption that Daniel was still in captivity in the border town of Azaz, where he had originally been detained. Therefore, they focused their efforts on trying to find key members of the complex network of rebel groups headquartered around the sand-coloured building where Daniel was believed to be held.

. * .

On the tenth evening of his captivity Daniel was moved and led up a flight of stairs, blindfolded and with his arms tied behind his back. He felt several hands search the pockets of his leather jacket and trousers.

'What's this?' asked a voice. Daniel guessed the guard had found the sheet of paper with his fictitious story.

'A story,' he answered, but he was allowed to keep neither the paper nor his leather jacket, which the guard ripped off his back, before forcing Daniel into a cross-legged position with his hands cuffed in front of him. Then he fastened Daniel's handcuffs to a radiator. Facing the radiator and with his back to the room, Daniel was able to lift the blindfold slightly with the inside of his upper arm and get an idea of his surroundings.

From the little he could make out without his glasses, it looked as if he was in some kind of large foyer with corridors leading off to other rooms. The room echoed when anyone spoke and he could see a wash basin, a window and a table in the middle. Daniel could hear people walking past the wash basin; some splashed water on their faces or filled water bottles, while others just walked through.

A man gave Daniel some water and an omelette. Once he had eaten, he dozed off in an awkward, cross-legged position. He was suddenly awoken by a violent kick in his side.

'Don't sleep!' came the order.

Daniel straightened up, but found it hard to stay awake, because everything was dark behind the blindfold. For a while, he managed to sit up whenever he heard steps behind him. But he must have keeled over at some point, as he was abruptly awoken by an excruciating pain in his back, as if he had been whipped with a cable.

It wasn't until he had heard several calls to prayer the next day that someone untied his aching body from the radiator and led him into another room. Once the blindfold was removed, he saw comfortable armchairs and a wooden desk. Behind the table sat a masked man, who turned out to be his interrogator.

Daniel was ordered to sit on the floor and answer questions that he had already answered several times.

'Who are you?'

'I am Daniel Rye.'

'Where do you come from?'

'Denmark.'

'Who drove you here?'

'Friends,' answered Daniel.

The voice behind the mask sounded very young; Daniel guessed they had put a twenty-year-old in charge of the interrogation because he could speak some English. The interrogator announced that he didn't believe Daniel.

'We know who you are. We know you're lying,' he stated, and Daniel was taken back to the radiator in the foyer.

After another night of sitting cross-legged with no water or food, he was taken back to the interrogator.

'Tell us the truth. We know what it is, but we want you to say it!' he shouted.

Daniel repeated the same information.

'I'm only here to portray the civilian suffering caused by the war,' he said, faintly registering some kind of rummaging going on behind him.

Before he had a chance to realize what was happening, more hands forced him down on to his back and a car tyre was pressed down over his bent legs, so his knees were sticking up through the tyre. A stick was then placed behind the backs of his knees, locking his legs in place. He was turned over on to his front, which exposed the bare soles of his feet.

He gasped for breath.

A searing pain surged through him as the guards began relentlessly hitting his feet with some sort of cable or pipe. Daniel screamed and a man pressed a stun gun against his ribs and shoulder. He screamed again. He couldn't hold it in.

'Who are you?' one shouted.

'I'm Daniel Rye Ottosen,' he stammered, and was thrashed again.

'You're lying! You're lying!' shouted the interrogator. 'Tell me who you really are!'

Daniel cried and screamed.

'Man up and stop crying!' one of them shouted.

Every time they lashed him, he screamed. If he didn't scream out loud for fear of provoking more lashes, he screamed inside, losing all sense of time.

When will it stop? What do they want? How long will this go on? Just as long as they don't break my bones or anything. As long as they don't cause any permanent damage.

At some point, the whipping and the pain ceased. Someone removed the car tyre, dragged him out to the radiator in the foyer and handcuffed him to it once more. A few hours passed. Then they started all over again.

It was on the third or fourth round that everything started to become a blur. The only thing he was aware of was that he was back in the interrogation room again.

'You're a gymnast?' asked the interrogator.

'Yes,' answered Daniel.

'Right, well, what can you do then?' he continued.

Daniel replied that he could show them some exercises if the handcuffs were removed.

'We can't do that,' said the interrogator, who sat behind the table with a couple of other men.

'Can you handcuff me in front of my body then?'

The interrogator agreed and his hands were handcuffed in front of him.

Daniel hadn't moved very much in recent days apart from writhing from pain. His body ached; his feet were swollen from the beatings; he was thirsty, hungry, tired and completely beside himself. He took a deep breath and looked up at the ceiling, straightening his posture and trying to feel his body.

And then he was off. He jumped as high as he could in the air and as he tucked his knees towards his stomach he flipped backward. His eyes scanned the stone floor to gain his bearings before he landed firmly on both feet. Pain surged through his body, but he had managed to perform a standing back flip and had stuck the landing – accomplished for the first time in his life with his hands cuffed.

The guards' initial reaction almost made him laugh.

'That's a pretty stupid thing to do,' one commented.

'I can also stand on my hands,' suggested Daniel, and he was allowed to show them another move to prove to the kidnappers that he wasn't a CIA agent, but an elite gymnast from Hedegård. Standing tall, he bent forward and laid his hands down on the floor. He wanted to slowly bring his legs upwards into a handstand, but his palms were too close to each other because of the handcuffs, so the result wasn't perfect.

The guards called him over to the table and placed a printed picture in front of him, which he had taken at the European Gymnastics Championships in Aarhus in 2012.

'Who are they?' asked the leader.

Daniel stared at the five men in the picture in their tight, white-, black-and-red gym suits. They were his teammates. He had taken the picture just before they took the floor at the final competition of the European Championships. They looked particularly determined: if they won this event, they would bring home the gold medal.

'They are Niels, Stefan, Andreas, Lasse and Steven,' said Daniel.

They beat him again. His answers didn't seem to make any difference.

When they were finished, he was dragged back to the radiator, which had become the symbol for respite. His feet were cold, sore and swollen. It must have been about three days since he had had any water or food. Or gone to the toilet.

. * .

'Helloooo Daniel. Are you ready for me now?' shouted a deep voice. Daniel didn't recognize the voice that echoed in the foyer that evening, but he would soon know to whom it belonged. The torturer who used the nom de guerre Abu Hurraya, meaning 'Father of Hurraya', was known as the prison's most brutal guard, reputedly taking genuine pleasure in torturing hostages.

'You have beautiful hair. Why did you even come here in the first place? It was really stupid, you should never have come. Follow me,' said Abu Hurraya in broken English as he stood in front of Daniel and fumbled with a key to the handcuffs.

Abu Hurraya was a tall, broad Syrian with long hair gathered in a ponytail. He lived on the first floor of the building, just above where Daniel was being kept. The other prison guards always knew where he was because of his distinctive voice, which they called 'heavy'.

The torture would take place either in the office, where other guards had seen him put a stun gun to a prisoner's body, or in special rooms, where a selection of chains and other instruments hung on the walls. Abu Hurraya was often summoned for beatings, which he performed dressed in ordinary trousers and a T-shirt. Unlike many of the other guards, he didn't look like a fighter.

Abu Hurraya released Daniel from the radiator and walked behind him towards a room that Daniel hadn't seen yet. As they entered, he noticed a man lying motionless in one of the corners. 'You'll look like that in twenty-four hours,' commented Abu Hurraya.

He wrapped some foam around Daniel's wrists and put the handcuffs on again.

'Reach out your arms,' said Abu Hurraya, stepping on to a chair. He pulled down some chains from a hook in the ceiling and looped them around the handcuffs. Daniel's body was now completely extended. He was standing on flat feet, with his arms stretched up towards the ceiling. The foam lining the handcuffs fell off and he felt the sharp iron dig into his wrists.

'See you tomorrow. You might be ready to talk by then,' said Abu Hurraya with a cheery voice, before walking out, leaving Daniel almost dangling from the ceiling. The feeling in his hands and arms quickly disappeared; it was replaced by a constant tingling pain that penetrated his entire body.

When he had entered the room Daniel had faintly made out a window with a balcony and now he could hear people outside the window – Syrians, who might be on their way home from work, if they still had a job, or were perhaps out shopping for dinner. He was thirstier than he'd ever been and dreamed of gallons of water.

The sound of the calls to prayer permeated through the window during the evening hours and again around midnight. When Daniel heard some footsteps outside the door a few hours later, he called out the Arabic word for water, which Ayman had taught him: 'Ma! Ma!'

A punishment was promptly issued. A man came in, whipped him a few times on his back and disappeared again. Daniel remained standing, stretched out from the ceiling to the floor, all night long.

He fell in and out of consciousness and discovered at some point that the man in the corner was gone. When sunlight hit him in the early morning hours, he heard the call to prayer once again, along with the voices of children – the sound of boys' high-pitched voices teasing him and shouting English words through the door behind him.

'Are you thirsty? Do you want some water? Are you hungry?'

Then they giggled and disappeared. Daniel was so thirsty and tired that he drifted off into a dream state: he was breaking into a 7-Eleven and drinking the entire contents of the store – milk, water, cola. He ran from shelf to shelf like a dehydrated thief, chugging drinks in a frenzy.

The stone patterns in the tiles underneath him began to blur and take on animal forms. The ground was teeming with vermin and he started to urinate. He felt the warm flow trickle down his leg. He shifted slightly to give his trousers a chance to dry; that way no one would notice, he thought. But that was ridiculous, because there was no one there. Only the creatures on the floor, his thirst and the urine. The light outside disappeared. He heard the call for prayer and the sound of children once again. He was almost pleased to be so thirsty, as it made him forget how painful and powerless it felt to stand there, like a taut bowstring.

He had been there for twenty-four hours when Abu Hurraya returned.

'I'm thirsty,' said Daniel.

'Relax, you'll get some water,' Abu Hurraya told him.

Daniel's brain danced around in a chaotic frenzy; he pictured himself being unshackled from the ceiling, his arms falling naturally down the sides of his body as he walked out of the room on strong, dignified legs.

Abu Hurraya stood on the chair and loosened the chain from the ceiling: Daniel crumpled to the floor like a rag. His body folded underneath him, a corpse washed away by the ocean, and he was swept weightlessly into a soft world of darkness.

. * .

Over many decades in Syria, torture had developed into an absurd art form. Creative and effective methods were given names which were familiar to most Syrians, even those who hadn't been exposed to the regime's prisons. Many could define 'The Tyre' or 'The German Chair', 'The Flying Carpet' or 'Shabeh'.

Daniel had endured one version of 'The Tyre'. The other version consisted of pushing the car tyre down over the head and legs to make sure the prisoner was unable to move away from the blows.

'Shabeh' was another well-known classic: the victim has his hands cuffed behind his back so that the chain hanging from the ceiling forces the arms painfully upwards. The method Daniel was subjected to, his hands tied above his head, was in fact a milder version of 'Shabeh'. The word has no real meaning, but some believe it comes from the word *shabih* or ghost.

Thousands of Syrians had been tortured by the regime and in military prisons. Torture was generally more the rule than the exception for inmates. Under President Hafez al-Assad's leadership from 1971 to 2000, torture became systematic, and this continued under his son, Bashar al-Assad, who took over the presidency from his father. Torture was the regime's trademark, which lived on in the newly dominant Islamist strongholds in northern Syria. Former prisoners who had been imprisoned by both the regime and the rebels described how the Islamists' torture methods were an exact copy of the techniques used in Assad's prisons.

In the government's notorious Sednaya Prison, just north of Damascus, the inmates, often political prisoners, were subjected to torture and humiliation. According to many eyewitness accounts and reports, prisoners often died from being tortured.

So it was no coincidence that Daniel was subjected to the same torture methods that his torturers had endured themselves. For instance, Abu Hurraya reported to Abu Athir, who had been put in Sednaya Prison in 2007 on charges related to terrorism, but was freed under President Assad's amnesty at the beginning of the revolution.

Abu Athir, a slim man in his early to mid-thirties with shoulder-length hair and a very thick, full beard, was known as one of

Sednaya Prison's hardliners. He was a radical Islamist who fell out with other jihadists and Islamists because his narrow and ultra-conservative dogma left no space for any other versions of Sunni Islam. Immediately after his release in the summer of 2011 he formed the rebel group the Sunni Lions in Aleppo and became a familiar face among Syria's armed factions during the civil war. In August 2012 his brother was killed and Abu Athir took control of his brother's brigade, the Mujahideen Shura Council.

Abu Athir's power grew significantly when he met ISIS leader Abu Bakr al-Baghdadi in Iraq later that year, and he became one of his most fervent and vocal followers in calling for an Islamic caliphate. Some months later, following a split between the two factions Jabhat al-Nusra and ISIS, he helped to ensure that fighters from Jabhat al-Nusra joined Baghdadi's ISIS, and made sure his own faction also endorsed ISIS.

In May 2013 Abu Athir became part of ISIS's Shura Council, a powerful organ under Baghdadi's control. Abu Athir was in charge of media relations and was responsible for the recruitment of foreign jihadis, while at the same time serving as the trusted and influential Emir of Aleppo.

. * .

Daniel's body slumped against the radiator, heavy and useless. Not even the cup of water and the roll of bread with falafel and tomato that he had been given could revive him after hanging from the ceiling for a full day and night. He had eaten only the tomato – his mouth felt too dry to swallow anything else. He drifted in and out of a restless sleep, dreaming of a kung-fu master who beat him and ran after him, until some guards woke him again, heaved him

up by his arms, and dragged him across the floor and back into
the interrogation room.

'If you don't tell us who you are, we'll hang you up for three
days with no food or water. Then we'll behead you and send a
video home to your parents!' a voice boomed at him.

Daniel lacked the strength to react. Instead he heard his own
inner voice as he allowed his body to be led into another room.

*Fuck, you can do whatever you like to me; hit the soles of my feet, whip my
back, just don't hang me up without water again . . . I'll die. I'll rot . . . I'll
just fucking rot and wither away from this. I'd rather die.*

The room resembled the one where he had previously been
hung up, except that there was a rubbish bag full of Coke cans
on the floor, a table and a broken wooden bed. A man held him
up so he wouldn't collapse, while the torturer grabbed a chain
hanging from a hook on the ceiling. The torturer wrapped it
around the handcuffs and padlocked it, locking the chain and
handcuffs to the ceiling. Daniel was left standing once again with
his arms stretched above his head. The torturer disappeared.

I can't! I can't! he screamed inside. *I can't stand here for three days
and then die afterwards.*

He looked around him. The table. It had been placed to make
sure it was just out of his reach. His wrist. He could bite through
his wrist so he could escape.

Water. He was so thirsty that his brain was about to dry out
and flashes of visions and images flickered past. It required
nothing of the guards to leave him hanging there. What if they
forgot about him?

He could neither sleep nor move to escape the constant pain. Every muscle in his body was being stretched to its breaking point. He was trapped in a never-ending hell, without a way out, without the slightest relief. Two, maybe three, hours passed before he regained control of his thoughts and once again focused on the table in the room.

If only he could move it closer to him. He grabbed the chain with his hands and held on tight as he swung his body in an arc above the floor. His big toe brushed the edge of the table, which made a clattering noise. Daniel paused momentarily, listening for footsteps in the hallway, then swung himself over and over again towards the table; each time it moved by a fraction. And each time he listened to see whether the noise attracted any attention. Finally, the table was close enough that he could pull it underneath him with his legs.

He stood on the table top. The most wonderful feeling flowed through his body as he sank his arms down from their outstretched position. The relief spread from his elbows to his shoulders. He stood there for a long time, enjoying this new sensation, until the thirst overcame him. Thoughts rushed through his head: *To be free from this world, to decide for yourself when you want to leave it. That's all I want.*

He bit his wrist hard. It started bleeding and a stab of pain rushed through him. He couldn't do this to himself. But imagine if he could just drink a little blood or escape. Or simply disappear.

He looked at the chain that hung from the hook on the ceiling above him. If it could be an instrument of torture, it could also be one of liberation. His hands reached for the cool metal and wrapped the chain around his neck, so it rested against his skin.

For a moment he frightened himself. He had lived a wonderful life, he thought to himself. Even if he hadn't had any children. The fact that he hadn't left his mark on the next generation suddenly meant much more to him than he'd ever expected. He recalled the day he had been kidnapped and thought about his Syria project. At least he hadn't just sat at home in indifference and done nothing. He rested his arms and felt the chain around his neck as he stood still for a brief moment. The thirst had disappeared.

Suddenly he sensed someone looking at him. As he turned his head, he could just make out the outline of a small figure in the doorway. It had to be a child. Daniel turned his head back – and jumped. He sprung off from the table towards the ceiling. He felt a violent jerk in his body and the plaster from the ceiling raining down on him. There was a tightening sensation around his neck and everything went black. He felt his body tingle and he urinated in his trousers.

He descended further and further into darkness.

. * .

Arthur was working undercover to locate Daniel. After extensive discussions in various towns along the Syrian border, he hired several locals to help him with the search. These included Alpha, whom he called his assistant and who had an extensive network, and Majeed, whose task it was to track down the group that had kidnapped Daniel.

Majeed was a local television journalist who had previously worked as a fixer for foreign journalists in Syria. When Alpha rang Majeed and requested his help, he agreed despite the high risk he'd be taking, not only for himself, but also for his wife and their three children. But he needed the money and he felt sorry for the vanished Dane. Even though Majeed didn't know Daniel, he got the impression that Daniel had travelled to Syria to tell people's stories through his photos. Perhaps Daniel was someone who thought everyone else was just as kind as he was – but Syria was no longer like that.

With a file in his bag containing information about Daniel, Majeed travelled around Azaz and the surrounding area searching for clues. He held countless futile meetings, until he finally succeeded in making contact with an influential ISIS figure in the area. The man went by the nom de guerre Abu Suheib al-Iraqi, which meant he came from Iraq. According to several sources, he was about forty years old and had been a soldier under Saddam Hussein. In other words, he was a former Ba'ath Party loyalist turned ISIS hardliner, now fighting in Syria and involved in kidnapping both foreigners and Syrians.

Along with a trusted friend, Majeed drove to the house where they knew that Abu Suheib was staying. A chubby man with a full beard covering his wide face greeted them with a bowl of fruit and an otherwise unwelcoming attitude. When Majeed explained that they were looking for information about a disappeared Dane, Abu Suheib spat out, 'You dare to come here and ask me about an infidel who has sullied the Prophet's name? We will slaughter him.'

'Who has sullied the Prophet's name?' asked Majeed.

'Denmark. Wasn't there a cartoonist in Denmark who sullied the Prophet's name?'

'You want to kill a Dane because another Dane has insulted the Prophet?' proceeded Majeed carefully.

'All Danes are infidels and we will slaughter them all, and because you have come here to ask about him, we ought to slaughter you too.'

The only positive outcome of the meeting so far was that Majeed had finally found someone who admitted that he knew of Daniel's existence. He tried to calm him down.

'What do you want?' asked Abu Suheib.

'We want to bring Daniel home to his family.'

'How many "notebooks" will you give me?' asked Abu Suheib.

Majeed didn't know what he meant by 'notebooks', but later found out that in Iraq a notebook is the equivalent of $100,000.

'It's impossible to put together such a huge sum of money,' objected Majeed. 'His mother and father and fiancée are the ones trying to get him home, not the state.'

'The man works for the intelligence service – he's admitted it.'

'He's a photographer,' answered Majeed, who wanted to show Abu Suheib his file with information about Daniel for proof. But Abu Suheib wouldn't budge. He demanded an ambulance to transport wounded ISIS soldiers and seven notebooks. When Majeed pleaded again, explaining that they couldn't pay so much, Abu Suheib asked him to leave.

Arthur viewed Majeed's meeting with Abu Suheib as a possible opening. Abu Suheib seemed willing to negotiate and he knew where Daniel was. More names began to emerge. On his notepad he wrote 'Abu Athir' and drew a square around the name as someone to be investigated in greater detail. The information suggested that Daniel was being kept under Abu Athir's control somewhere in Aleppo, even though it was likely that Abu Suheib's local ISIS group in Azaz had been the ones to kidnap him.

. * .

Daniel had now been missing for more than two weeks. After the first week, Susanne and Kjeld were trying to get back to their normal routines. On Sundays Kjeld rode his bike to clear his mind. It helped to calm him. Every morning Susanne wrote a few lines in her diary and researched uplifting quotes online, which she used to look up for use in greeting and birthday cards.

On 25 May she wrote in her diary: 'I survived the time before last and I survived the last time, so I will have to survive now to survive next time.'

They finally told their immediate family that Daniel had been kidnapped. They also told Christina, whom they had put off with white lies until now. She wept and made herself refrain from googling stories about Syria. It was too frightening.

. * .

Daniel felt hands on his neck and shoulders. Some people were holding him up, others fiddled with the chain. For a brief moment he thought God's hand was lifting him up towards the light – until someone threw cold water on his face. He was reluctant to wake up, but moved his head instinctively when a boot threatened to step on it.

The guards broke out in cheers: their hostage was alive and kicking. They celebrated by beating him with a plastic tube, which bent around his tormented body, and then they left him tied to the radiator in the room.

They had tortured, starved and drained him of all humanity. He was no longer himself. He had jumped as high as he could so that the chain would break his neck, but his head remained intact on his shoulders and the guards were celebrating because he was still alive. Had the child in the doorway given him away? Maybe they wanted to kill him themselves? Maybe he had actually wanted the child to raise the alarm? He didn't know.

Once he was alone again, he tried to reach the bag filled with cans of Coke in the hope that he might find something to drink.

His feet could just about touch the bag, but he couldn't move it. Over by the bed, he saw a half-filled water bottle, which lay there shining like a miracle. Water. Using the outer edge of his big toe, he managed to reach it. He drank the few gulps that were left in the bottle, looked around the room and suddenly realized that there was no glass in the window frame.

Instead, there were rolled-down metal shutters on the outside of the window. They were partially destroyed in one corner and a piece of cardboard had been pasted over to obscure the view of the outside world. He also caught sight of an old lampshade in the nearest corner. It resembled the lamp his grandmother had at home with a fringe dangling around the bottom of the shade.

Before leaving for his trip to Syria he had seen the film *Rescue Dawn* starring Christian Bale as an American pilot who is taken hostage during the Vietnam War. In the film Bale uses a nail to work open his handcuffs, allowing him to escape the torture camp.

Daniel thought of this scene as he contemplated the old lampshade on the floor. He pulled it towards him with his feet. Perhaps things could work out in real life as they did in the movies.

He took his time jiggling and fiddling with the lampshade's metal spokes and eventually managed to break a piece off the shade that was about seven centimetres long. He inserted the end of the metal into a hole in the handcuffs so he could bend it slightly. It formed the shape of a key, which he might be able to use in the same way as Christian Bale's nail.

Daniel stuck the metal into the handcuff lock and turned it. He fiddled with it for several hours at different angles until finally, he heard a click: the lock was open.

He sat quietly for a moment. The only thing he knew for certain was that he was on the first floor and could jump out of the window, but he had no idea how far down it was, nor what was outside the house. It didn't matter. He just wanted out. Better to die on the run than live under torture.

Daylight penetrated the holes in the metal shutters, forming cones of light on the floor. Daniel heard the day's first call to prayer as he removed the cardboard and climbed through the corner of the window frame where the shutters were broken. He pushed himself through until he was finally standing on a small balcony.

It was low enough for him to jump, so he crawled over the railing, stretched himself out and dangled his legs in the air before he let go and landed on his bare, swollen feet in a pile of branches.

He scanned the horizon for somewhere to run for cover, but could see only gangly, leafless trees and an empty building to the right. Next to the trees was a dirt road and he chose this as his escape route, even though he was well aware that he would practically light up like a beacon in the middle of the flat, light-brown landscape with his blue shirt and black jeans that stank of dried urine.

When he had run a short distance, Daniel could make out something that looked like a leaky old water tower. Instinctively, he headed towards the water jet that was leaking out of the tower. He stood under the water, drank it and became soaking wet. Time was of the essence, but he wouldn't last long as a prisoner on the run without any water.

He continued down the dirt track for a while, but the buildings on both sides were surrounded by tall walls, which made it impossible to hide. The road split and as he made a left, he could see a man watching him from a window. He also passed two women who tried to make contact with him and he shouted as naturally as possible '*mafi mushkila*', 'no problem', before he followed the wall around the corner to the right. The stones cut his feet. It felt surreal to be free.

Around the corner he caught sight of a hole in a wall, where there was just enough space for a body of his size to squeeze through. He crawled through it and came out in a garden with tall grass in front of a house. For a moment he stood still and breathed deeply. In the grass in front of him was a pair of old trousers filled with what looked like sticks of dynamite. A feeling of panic set in, he felt trapped. The women could have alerted someone about the blond man they had seen running around barefoot in the neighbourhood.

He clambered back through the hole and ran further down the dirt road towards a more open landscape. His scratched feet left a bloody trail behind them, and the neighbourhood was about to wake up. He could make out a few scattered settlements on the horizon, but he knew that he wouldn't be able to run for several kilometres. Instead, he ran out into a cornfield, where he threw himself on his knees and took off his blue shirt to camouflage himself and proceeded to crawl forwards on his elbows.

He could feel the dry earth clods and rocks scraping against his naked torso. However, he couldn't carry on in a straight line because the corn was too low in some places to conceal him.

Suddenly he heard voices from somewhere behind him. He stopped crawling and lay completely flat on the ground for a moment, before he curled up in a foetal position and waited for the voices to disappear.

It sounded as if several men were talking together as they stamped about in the corn. Daniel leaned forwards slightly to see where they were and discovered that there was a man standing right next to him. When the man looked at him, straight in the eye, Daniel leapt up in a split second and sprinted further into the cornfield.

The men behind him were now shouting loudly in Arabic, and his legs were heavy, as if he were running on a cushion. He heard gunfire. Bullets whizzed past his ears. Daniel threw himself to the ground in a mixture of exhaustion and fear of being hit. Men he didn't recognize bent over him.

'I am Daniel, from Denmark,' he panted, and he told them they would get money if they helped him over the border into Turkey. A short, fat man tied his hands behind his back and lost control of his gun, which went off into the ground. Daniel almost smiled. If they were such amateurs, he thought, he might be able to persuade them to drive him towards Turkey.

They put him into the back seat of a car parked on an adjacent road and drove in the direction he had just been running from.

The car stopped at a sand-coloured house surrounded by a wall. They led him down into a cellar, where they provided him with a bottle of water that had been in the freezer and a cigarette.

Daniel inhaled the cold water and cigarette, while he showed them the bruises on his torso and neck. They didn't speak any English, but seemed to understand. Did they also understand that he wanted to go home?

They threw him back into the car, in the trunk this time, and drove for quite a while. They made short stops along the way – it sounded like they were buying groceries.

They pulled him down into another cellar – a kind of banqueting hall, where weddings might be held. There were oversized Arab sofas lined up against the walls. Daniel was allowed to have his hands untied to go to the toilet and wash himself. They gave him an extra-large pullover to wear.

A couple of kind older men came by with chocolate, coffee, biscuits and water. Daniel began to believe he might see his mother again. Some boys came along wearing Arsenal jerseys and studied him closely, along with the rest of the gathering, as he once again displayed his various marks and scars. Until a voice made him shudder.

'Helloooo Daniel. We've missed you. Where have you been?'

His tormentor, Abu Hurraya, stood in the doorway, handcuffs at the ready.

. * .

A piercing pain jolted Daniel's body. The handcuffs had been tightened so much that they cut into his skin, while the torturer led him to a water pipe that ran vertically between floors.

'Welcome back!' shouted Abu Hurraya.

Daniel's escape had been a total failure. He had been driven back to the building where he'd been detained. The biscuits and water had been only a fleeting pleasure. Ultimately, someone had called Abu Hurraya. Maybe they didn't dare take the risk of helping a foreigner. Perhaps the locals were also afraid of ending up like him.

Abu Hurraya's men put shackles around his left ankle and locked it to the pipe, while his upper body was fastened to the pipe with thick chains. A prison guard put a plastic fastener of the type electricians use to hold cables together around Daniel's neck and tightened it. The plastic strip pierced his skin in the same way as the handcuffs. He had difficulty breathing and soon passed out, so the guard took it off.

The following three days he spent chained to the pipe merged into a blur. He had reached a state of total exhaustion. Three weeks had now passed since he had been captured and he was starving, thirsty and urinating in his trousers. His body simply couldn't take it any more. The heavy chains forced him into an awkward, half-standing position. The kicks and blows that he regularly received to his ribs no longer hurt, but the handcuffs did. It felt as if the metal had cut through his skin and was now directly scraping against his open wounds.

The guards turned up in groups and egged each other on, shouting and screaming that he was going to die. They played games in which they kicked, beat and whipped Daniel across the chest until he finally confessed that he was a spy, which they so badly wanted to hear.

Daniel fainted. When he woke up, he thought he was at home with his grandmother at her yellow house in Hedegård. Then he lost consciousness again and dreamed that he was going to be killed by gunfire out in the cornfield.

At one point he stirred at the sound of chairs scraping around him and he could hear an unfamiliar, deeper, slightly older voice. Maybe this was who the others had been waiting for. Maybe now he was going to find out what real torture felt like.

The voice spoke Arabic with a different and lighter tone. The older man suddenly moved towards Daniel and loosened the chains, so he could sit. Daniel wept with joy. Tears streamed underneath the blindfold and down his cheeks as he slumped on the floor. It was confusing to think someone was being nice to him.

'Water,' asked Daniel.

The kind man filled a water bottle, which Daniel finished, then asked for more. Daniel was also given a couple of puffs on a cigarette – the other captors usually didn't smoke. He knew that the man was sharing his cigarette out of kindness, without his superiors' knowledge.

Daniel ate what seemed like life-saving biscuits until his mouth was dry and he had to drink more water. Then, lying on the floor, he drifted into a nightmare-free sleep. He awoke to a beating by Abu Hurraya. The friendly man had disappeared, leaving only the torturer in his stead.

Abu Hurraya ordered him to stand on one leg, but Daniel could not and collapsed on the floor. Then he had to lie on his back and stretch his legs backwards over his head and get up on his feet again. Abu Hurraya opened Daniel's trousers, pulled them down and pressed something that felt like a candle against Daniel's buttocks. Daniel was on the verge of fainting from fear. Abu Hurraya spoke Arabic and Daniel sensed that he was talking about his genitals while he squeezed one of his testicles very tightly.

Daniel screamed and the fear turned into rage. He wanted to kill him. It was the first time that he had ever wanted to kill someone.

'Daniel *jahass*!' shouted Abu Hurraya, using the Arabic word for donkey or mule, while he pulled Daniel's trousers up again and disappeared.

Daniel pissed himself and someone came to mop up the floor.

. * .

It was the middle of the day and the heat was rising from the asphalt. Daniel was led out of the building blindfolded and thrown into the back of a box van. Soon, more prisoners were piled into the van on top of him.

They all reeked of sweat and their weight pressed on to his hands, making his handcuffs dig even deeper into his raw flesh. He tried turning to spare his wrists, while the van bumped along, but it hurt so much that he decided he would rather be knocked about.

When the van stopped, he was led into a room with a toilet. A chain was hung around his neck and chest and he was locked to a sink. He enjoyed his solitude away from the busy foyer, where he had felt he was constantly being watched. In the following four days he drank foul-smelling but vital water from the toilet bowl. No water came out of the tap.

The pain from the handcuffs permeated his sleep. In his dreams he lived in a cycle of failed escape attempts. He ran into things, couldn't get up, fell down; people lied and laughed and wouldn't remove his handcuffs as they had promised.

He woke up in pain and shifted his position from right to left without finding relief.

It was around 10 June when a prison guard came to move him again. His next destination was to be the basement of the torture centre where some other western hostages were already being held captive.

The Hostages under the Children's Hospital

Daniel was standing in front of a mirror that hung on the wall in the toilet of his new prison. The handcuffs and the blindfold had finally been removed and he had been given some clean clothes. He was looking at himself for the first time since he had been kidnapped twenty-four days earlier.

The skin around his eyes was not just blue, thought Daniel, but black as the night. There were marks that hung like a chain of oblong, grey beads around his neck, testifying to his suicide attempt. He leaned over the sink towards the mirror and looked himself deep in the eyes. There was no life in them. His cheeks were white and sunken. It was like looking at a dead man. He realized that the water he'd been given in the last few days might have actually saved his life.

Because of the blindfold, he hadn't seen his hands since he had been caught in the cornfield and had smoked a cigarette in the banqueting hall with the boys in the Arsenal jerseys. They had swollen to twice their normal size, as if he were wearing ski gloves. When he went to wash the wounds on his wrists, he understood why the pain was so excruciating. Through a bracelet of reddish-brown gunk in the wound, he could see his bones and tendons. He tried to clean the wounds and washed the smears of blood and dirt off his body, which stank of stale sweat and fear. Then he put on the clean blue underpants and the camouflage uniform that the guards had given him.

Daniel was led into a large basement room. A heavy black metal door separated him from the corridor. The whitewashed walls of the cellar were made of concrete and the only sunlight that reached down into the room came through a small window in the toilet. Clinical white tiles covered the floor.

Daniel was able to walk freely around the room without a blindfold or handcuffs, and he had been given a blanket and a water bottle. He was fed a couple of times a day. He tried to get body and soul together again. He'd had ongoing gastrointestinal distress, which was made no better by the new, luxurious surroundings, even though he could now clip his nails and keep himself reasonably clean.

. * .

It was the torturer Abu Hurraya who had delivered Daniel to the basement of the building, which was known as the children's hospital in Aleppo.

The hospital had served as the unofficial prison of various rebel factions since the war had begun. The rebels were fighting among themselves for control of the area and there were periods when several factions shared the hospital buildings between them, so prisoners of Jabhat al-Nusra were in one wing, while ISIS prisoners were held in the other.

The prison was at that time under the daily leadership of the ISIS head of security in Aleppo, who went by the nom de guerre Abu Ubaidah al-Maghribi. The surname al-Maghribi indicated Moroccan ancestry, but he was by all accounts a citizen of the Netherlands. In a picture that was taken of him before he went to Syria, his almost feminine features are remarkable: a narrow face with a beauty mark on his left cheek and curved, full lips; round, dark, smiling eyes under bushy eyebrows; clean shaven with short hair, slim and tall.

Once in Syria, he had let his beard grow, but it was thin and barely covered his chin and cheeks. He never shouted and spoke in a friendly manner in several languages, including Dutch, French, English, German and Arabic.

According to several sources, Abu Ubaidah had studied computer engineering at the University of Amsterdam and now held a senior position in the ISIS organization. He had apparently married and had a child in Syria, all while holding prisoners in the basement of the children's hospital.

. * .

'Psssst, Daniel . . . Daniel . . .'

He woke up and looked straight at two western-looking men. One of them had short grey hair, while the other had longish, tousled brown hair.

They looked at him with concern in their eyes and introduced themselves as the French journalist Didier François and freelance photographer Edouard Elias. Didier was in his early fifties and an experienced correspondent, while Edouard was in his mid-twenties like Daniel. The Frenchmen already knew his name.

They had heard Daniel screaming while someone had been shouting his name.

'We could hear that they were treating you very badly,' Didier remarked. Didier and Edouard had been kidnapped only four days ago and had no visible bruises.

Daniel felt a paradoxical relief that he was no longer the only westerner. The presence of the Frenchmen could be his chance of survival, since the more foreigners there were the more focus there would be on finding them, he thought. And he had been longing for human contact with someone who spoke English.

'I was captured three weeks ago,' said Daniel and he told them briefly about what his torturers had done to him.

The sight of Didier and Edouard brought home to him again how dehydrated, emaciated and bruised he was. He had been reduced to a defenceless, dirty animal and he sensed that his wretched physical and mental condition was disheartening to the newcomers. The Frenchmen didn't say much, as if Daniel were the symbol of what could happen to them. He could well understand their reaction.

When Didier asked him for advice on how to stay active while they were locked up, the mood softened a little and Daniel showed them a couple of abdominal and back bends that they could do to keep their bodies in shape.

After a few days they were all moved to a small boiler room further down the corridor. Two cisterns filled most of the room, but they were allowed to take their blankets with them and they were fed at noon and 6 p.m. Daniel was struggling with the open wounds on both his wrists and with his violent diarrhoea, which he had to control somehow, because there was no toilet in the boiler room.

When the prison guards knocked on the door and shouted *hamam*, the prisoners got to their feet and put on their blindfolds. They grabbed a water bottle with one hand and held on to each other's shoulder to walk single file to the toilet. When they got there, Daniel hurried to use the toilet and fill his water bottle while the guards pounded aggressively on the door.

After only a few days in the cistern room, they were moved back to the large basement room. Daniel became increasingly ill and couldn't keep anything down. He was lying on the floor and could feel pain all over his body, when a prison guard came in.

'Do you think we can get a million dollars for you?' he asked.

Daniel momentarily forgot his discomfort. The question was the first indication that the kidnapping could be about money and that he wouldn't be sitting in this basement for ever. He remembered that his insurance would pay only five million kroner (about £530,000), but that was secondary right now.

'I don't know, but maybe,' was his response. Daniel had been given a glimmer of hope to cling to.

The three western prisoners were soon separated from each other. Edouard was to remain in the basement room, while Didier and Daniel were moved to a smaller cell. There were already a couple of Syrian prisoners in the small cell, and this one didn't even have a toilet.

For Daniel, the following days were a living hell.

He was terrified of what the guards might think of doing to him if they had to constantly take him to the toilet because of his diarrhoea. He didn't dare knock on the door and ask permission to go. Suddenly he noticed faeces leaking out through his trousers and down on to the blanket. He tried to act like it was nothing, but when one of the Syrian prisoners smelled Daniel's diarrhoea, he immediately hammered on the door and shouted to the guards that he didn't want to sit in that stench.

The guards hustled Daniel out to the toilet, where he was ordered to wash himself and put on a clean pair of trousers. Then they put a large, empty yoghurt container into the cell, which Daniel was supposed to use as a toilet. But the bucket wasn't deep enough and his faeces splattered out over the wall.

The other prisoners were irritated and so were the guards. When one of them, a short, fat man, discovered faeces on the wall, he went berserk and hit Daniel on the head and shoulders with a stick.

He then took Daniel to the bathroom, where he drew his pistol and pointed it threateningly at Daniel's face.

'You have to pull yourself together,' said Didier to Daniel afterwards, with reference to the fact that the smellier and the more frightened and submissive he became, the more he was reducing himself to an animal that the guards thought they had the right to beat.

He was so weakened by the beatings and the diarrhoea that he often fainted when he stood up and he didn't have the strength to eat. Didier hid flat bread for him under the blanket and asked for diarrhoea pills.

But it was the wounds on his wrists that most worried Daniel. He was terrified that they would become infected, that he would get gangrene and die. The bracelet of pus and fluid hardened, fell off, and became slimy again. He tried to protect his wrists from the hairy blanket he was lying on by placing a piece of fabric between it and his hands. When he finally dragged his body to the toilet, he held back from washing afterwards for fear of germs and just shook himself dry.

The fat little man often came to visit, sometimes with food and a young boy – whom he was clearly looking after and who could be heard shouting nonsense out in the corridor – and at other times just to amuse himself by humiliating Daniel.

'Make a noise like a dog!' shouted the fat man, who laughed loudly when Daniel barked.

'Make a noise like a donkey!'

Daniel didn't dare disobey.

'When I say "Daniel", you say "*jahass*",' came the order.

'Say it as if you are sad,' he continued and Daniel said '*jahass*' in fifteen different ways.

'As long as they don't beat me again,' he thought as he went through all the sounds of the animal kingdom.

He had become a dog himself, one that did what it was told, and lay down on his back with his legs over his head. He was afraid of shitting in his trousers in front of the little fat man.

There wasn't any peace at night, either. Daniel lay listening to prisoners being dragged out of other basement rooms and beaten. The screams and blows of the whip reached into the cell, where he counted them to shut out his anxiety. Counting helped. The victims howled and whimpered, sometimes for maybe fifteen minutes, other times for several hours. The torture made Daniel sleepless and paranoid.

On 20 June, after more than a month in captivity, a guard came to fetch him and told him to follow. Daniel crossed the hallway and was led into the guards' room. It was a long room with a television and a table at one end, where two guards were sitting. One of them was a burly man with a long beard, who stood ready with a camera on a tripod. The burly man told him to sit on a chair by the wall. Daniel was going to appear in a video.

'It's to your government,' he was informed.

Daniel sat in a camouflage jacket and tried to look at the camera, even though it was too far away for him to see it properly without his glasses.

'Pull your sleeves down over your wrists,' said the cameraman, adding, 'and hold them down between your knees.'

Following instructions, Daniel said who he was and that he wouldn't be released unless the Danish government paid a ransom. 'Please pay so I can come home,' begged Daniel, followed by greetings to his family: 'I'm well. I miss you. I love you, Mum and Dad. I love you, Signe.'

Then they turned off the camera.

'Thank you,' said Daniel, relieved that a video message would finally be sent to Denmark.

'You should thank yourself,' said the burly man, blindfolding him and taking him back to the cell.

. * .

More than a month had gone by since Daniel disappeared. It became a permanent part of Susanne's morning routine to follow the news about Syria and write in her diary.

She also developed habits she had never had previously. Every evening she said a prayer, asking God to take care of Daniel, no matter where he was or what he had done. In the bedroom she had placed two wrought-iron hearts containing strings of lights, which she lit every evening at dusk. She also began taking the time to chase flies out of the window to freedom instead of smashing them with a fly-swatter as she usually did.

Susanne and Kjeld were both spending a lot of time on the phone. In the space of a few weeks a previously unknown man had become the most important person in their lives. Arthur was their lifeline to Daniel and he called them frequently from Turkey with new information.

'Daniel has probably been brought before a sharia court in Aleppo,' he reported in a loud voice. 'It's being said that he has been accused of having brought pornographic images.'

Arthur explained that, within his network of informants, rumours had flourished at first that Daniel had been sentenced to death and that the sentence had already been executed. Shortly afterwards it was reported that he was alive and could escape sentencing if the family paid a sum for his offences. Arthur suggested that, with his help, Susanne and Kjeld should write a letter to the sharia court to influence the judges to release Daniel on payment of a fine. It was still unclear whether the information had come from influential sources in the hierarchy around Daniel, yet Arthur sent word to his network that he wanted to get proof that Daniel was still alive and to start negotiations. The hope was that this message would also confirm that Daniel had been detained in Aleppo as alleged.

An amount of approximately $700,000 had been mentioned by Abu Suheib, according to an intermediary. This was money that would have to be paid by Daniel's family, because Denmark doesn't pay ransoms to kidnappers. The political parties in parliament had rarely been more steadfastly in agreement than they were on this issue. They didn't want to incite terrorist organizations and other criminals to take more Danish hostages. Denmark thus belonged to the group of countries that was trying to curtail the hostage industry by slamming shut the cash box. The State didn't want to become involved in what the ministries behind closed doors had dubbed the 'Daniel affair', either by paying a ransom or any other costs associated with the search for him.

On the other hand, the Foreign Ministry was willing to play a liaison role and made rooms available for meetings between various actors in the case. It was also incumbent on the Ministry's Citizens Advice Bureau to provide information to Susanne and Kjeld, who, along with Anita, regularly attended meetings at the Ministry concerning Denmark's position on the case and the latest news about Daniel, although very often they had already received this information from Arthur.

There was no doubt that the network that had taken Daniel was just as ideological as it was money-grubbing. The hierarchy among the suspected kidnappers slowly became clearer to Arthur and it led straight to the top of the ISIS leadership. At the bottom of the hierarchy sat the Iraqi ISIS leader in Azaz, Abu Suheib, who was most likely the one behind Daniel's kidnapping in the first place. Further up was the head of the prison in Aleppo, the Dutchman Abu Ubaidah. Operationally, they shared the same boss, Abu Athir, who was the Emir of Aleppo and was at the top of the hierarchy as a member of the Shura Council under Baghdadi.

All lines of command led to Abu Athir and Arthur learned from his network that it was he who decided whether hostages should live, die or be brought before a sharia court.

The family couldn't take the risk of not trying to raise the $700,000 that might bring Daniel home. Kjeld contacted the family's banker and on 20 June Susanne overcame her misgivings. She and Kjeld signed for a loan of 3.7 million kroner, guaranteed by Daniel's insurance. Susanne dropped off the signed loan documents at their local bank branch before going to work at Legoland, where she earned $23 an hour.

She told herself that the staggering amount they had borrowed was just a number on a piece of paper.

. * .

No one ever saw the video in which Daniel appealed to the government to pay a ransom, because it was never sent to Denmark.

Daniel, who was unaware of this, survived on the slim hope that the appeal would help to get him out. In the meantime, he had been moved back into the large basement room, without Didier. The cell was now full of Syrian prisoners, who had placed their blankets as far from the toilet as possible. The atmosphere in the room was sultry and stagnant and the only fresh air that occasionally reached them came from the small toilet window.

Daniel lay between a thin man, Bashir, who was in his fifties, and his stout friend Mohammad, who had sixteen children; there were a lot of medicine bottles by his blanket, because he suffered from diabetes. They welcomed Daniel and let him eat more than them.

In the morning the Syrian prisoners got up early to pray, while Daniel usually slept until the first meal, around midday. He tried to establish daily routines to regain his strength. He felt weak when he tried to walk around in the cell, but reminded himself that if he got some exercise his body would begin to absorb nutrients rather than expel them. He counted eighteen steps back and forth across the cell floor.

Bashir smiled at him and told him in English about his son, who was at university, and his two wives, who were good friends, even though they shared a husband. The guards told Bashir that they had imprisoned that son and one of his wives. He cried every time he prayed, fearing the worst.

'They aren't real people. They are insane,' Bashir sobbed. He was convinced that he would never get out alive. 'I wish the revolution had never begun,' he said. 'The only ones still fighting are the bandits. The good people left long ago.'

The walking helped and, soon enough, Daniel was pacing back and forth on the floor for hours talking to himself. He played several voices at once, and he imagined that God was one of them.

Good morning, Daniel.

Good morning.

How are you?

I'm fine, thanks. I'm in a room where there is plenty of space and I get food twice a day. I can go to the toilet when I want to. My stomach feels better and I have a wonderful family and girlfriend.

What would you like to do when you get back home?

I would like to see my family and Signe first, of course. And then I would really like to find a permanent place to live in Copenhagen.

How would you furnish it?

I want to buy a printer, so I can print some photos. Then I could build some cushioned stools and a big, beautiful wooden desk. I would give my younger sister a rail pass for her birthday, so that she can come and visit whenever she wants. Signe could move in with me and then my family can come for Christmas.

What will you eat?

Well, I'd really like to learn how to cook duck. My mother could teach me her recipe.

When he felt pain in the back of his knees, he lay with his legs up the wall and observed the motley crew of prisoners, who were regularly being replaced with new people. Two Kurds had been captured and were accused of having shot some Islamists. One of them was small and lively, the other one thin and frightened and Daniel couldn't help but look at a strange hole in the base of his nose where mucus leaked out. *He reeks of beatings*, thought Daniel, who had learned first-hand how torture makes the body smell.

A hierarchy quickly formed among the prisoners, which made Daniel uneasy. They behaved like guards towards each other, where the strong ones made decisions and the weak ones were exploited. The smelly Kurd was treated like a slave and forced to massage the superiors and wash their plates. In general, Kurds were always at the bottom of the hierarchy, purely because they were Kurds. Daniel enjoyed a certain status, because he symbolized a ticket to the West and also because he had been imprisoned the longest. But the hierarchy could change in a flash. If a prison guard selected one of them as a scapegoat, the others kept their distance, so as not to be associated with him. Bashir was always at the top, though, because he had the greatest reserves of energy.

Occasionally, the internal pecking order would be replaced by a community of equal standing, like the time when a new prisoner was thrown into the cell. He was about eighteen to twenty years old. His body was black and blue; his clothes were torn to shreds and he couldn't walk or eat. Together they dragged the new man into the bathroom, where they washed him and his clothes. Survival sometimes depended on forgetting one's own suffering and helping others who were worse off.

. * .

In order to pay the $700,000 that Daniel's family had borrowed from the bank, they needed a proof of life, so as to be certain that those who were demanding the money really had Daniel – and that he was alive.

Arthur's local assistant, Majeed, was trying to get permission to see Daniel in the prison and to take a photograph of him. Majeed drove to Aleppo on numerous occasions, until one day he was finally allowed to meet the Dutchman Abu Ubaidah.

Abu Ubaidah was slight, calm and subdued. He listened more than he spoke and when he opened his mouth he chose his words carefully, which Majeed found unusual in such a setting. Abu Ubaidah didn't reveal whether or not he knew of Daniel, but told Majeed he would have to wait to talk to Abu Athir.

Majeed waited for two days. When Abu Athir finally showed up, his bodyguard, who wore a suicide vest, immediately took Majeed aside and said, 'How dare you approach the Emir of Aleppo!' The bodyguard dragged Majeed down into a basement,

THE ISIS HOSTAGE 113

where he was frisked before being allowed to speak to the emir.

'Have you come here to ask about an infidel?' asked Abu Athir suspiciously.

Majeed explained that he wanted to take a proof-of-life photograph of Daniel; Abu Athir consented.

On 30 June Majeed was driven to the prison under the children's hospital. When he arrived, he wrote down his name and the date on a piece of notebook paper, which he handed over to Abu Ubaidah. He wasn't going to be allowed to take the photograph himself.

. * .

A masked man wearing a tracksuit came into the cell. He held a camera and a piece of paper. He made Daniel stand against the wall and ordered him to hold the piece of paper in front of him, on which a name and date were written.

30/6/2013. Majeed.

There were a couple of clicks from the camera and the masked man disappeared just as quickly as he had come.

Daniel had no idea who Majeed was.

. * .

The proof-of-life photo of Daniel with Majeed's note was delivered to Arthur on a USB memory stick. It was the first tangible proof that the people they were dealing with had access to Daniel. It was now more than fifty days since Daniel had been kidnapped.

Arthur asked the crisis psychologist who had been allocated to

Daniel's family to drive to Hedegård and show them the photograph. Kjeld, Susanne, Christina, Anita and Anita's boyfriend were sitting around the table in the kitchen when the crisis psychologist placed it in front of them.

'He's alive,' thought Susanne when she saw the photograph of Daniel. 'He's alive, but his eyes are dark and tired.'

Christina began to cry and looked at the others' stony faces. As the tears ran down her face, it irritated her that she was the only one who was crying.

Daniel had become thin. His shoulders had almost disappeared and his chest was flat under the camouflage jacket, but the family reassured themselves with the thought that it was most likely Daniel's muscles that had shrunk. As Susanne wrote in her diary, 'Everyone knows that the muscles disappear quickly, and fortunately he is in really good shape.'

The psychologist emphasized Daniel's clean nails.

'It's a bad sign if he isn't able to keep himself clean,' she said. Susanne thought that Daniel looked frightened and tired, but the psychologist pointed to the whites of his eyes. It meant he was getting enough fluids.

It was also comforting to know that by sending the proof of life, the kidnappers apparently believed that Daniel was worth a lot of money and they weren't about to risk losing thousands of dollars.

No one mentioned the visible wounds on his right wrist and the scars discernible on his neck; at least, not out loud. Anita didn't talk about the wounds until she was sitting in the car with her boyfriend on the way home to Odense. That was when she realized for the first time how serious the situation was. Or, as

Susanne wrote in her diary that evening: 'If the seriousness of the situation hadn't been clear to us all before, it certainly hit us the moment we saw the photo.' She didn't write anything about Daniel's wrists.

. * .

Tomatoes. Onions. Cucumbers. Olives. Daniel greedily ate the vegetables that Bashir had earned for the cell. When he washed the metal plates in the bathroom after meals, the guards gave him extra food, which they all shared. Daniel's day consisted predominantly of his walks in the cell and long talks with Bashir. It was no longer Daniel who was beaten by the guards, but his fellow prisoners. He sat facing the wall and waited until the beatings of the Kurds and some of the others were over. He got nothing more than a few punches in the ribs or a slap around the head, and he got the feeling that the guards had been told not to beat him.

His body was beginning to recover and he was comforted by the fact that he had participated in one proof-of-life video and had had his photo taken. There was something happening around him that he only got confirmation of when a guard came into the cell one day and said, 'Daniel, you're on your way out.'

Almost every day something happened in the cell which made it difficult for Daniel to find peace, and his mood swung up and down. One day the door opened and the guard spoke in Arabic with Bashir and his friend. Afterwards, Bashir sank down on the rug, clearly affected by the conversation. Daniel went over and asked him what had happened.

'We have to make a video,' he began. Bashir talked about his possible death sentence. He and his friend would have to claim their allegiance to the Syrian regime in a video. They would have to say how they had helped in the bombing of civilians in Aleppo. The guard said that they would be killed if they didn't cooperate in the propaganda video, which was intended to show that the kidnappers had imprisoned some of the regime's supporters.

The video would lead to Bashir's certain death, whatever he did. If other rebel groups saw it, they would kill him for supporting the regime. If he refused to appear in it, he would be shot by his captors.

Before Bashir left the cell, Daniel asked him for a favour. If Bashir were released, he was to write to Christina and Signe and say that Daniel was fine. They exchanged email addresses and Daniel repeated Bashir's to himself over and over, so that he would remember it.

Bashir and his friend were taken away and Daniel never saw them again. He feared for them; he missed their company and felt lonely and far away from everything familiar. All his doubts resurfaced. Maybe he wasn't on his way home after all.

Instead, the prison guards started to worry about his wrist. A doctor rubbed iodine on it and bandaged it and while Daniel stood with his hands against the wall, they exposed one of his buttocks and gave him a shot of antibiotics. They were clearly interested in keeping their hostage alive, but how long would they hold him?

Daniel was trying to walk away his worries, eighteen steps back and forth, when he suddenly got an unexpected visitor from Denmark.

The heavy metal door opened and he was ordered to put on

his blindfold. He tied it as loosely around his head as possible.

'Come with me,' said the guard.

Daniel was made to stand against the wall in the corridor, where he could just make out the toes of four boots under the blindfold, standing right in front of him. Suddenly someone spoke Danish to him.

'Where do you live in Denmark?' asked a voice, which sounded young.

'I live in Copenhagen,' said Daniel.

'Do you have any brothers and sisters?' asked another voice that sounded just as young – from his accent, Daniel suspected the man had been born and raised in Copenhagen.

'Yes, I have an older sister and a younger sister.'

The Danes seemed to be carefree and in high spirits; they were chuckling and Daniel was irritated by the thought that they had come just to see the Danish zoo animal in the basement.

'Do you think we can get two million euros for you?' asked one.

'The Danish government doesn't negotiate,' said Daniel, and he told them that his father was a lorry driver and his mother a hairdresser. Two million euros was a massive sum for them.

'I really don't think you can get that much,' added Daniel.

'Is there any information you can give us about your family?' demanded the other one.

Daniel gave them the information that he could remember; telephone numbers for Susanne and Kjeld and email addresses for his sister and Signe. He tried to make sense of the fact that there were two Danish-speaking boys in an Islamist prison in Syria, quizzing a kidnapped compatriot.

'What about your elder sister?' asked one of them. 'How old is she?'

'Thirty-two.'

'OK, do you think we can get married to her?'

'You'll have to talk to my father about that,' said Daniel.

'She's blond, isn't she?'

The question sounded more like a statement and the two Danes disappeared.

Daniel had noticed several Europeans in the network that was holding him captive. Even though he had been kidnapped by Islamic extremists in the midst of a civil war in Syria, a number of those whom he saw wearing hoods spoke French and English – and even Danish. The torturers, the guards and the kidnappers were either a product of the Syrian regime, the Iraq War or of life in Europe. Several thousand Europeans, such as the Belgian Jejoen, had travelled without the slightest hindrance over the border from Turkey, and some ended up working for the same man who was making the final decisions about Daniel: Abu Athir, the Emir of Aleppo.

In other words, there was a four-lane motorway from the heart of Europe to the caliphate.

. * .

The background of the photograph of Abu Athir was bursting with bright-green fruit trees. The sun was shining and at the emir's side was one of his European disciples. It looked as if they were at an idyllic spot in the Syrian countryside as they stood next to each other, smiling for the camera. Abu Athir's black hair billowed and disappeared behind his shoulders. His face was wrapped in an abundant, thick beard, broken only by a wide smile that exposed a set of snow-white teeth with two pointed canines in his upper jaw. His tight-fitting, black wool hat made him look like a hipster and his eyebrows formed a slight unibrow over his wide nose. The day the picture was taken Abu Athir was wearing a beige tunic unbuttoned at the neck, with a grey shirt underneath and practical outdoor trousers from the Swedish brand Fjällräven. He was much taller than the Frenchman beside him. The Belgian combatant Jejoen, who had come to Syria to take part in the war under the emir's command, looked at the picture for a long time. He was fascinated by Abu Athir and there was general agreement among the Europeans that the emir was especially tough, but approachable.

You had to earn his trust, however, which is where Jejoen was having problems. Abu Athir was suspicious of him, because Jejoen's father Dimitri was travelling around Syria looking for his son, which meant that Jejoen's Syrian comrades suspected him of being a spy. They had found a message on Jejoen's mobile from his father, who had mentioned some Israeli contacts. At the risk of his own life, his father had visited one rebel leader after another, including the great emir Abu Athir, who briefly detained him.

No one understood how he was released alive, but the messages and his father's search raised suspicions about Jejoen, who was placed under house arrest in Abu Athir's prison in the basement of the children's hospital.

. * .

Daniel was trying desperately to get a message home to Hedegård. There was a new Syrian prisoner in the cell. He had been accused of having sex with his brother's wife, because he had been seen alone with her. The judge had looked mercifully on this transgression and the Syrian was to be released once he had received his punishment: a whipping.

Daniel tore a piece off a box of penicillin tablets and wrote a message to Signe and Christina with a pen borrowed from one of the other prisoners. He wrote that he was fine, was being fed every day and had access to a toilet. They shouldn't worry and he was sorry that he had put them in such a situation. Daniel gave the Syrian man their email addresses, so he could send the Danish message to them if he ever got the chance.

He folded the fragment of paper and the Syrian stuffed it in his back pocket.

'What about in your underpants or socks?' suggested Daniel. 'A less obvious place?'

A few days after the Syrian had been released, the guards moved Daniel to a new room further down the corridor. It was a boiler room directly opposite the toilet that prisoners used if their cell didn't have one.

It was around 17 July and Daniel had been imprisoned for two months.

. * .

Susanne and Kjeld's bank loan of 3.7 million kroner had been converted into US dollar bills by the Danish National Bank. They were now stacked and ready for payment with Arthur in Turkey, who, with cash in hand, was going to get Daniel back home.

But the communication with to the kidnappers had cooled. Despite intense pressure, Arthur couldn't get the practical details in place on how the money should be handed over. It seemed to him as if those responsible had lost interest in closing the matter, and his network wasn't having any luck in obtaining clear answers.

The reason was probably that the relationship had become strained between Abu Suheib, the Iraqi head of ISIS in Azaz, who had taken Daniel captive, and Abu Athir, the Emir of Aleppo. For Arthur, it was crucial that the person he was negotiating with also had the keys to Daniel's cell. He sensed that the Iraqi was interested in negotiating a release, while Abu Athir seemed to want to hang on to Daniel. And Abu Athir had the keys.

At the same time the war was raging in and around Aleppo, where Daniel was being held. The insurgent groups were fighting among themselves and against the Assad regime, which continued to bomb the populous city.

An increasing number of reports were coming in that poison gas was being used against the rebel-controlled areas. In Raqqa, a city north-east of Aleppo that the rebels had taken control of in March 2013, there were rumours that ISIS was winning more influence and had pushed out Jabhat al-Nusra and the other factions.

Susanne and Kjeld followed the news from Syria and feared for Daniel, sitting imprisoned in the midst of war. They watched powerlessly as the bombs fell on Aleppo.

. * .

Daniel was in the boiler room with seven Syrians. A couple of them were in their teens, while others were family men in their forties who didn't speak a word of English. However, there was one young man in his twenties with whom Daniel could communicate and play games. They scratched out a chequerboard on the concrete floor with a nail and used stones to represent the chequers. One player's chequers were large stones, the other's small ones. Daniel tried to disappear into the game and forget about the cords dangling from some pipes in the ceiling, and what they might be used for.

'Sometimes they torture in here,' his fellow prisoner told him. Daniel shuddered at the thought of sitting in the room where the torture took place. Occasionally he and the other prisoners were taken to the toilets across the corridor while someone screamed for fifteen minutes inside the boiler room. Daniel was paralysed by the screams, while his fellow prisoners took the opportunity to wash their clothes in the sink or go to the toilet.

Daniel didn't dare spend too long urinating. If the guards had worked themselves up after beating a prisoner, it could mean a beating for him if he wasn't finished in the toilet by the time they came back.

There was often noise in the corridor, because the toilet and wash basins lay directly opposite the boiler room and prisoners were constantly being led in and out. Daniel discovered a small hole in the boiler room's metal door and when he looked through it he felt the breeze that filtered through. His poor eyesight became noticeably better when he looked through the hole towards the door to the toilets. His eyes could suddenly focus like a camera through the small opening. He was soon using it as a way of passing the time, by keeping up with what was going on outside the room and seeing who walked by. And he knew he was unlikely to be discovered, since the guards would have to first unlock the door, giving him time to move away from it.

One day he heard voices speaking English in the corridor. From his vantage point, he could see that there was a group of prisoners in a queue for the toilet.

'WHAT'S YOUR NAME?' shouted a guard. The answer came loud and clear.

'MY NAME IS JAMES FOLEY.'

The guard repeated his question to three other prisoners, and Daniel heard them answer: John Cantlie, David Haines and Federico Motka.

He moved away from the door, dumbfounded. *How many of us are there?* he thought. He watched through the hole on a daily basis when there was noise in the toilets.

In particular, he was surprised that James Foley was in the basement. The last news he could remember about the missing American was that he had been imprisoned by the regime in Damascus.

It wasn't long before he spotted two men he also hadn't seen before. One of them was in desert boots, jeans and a white shirt. The other one wore a checked shirt and trousers, where the lower part can be zipped off. Daniel smiled when he saw that the man was wearing boat shoes. They had to be westerners too.

Daniel began counting. There were the two Frenchmen, Didier François and Edouard Elias, whom he had shared a cell with, but had not seen for a while. There were the four men who had been asked to say their names by the toilets: James Foley, John Cantlie, Federico Motka and David Haines. And then the two men in boat shoes and desert boots, whose names he didn't know. And then there was him.

I'm obviously not the only idiot, he thought, and suddenly became optimistic. The more of them there were, the more focus there had to be on their release. He wept with relief.

When he had been in the boiler room for five days he was led into the guard room, where Abu Ubaidah sat in jogging trousers at a table with a computer in front of him. Also on the table was the message that Daniel had tried to smuggle out with the Syrian prisoner.

'Why would you do such a thing?' Abu Ubaidah said quietly in English. 'We're treating you well, aren't we?'

Daniel explained that he hadn't told them where he was and offered to translate the letter from Danish to English.

'No. We've already had it translated,' was the reply.

A few days later he was taken into a dark room with a wooden door. Sitting there was the man in the white shirt and his partner with the boat shoes.

Pierre Torres and Nicolas Hénin introduced themselves and gave Daniel a proper hug as a welcome. Pierre had longish dark hair, a broad white face and a wide, open smile. 'Welcome to our room,' he said kindly, and Daniel felt overwhelmed by this warm reception.

The two Frenchmen had each been kidnapped separately in Raqqa more than a month ago, on 22 June. Pierre was a marine biologist, but had become a freelance journalist after the Arab Spring. The movement had awakened his activism and he had been in Egypt, Libya and Syria several times.

At the end of May he had gone to Raqqa, where he was living with a family. ISIS was gaining ground in the town, but not without resistance. There were daily demonstrations against Jabhat al-Nusra, whom people called the Islamists, but Pierre's experience was that most of the combatants had already switched their allegiance to ISIS. Raqqa was full of hooded Islamists, but also democracy-hungry activists rebelling against the Islamist hegemony, which they didn't want to replace the tyrannical regime. Pierre was fascinated by these ideological clashes.

The day he was kidnapped he had had an upset stomach, but was nevertheless walking to the city centre to witness another demonstration against the Islamists. A few blocks from the governor's building a small car drew up beside him. The men wore hoods, which didn't concern Pierre very much because most of the fighters did. However, when they pointed their weapons at him, he was afraid that they belonged to one of the regime-backed militias. He resisted and tried to escape, but each time he pulled away they slammed his head on the roof of the car. Eventually he was thrown into the back seat with blood dripping from his forehead and driven to a house outside the city, south-east of Raqqa. There he met Nicolas Hénin, who had been taken the same day.

After two weeks they were moved south to the children's hospital in Aleppo, where Daniel was the first westerner they had met, although they were aware that there were others.

They had communicated through a hole in the wall with Didier and Edouard, who were sitting in the next cell. They also knew that the aid workers David and Federico were there.

Daniel immediately took to Pierre, who, as a marine biologist, could give him advice about nutrition and bacteria.

'You're far too thin,' he said to Daniel, who looked like a scarecrow. Daniel's eyes stared out from deep, dark holes and Pierre felt he could see all the way into Daniel's brain.

'What happened to your wrist?' asked Pierre, and Daniel felt the urge to cry over someone wanting to hear his story.

The ceiling fan made such a noise that they couldn't hear what was going on in the corridor. It was hard to tell if it was day or night, because the only light came from a naked light bulb. Unlike Daniel, Pierre and Nicolas spoke to the guards quite a lot. The Frenchmen hadn't been exposed to as much violence as Daniel and therefore dared to express their needs. For example, they asked the guard (whom they called 'Abu Gold Watch' between themselves, because of his big gold watch) if they could have toothbrushes. Even though the answer was no, Daniel was surprised that they had asked. Most of the time, he tried to make himself invisible to the guards, who nevertheless singled him out by asking him to perform such actions as banging himself on the head with a shoe a hundred times.

Pierre advised Daniel not to play along with the guards' humiliations.

'You have to be more boring and pretend you don't understand anything.'

'I can't just start ignoring them from one day to the next,' said Daniel.

He realized that Pierre was trying to make him stronger and thus less subject to the whims of the guards. One day, when he wanted to teach Pierre the proper technique to do a push-up and couldn't even lift his body off the floor, he knew he had to regain his strength to survive.

He started training. Before lunch he strengthened his torso and before dinner he exercised his legs. Pierre took part in the exercises and at night they lay side by side on their blankets and talked.

Their daily training was interrupted briefly by a guard who wanted to photograph Daniel.

'Could you two exchange clothing for a moment?' asked the guard, pointing at Daniel's military clothing and Pierre's white shirt, wand can you do something about your hair?'

Daniel pulled Pierre's shirt over his head. It was too big for his narrow shoulders, but looked nicer than the military jacket, which gave the impression he was a combatant.

He was taken out to the corridor and had his photograph taken. There were no questions and no label, so he was unsure whether the photo would be used as proof of life. Nevertheless, he tried to send a message home – a smile. He hoped that the smile would reassure his family in Hedegård if they ever got to see the photograph.

Daniel and Pierre had just managed to work out an exercise routine when they were moved to a larger cell under the children's hospital, where there were four more western hostages: Didier and Edouard, and David and Federico. There were now a total of seven westerners in the same cell. It was the first time that Daniel had met the two aid workers.

David was British, while Federico was Italian. They had come to Syria together as aid workers to find suitable places to establish refugee camps for the rapidly growing number of internally displaced refugees. In the spring of 2013 they had been attacked by masked men on a road in northern Syria and they hadn't stood a chance.

David was thin and had such a full beard that he reminded Daniel of a caveman. Federico was young and taciturn. They told him that they were receiving much better treatment than they had before. Neither of them went into further detail about what had happened to them.

Finally, after more than two months in captivity, Daniel no longer stuck out as the blond westerner among the Syrian prisoners; at last he had some people to talk to who understood him. Together they could try to make the best of the terrible situation they were in. But after a few days, Daniel saw that any solidarity had been replaced by an internal hierarchy, just as it had been when he sat in the cell with the Syrian prisoners. In the cell, the seven hostages arranged their sleeping areas along the walls. Daniel was given a place closest to the door and right by the buckets where they shat. He knew he belonged to the lower half of the hierarchy, otherwise he wouldn't be forced to sleep by the toilet buckets, which was regarded as an almost radioactive area in the cell. Moreover, it was unpleasant to be close to the door and the unpredictable guards who barged in several times a day. At least Pierre lay next to him, which made Daniel feel safe.

The ranking was also defined with the help of the kidnappers. The guards ordered the cell to appoint an 'emir', who would speak on behalf of everybody. The title went to the Frenchman Didier, because he was the oldest among them. One of his tasks was to decide what the prisoners should try to get the prison guards to deliver.

'We should ask for more food,' suggested someone.

'No, what about soap? We must show that we care about our hygiene,' said another.

'Toothbrushes!' shouted a third.

Daniel said that he didn't need anything.

'I'm just happy not to be hanging from the ceiling,' he remarked. 'For me, it's important to regain my strength and get some exercise.'

The heat in the room was oppressive. Even though there was a fan, the air felt so still that some of Daniel's co-prisoners complained that it would be dangerous for them all if he began exercising and sweating too much in such an enclosed space.

He disagreed, but worked out a plan. When the morning sun hit the fan, it cast an orange beam of light on the wall just above him. Then he got up and did strength and balance exercises on his blanket, while watching the beam move from the wall above him and down across the floor. When it hit Nicolas's feet, Daniel would have to finish his gymnastics, because the others would begin waking up. The complaining stopped.

Outside the cell, there was more and more fighting. They could hear the deafening sound of bombs and firing near the children's hospital. The war was moving closer, but Daniel didn't care. He devoted all his energy thinking about mealtimes, when he would suddenly see sides of himself he didn't much like.

They were given too little to eat and he felt a constant gnawing hunger that was driving him mad. If the guards forgot to come with food, his whole body filled with anxiety. Lately, some French-speaking fighters had been in charge of taking care of the prisoners and they had not been generous types. They sometimes withheld meals, so Daniel ate like a dog, hoarding and grabbing things from the other rations when the food was finally brought in. Heated arguments arose about who was stealing food from whom, and Daniel invented a technique whereby he swallowed the food almost instantly to hide how much he was eating, and defended himself by saying that he was too thin. He greedily licked his metal plate for the smallest crumb, while others became surly, withdrawing from the disagreements and refusing to eat. Several of them pointed to Daniel as the villain.

The only peace around mealtimes came when seven chunks of bread and seven boiled eggs were handed out.

The prisoners in the cell had been given a pen to share and rules were soon agreed as to when it might be used and for what. Daniel was given permission to use it to design a chess game, which he sat in a corner to make. He broke small pieces off the penicillin package that he had brought with him from cell to cell. He used the pen to draw the king, queen and pawns, but when he wanted fill in the black pieces, some argued that it was an unnecessary waste of ink.

The chess set was his new pastime and at night Daniel and Pierre lay close to each other on their blankets and played, while having whispering conversations about their lives and families.

Pierre spoke about his elderly Spanish father, who had lived through the Spanish Civil War. His parents' house was an hour's train journey from Paris in an abandoned factory that had been Pierre's childhood home, surrounded by fruit trees and the roar of the river that flowed past at the end of the garden. Pierre had left home several years earlier, but Tonton the donkey still lived in the garden, and Olaf the dog also ran around among the free-range geese that often peeked into the living room through the garden door.

Daniel didn't know what he would do if Pierre disappeared. Their talks kept the fear and the madness at bay.

. ✻ .

On 4 August Kjeld was sitting in his lorry when he received an email from Arthur with an image file attached. He waited until he went home to Susanne before downloading the file.

Arthur had written in the email that it was a new photo of Daniel. Kjeld and Susanne agreed that this time they didn't need the crisis psychologist to be present. They felt able to see the image alone and besides they wanted to save on the cost of the psychologist, who would surely be needed when Daniel came home.

When the photograph appeared on the computer screen in their study, they went completely quiet. A wild man in a white shirt was staring directly at them through round, sunken eyes. He had a beard and hair that stuck out all around his head.

Susanne and Kjeld wept, while staring at the picture. Their son looked so abject, as Susanne described it, and he had some ugly marks around his neck. They could no longer be ignored; the marks were even clearer than in the first picture they had received.

'Do you think they've tried to strangle him?' asked Suzanne. Kjeld didn't dare answer.

It was only when they had been looking at the photo for quite a while that they noticed the smile. Daniel was trying to send a message that he would be all right, thought Susanne.

When Daniel's elder sister Anita saw the photo, she thought he looked exactly like their father when he had been ill with cancer, with his prominent cheekbones and hollow eyes. She said that the marks around his neck could be a fungal growth, which you could get if you were malnourished.

'I'll take that her word for it,' Susanne wrote in her diary. There was so incredibly little for the family to hold on to.

Two photos in more than two months, when they had neither heard Daniel's voice nor had any idea what was going to happen to him. At the same time there was the forced silence. Daniel's disappearance was a secret outside the family's inner circle.

Susanne had told only three trusted colleagues at Legoland, otherwise she couldn't stand talking about it. It was hard enough already. While visitors rode the carousels at the theme park, she stood in the staffroom and received calls from Arthur and the authorities, who had questions or new reports about her kidnapped son. Sometimes she wept; other times she felt hopeful.

'Tell lies which are as close to reality as possible,' Arthur had advised them when Kjeld and Susanne recounted how they were getting lost in the web of lies they told to everyone else about Daniel's whereabouts.

They had cancelled going to a party, because they couldn't handle lying to their friends. They excused themselves by saying they had the flu. When the host asked them some weeks later about their illness, they had no idea for a moment what she was talking about. Kjeld and Susanne were living a double life.

. * .

On the same day as they received the photograph of Daniel in Hedegård, he and the other six prisoners were joined in their cell by another hostage.

'We have a friend for you,' announced a guard.

The American journalist Steven Sotloff lay down in the only place there was room – the middle of the floor. He said that he had been captured shortly after crossing the border from Turkey and that the many checkpoints on the roads in the area were no longer controlled by the original Syrian rebels. Now ISIS fighters were standing there.

There were now eight westerners in the same cell. Somewhere else in the basement under the children's hospital were James Foley and John Cantlie. Daniel had seen them, but would not meet them until several days later. It finally happened when the prisoners were going to the toilet.

As always, they were ordered to go in single file down the corridor, blindfolded. Daniel never knew if anyone was standing there ready to give him a slap. They didn't take their blindfolds off until the door to the toilets was closed and locked behind them.

James was standing between two sinks and first greeted Federico and David, whom he knew already, after which he presented himself to Daniel, who kept a little in the background.

'Hi, I'm Daniel,' he replied.

'We've heard a lot about you,' said John, and James smiled broadly. James had a bit of an underbite and a beard on his chin. During his imprisonment, he had converted to Islam and wore a long tunic. Daniel couldn't take his eyes off James, who was finishing at the sink. A grown man, thought Daniel, who washed himself calmly as if he were standing in his bathroom in the United States.

'See you,' James said to the group, before a guard led him away.

When the other hostages returned to their cell, they talked a little about James and John.

'They look much better than they did when we were in the Box,' David remarked and Federico nodded in agreement. The Box was the nickname for the prison the two of them had previously been in with James and John, near the city of Atme in Idlib province.

While there, they had been under the control of three British guards. David and Federico were reluctant to talk about what these three men had subjected them to.

James and John were in a cell at the end of the corridor with a German and, for a few weeks, a fourth fellow prisoner. He wasn't exactly a hostage in the same way as them. He had privileges. The Belgian fighter Jejoen was under house arrest, part of the time in the same room as the three westerners, but every now and then Abu Athir gave him permission to move freely around the building.

The others in the cell were also treated well. They were given copied pages from books about Islam and a French guard, Abu Mohammad, gave James permission to take a bath, which was unusual. Abu Mohammad would also sit in the cell occasionally and talk to them. An Iraqi guard, Abu Mariyam, bought cakes for them in the market and Jejoen joked around with James and John.

Jejoen had a good relationship with the Dutch prison warden, Abu Ubaidah, so sometimes he went into the kitchen and cooked, while also watching Abu Hurraya beating prisoners in the office or blasting them with the stun gun.

Jejoen noticed the piles of clothes that had piled up under the stairs to the ground floor. He was convinced they belonged to executed prisoners, because he had seen some prisoners being led away one day and the next day he recognized one of their shirts in the bundle.

His trip to Syria was far from being the adventure he had

dreamed of. All he wanted was to go back to Belgium and to his father, who was still looking for him.

. * .

In the second half of August 2013 Arthur's assistant Majeed met Emir Abu Athir and the prison leader Abu Ubaidah in a building close to the children's hospital in Aleppo. He had bought a small camera in Turkey, so that he could record a video of Daniel.

It seemed that Majeed had won over their confidence a bit, because they told him that Daniel had tried to commit suicide by hanging himself from a chain to which he had been shackled to the ceiling. The guards had heard a loud noise from inside the room, hurried in and found Daniel dangling from the ceiling. They had arrived just in time to save him. But Majeed was also lied to.

'Daniel has converted,' said Abu Ubaidah in his quiet voice. 'He is now called Abu Aisha.'

'As he is now a Muslim, let us get him home to his family,' said Majeed, but Abu Athir rejected this.

'His conversion is a lie built on fear,' said Abu Athir, who was still convinced that Daniel was working for the intelligence services and the army. 'There are several prisoners here who have converted, because they think it can get them out.'

'He's very athletic. He does gymnastics in the cell,' explained Abu Athir.

Abu Ubaidah was more reserved with information and never spoke badly of Daniel.

'Your friend is very smart,' said Abu Ubaidah. 'He always knows what to say.'

Majeed didn't know what he was supposed to make of that.

Majeed's visit to the children's hospital took place under high security. They tied a scarf around his face and drove around the streets for about an hour to confuse him, before he was led up and down the stairs. He sensed that he was in a basement when he heard a voice over a walkie-talkie: 'Is there anyone who can come over to the hospital?'

They went down a long corridor and turned into a room where the air was heavy and stuffy. Someone made a small opening in the scarf, so Majeed could peer out.

'Can you see him?' he was asked.

Majeed saw a thin, fair-haired man with tired eyes in a sunken face.

'Yes,' said Majeed, and his eyes were covered over again while he was dragged back along the corridor, where he waited for them to record a video of Daniel. He wasn't allowed to have the camera back, because the guards feared that it had a built-in GPS, so instead he was given a USB memory stick, which contained the video.

When Arthur heard that Daniel had tried to commit suicide, it put him in a tight spot. He usually shared most of his information with the family, but in this case he hesitated. The information could be an attempt to push the price for Daniel higher. It could also be a lie. But since there were no longer any real negotiations going on for Daniel's release, Arthur, in consultation with the crisis psychologist, chose to conceal Daniel's attempted suicide from the family; it was unconfirmed information and wouldn't benefit them in any way at that point in time. He saw it as part of his job to protect them from any information they didn't need to know.

. * .

Daniel stood against the wall in the guards' kitchen, while a guard filmed him. He was told to repeat precisely: 'My mum's name is Susanne. My dad's name is Kjeld. My girlfriend's name is Signe. It's the twenty-first of August and the guy who helped me is Majeed.'

A few days later the guards brought good news to the four Frenchmen. The French government would negotiate for their release, said the guards, but the opposite was true of the Danish government.

'If they won't negotiate, you'll be sent home in a body bag,' was their message to Daniel.

Pierre and the other Frenchmen were exhilarated and their mood changed, as if they were already on their way home. The hostages believed that real negotiations were taking place; that the kidnappers had contacted the authorities.

Daniel was frightened and confused. Had the insurance company refused to pay out? Did his parents not realize the policy existed? He lay next to Pierre, took his hand and wept at the thought that the Frenchmen were going home to their families, while he would be left alone in the cell with David, Steven and Federico.

Outside, the fighting had become more intense and they were getting even less food. Pierre understood the seriousness of the situation and held Daniel's hand for hours, while they lay staring up at the ceiling.

'If I am released, I will make contact with your parents, the Foreign Ministry and the insurance company,' promised Pierre.

Daniel squeezed his hand, but couldn't fall asleep.

Some days later, one evening towards the end of August,

everyone in the cell was told to stand up against the wall, after which they were handcuffed and blindfolded. The only thing in Daniel's mind was not to be separated from Pierre and the other Frenchmen. Being French meant hope. Being Danish could be a death sentence.

Daniel and James

Early in the morning of 23 August another email arrived in Kjeld's inbox. He was already on his way to work, but pulled his red truck over to the side of the road to read it. There was a video attachment. He called Susanne and they agreed that they would watch the video, which was probably of Daniel, when they were home from work.

In the evening the family downloaded the file and Daniel appeared on screen, wearing a camouflage jacket. He stood up against a blue wall and said: 'My mum's name is Susanne. My dad's name is Kjeld. My girlfriend's name is Signe. It's the twenty-first of August and the guy who helped me is Majeed.'

Daniel was staring into the lens. His round eyes glowed orange in the light from the camera. In the background could be heard the sound of cicadas. When he had to name the man who was helping him, he looked down at a spot under the camera, as if he couldn't remember the name, and then said 'Majeed'.

The video lasted only fifteen seconds, so they played it several times, looking for various signs of torture, starvation and lack of hygiene. Susanne felt relieved to finally hear her son's voice. He seemed composed on the video, but at the same time the situation was so scary that it felt surreal.

Christina felt that no one dared to talk about the fears they all shared. In Hedegård they didn't talk much about their feelings, given the difficulty of articulating what they all feared – the unspeakable situation that was permeating their everyday lives. Would Daniel die? Would he ever come home?

Daniel still looked thin – and then there were those frightening marks on his neck. He was no longer the Daniel they knew. He was a hostage, who had been told what to say and how to say it. They couldn't decipher his facial expressions, which were almost non-existent.

The video was saved on the family computer and Christina sometimes watched it when she was home alone; so did Kjeld and Susanne, but none of them spoke about it.

The worst part was that the nightmare had only just begun. The negotiations had gone cold and it could take a long time to get Daniel back.

The video was the latest sign of life and it was also the most recent indirect contact with the kidnappers, but no demand or proposal came with it. No one showed any interest in coming to a definitive agreement, so the video was just a message to reassure the family that Daniel was alive. It had nothing to do with getting him released.

Arthur had begun to doubt whether Majeed still had access to the hospital and Daniel's kidnappers. He advised the family to find new ways to establish contact. He helped them formulate a letter to Abu Athir, the Emir of Aleppo, in the hope that the family would be able to build a relationship with him that could bring Daniel home.

'Dear A. A.,' began the letter. 'We very much hope that your health has improved and we wish you a continued speedy recovery.' They were referring to Abu Athir's leg, which, so they had been informed, had been injured by shrapnel.

> We understand that Daniel violated your regulations while carrying out his work. We are very sorry about that and we offer our deepest apologies for his wrongdoings. We in his family are very unhappy and afraid about his situation. Two of Daniel's grandparents are still alive; they are both elderly and very sad and worried about what has happened to their grandson. It is very hard for both of them and we are very concerned that they may die of sorrow. Daniel is our only son, the one whose role is to maintain the continuity of the family. He is a good son and a loving brother to his two sisters, who are inconsolable. He is the kind of son who looks after and takes responsibility for the family. We beg you sincerely and with all our hearts to let Daniel come home.

The letter, which was translated into Arabic and signed by the whole family, ended with yet another apology for Daniel's actions.

. * .

In northern and eastern Syria a storm was brewing. ISIS had been officially formed five months earlier and the organization's fighters were advancing rapidly. They were expanding into cities and villages that the other Syrian rebel groups had recently seized from the Assad regime. As the *Washington Post* reported on 12 August 2013, ISIS was 'carving out the kind of sanctuaries that the US military spent more than a decade fighting to prevent in Iraq and Afghanistan'.

At the same time Baghdadi's ISIS faction had as good as seized power in Raqqa in an internal struggle with Jabhat al-Nusra. ISIS fighters kidnapped civilians and rebels who opposed the strictness of their order, including the local commander, who had led the fight against the government forces in Raqqa in March 2013. Many fighters from Jabhat al-Nusra had switched over to ISIS, which was also growing thanks to foreign fighters from throughout the Middle East and western countries. In the city of Adana, not far from Aleppo, they shot demonstrators and cut the throat of the local leader of the Free Syrian Army, which consisted of more moderate rebels.

The Syrian rebels were no longer fighting only the Syrian military and the regime's militias. They were also fighting ISIS and were therefore under pressure from two fronts, a situation which strengthened President Assad. The Syrian regime continued its bombardment of areas controlled by moderate rebel groups, while there was rarely an attack on ISIS in Raqqa.

ISIS's struggle was also about winning hearts and minds. But in many areas where ISIS fighters were surging forwards, the locals didn't care for their brutal methods. Even so, it was difficult to rebel against such an organized force. ISIS didn't tolerate any criticism and they shot anyone who contradicted them. In a video posted on YouTube in August 2013 it still looked as if they were trying to win the trust of the locals; it showed a religious holiday and ISIS fighters were handing out toys like

Teletubbies and stuffed animals. ISIS was also strengthened by the fact that a number of former military officers and Ba'ath Party members from Iraq were leading the group; they had experience in organizing fighters and disciplining populations. ISIS had emerged directly out of the political situation in Iraq left by the American invasion in 2003.

The organization deliberately used the Internet as an effective tool for spreading its message. ISIS was circulating slick propaganda and recruitment videos, produced with modern camera equipment and skilful graphics and editing techniques.

In one of the videos, none other than Abu Athir appeared, undisguised, along with the Chechen military leader born in Georgia who used the name Omar al-Shishani. The half-hour long video began with a caption showing the 'military operations room for the attack', after which Abu Athir discussed the strategy for a number of operations intended to pave the way southwards towards the towns of Hama and Homs. The shadow of his thick, curly hair moved in the light of a Google map projected on to a white wall, while a soldier zoomed the image in and out as Abu Athir reviewed the military situation around some of the villages. Sitting in a camouflage shirt, he pointed to a yellow pin that was labelled 'depot'.

'Here is the Air Force base,' he said, referring to the base held by the regime's military forces. 'If we take that, we open up the whole area,' he continued, pointing to some villages inhabited by loyal citizens from the president's own Alawite sect and guarded by regime soldiers.

'In each village, there are perhaps only one or two tanks, so, God willing, it won't be difficult. It will take them at least a day to assemble their troops if they want to send reinforcements. So the first day will be easy. The problem will come on the second day, but we are getting everything ready and giving our brothers mines and whatever else is available.'

His black hair looked purple in the light of the projector as he went on to talk about their arsenal.

'We have what we need. Don't say: Why haven't you given us this or brought us that? Put your trust in God. We haven't been able to procure more than that and the rest is up to God. As I always say to my brother: If you have just a single cartridge, kill someone with it; don't let it cause you to lose heart. If God wishes it, one bullet will protect you, I swear. We once resisted a full army, which had tanks and rocket launchers and all kinds of things, with just three Russian cartridges. It isn't a matter of having anti-tank missiles; it's a matter of faith and putting your trust in God and nothing else. I swear, three rounds,' concluded Abu Athir.

Not only the emir but also a group of young jihadists showed their uncovered faces on the video, which was intended to demonstrate how advanced the organization considered its operations to be. It was probably also the reason why the video was removed from the Internet after a short time.

ISIS's growing strength should be seen in the light of the fact that the Syrians who lived in the newly ISIS-controlled areas had already been traumatized by the war and the state of emergency. They dared not oppose the new rulers, nor were they in a position to rebel against them. For these Syrians it was about surviving the bombs that were being dropped on them and making do with the limited food available.

ISIS was taking root in a state of chaos, while Syria's infrastructure was being bombed to pieces. The organization sought to establish its dream – the Islamic Caliphate – on the ruins of Syria.

. * .

It was after dark when the eight hostages were to be moved from the basement under the children's hospital. Daniel stood handcuffed and blindfolded. His bare feet protruded beyond the size 34 turquoise sandals he had been given.

They were escorted out to two cars. Daniel heard Pierre's voice and was relieved that he was in the same car. After about half an hour the car stopped and their handcuffs and blindfolds were removed. They were thrown on to a chilly concrete floor in a dark kitchen and given a sandwich.

They were not offered any blankets and Daniel was freezing cold during the night. He was annoyed with himself for forgetting to bring the socks he had snatched one day during a toilet visit. There were sometimes discarded clothes out in the toilet, which the prisoners stole and took back to their cells. Despite the cold and the hard floor, he finally fell asleep with his head lying on one of Pierre's desert boots. The next morning the prisoners were woken up, blindfolded again and herded down a concrete staircase, while tied together in a long line. Daniel was afraid of falling, because those at the front of the human chain were dragging him down. He felt the gravel under his heels, which were sticking out of his sandals, as he carefully put one foot in front of the other, until they were led into a room with two oblong basement windows and a tiled floor.

At the time the prisoners weren't aware that they had been

brought to the industrial district of Sheikh Najjar, a couple of miles beyond the north-east suburbs of Aleppo. Before the war the area had housed hundreds of factories and businesses, producing things like medicine and cement for the construction industry. But the fighting between rebel factions and the regime had laid waste to the area and forced most of the businesses to shut down. In some areas Sheikh Najjar had become a spectral neighbourhood.

They were given water bottles and two blankets to be shared between eight prisoners. They also requested the most important thing: a bucket they could use if the guards forgot to let them go to the toilet.

When the blankets were distributed, a debate about lice arose. In the cell under the children's hospital Daniel had discovered some lice and lice eggs along the edge of his blue underpants and this had caused panic among the prisoners.

They asked him to check if he still had body lice. He found the small black insects and white eggs in his clothes, and when Pierre inspected his own clothing he discovered a large colony as well. The rest of the group refused to have lice near them, so Daniel and Pierre were sent to a space at one end of the cell, because there was an unwritten rule among the prisoners that the spread of diseases and pests should be avoided. If he tried to move into the 'lice-free' end, Daniel would immediately be asked to go back to his area. He protested loudly that they were treating him as if he was dirty and should be expelled from the group.

'Check your own clothes,' he said. 'It just can't be true that you don't have lice. If Pierre has them, then it's likely the rest of you have them too.'

It turned out they all had body lice, except for the newcomer, Steven, who lay without a blanket in the middle of the hard tile floor to keep as far away as possible from the others. Daniel was relieved that they were all infested. Lice had suddenly become common property – and they were also the world's greatest pastime. Daniel and Pierre sat beside each other for hours squashing the small insects and debating whether it was enough to squeeze them flat or whether they should have their heads ripped off. Pierre was good at finding them with his long nails; every day they counted how many they had found and compared their size and colour.

They also talked about what might be happening outside the basement room. They could hear that someone was sawing, hammering and drilling, and by peeping out through the keyhole, they could see that a group of workmen was busy building something. They couldn't see what it was, but it was clear that the guards didn't want the workmen discovering the eight hostages in the cell. Toilet times were limited to early morning and late evening, when the workmen weren't there. The guards also impressed on the prisoners that they should be quiet inside the cell during the day.

After almost a week, the guards elected to move the hostages upstairs to a room the prisoners began calling the Cigar Box. It measured just 6 feet by 13 feet, and the eight hostages had to lie in a row across the room, even though they were still sharing just two blankets.

'If you look at us, you will be executed,' said one guard firmly before closing the door.

The air didn't circulate in that claustrophobic room, which had only a small window overlooking a wall, and the prisoners were so closely clumped together that they all knew everything about everyone else.

When Daniel and David were whispering about opening a kind of stress centre together, in a country house with lakes, trees and animals, one of the others interrupted them.

'Shut up, you two. What a stupid idea. What do you think you can do with your skills?'

'Stay out of our conversation,' said Daniel, who felt he was about to explode. After all, he didn't grumble when the others talked about their travels around the world.

And when Nicolas later got up and pulled himself up into the cell's small window to look out, some of the others dragged him down roughly.

'Don't fucking do that again! You constitute a security risk,' said Federico, reminding Nicolas that they had been given strict orders not to look at the guards. There could have been a guard standing there, staring at the window.

Frustrations grew in the unbearable heat of the Cigar Box, where they were all hungry and mentally exhausted. They were often given only a biscuit or a plate with a thin layer of hummus for sharing and the guards drained them psychologically with false promises. They called on the hostages to choose two or three among them to talk to a doctor from the Red Cross as part of a possible negotiation, but nothing happened. They realized it was a false hope that the guards had planted in their minds so that they wouldn't try to escape.

As a defence against the tension, hunger and mental games, Daniel passed the time by playing the tour guide. The idea was that the hostages would visit each other for a few days when they were released. They would each tell the others about what they could offer in the way of experiences.

'After you land at the airport in Billund, we'll drive to my parents' summer house, where there are exactly eight beds,' began Daniel. 'My mother, Susanne, will come and prepare meatballs, gravy and potatoes. Then we'll go to my old boarding school and bounce on the trampoline and go canoeing on the lake and make a camp fire.' They would grill and drink beer and Daniel's cousin would serve her special chocolate layer cake.

'We'll also go to Legoland, where my mother works,' said Daniel.

Pierre played along and told them that it would be best to visit him in the autumn.

'This is my favourite time of the year, because then there are apples on our apple trees,' he said. They would pick apples and make cider and cakes, which they would enjoy in the garden.

The game eased the atmosphere, as did the industrial fan the guards put into the cell. It made so much noise that some of them got migraines, but under the cover of the noise, the prisoners could talk together in pairs without everyone being able to listen in on the conversation.

Someone knocked hard on the door – harder and faster than usual.

'Hands on the wall!' shouted a man with a British accent.

Daniel noted that he had a much firmer tone than the French guards who were the most frequent visitors. He found it both frightening and dangerous, because the man spoke fluent English and he understood every word.

The prisoners weren't allowed to turn around towards the

British man, who demanded answers on how often they were given food and if they were allowed to use the toilet.

'We don't get much food,' said one of the prisoners.

'You should be happy with what you get,' said the Brit, adding on the way out that they would soon be under his custody.

When the door closed, the hostages turned and faced each other. Federico and David were deathly pale and their hands were shaking. They recognized the voice and the British accent.

'There were three Brits when we were in the Box,' they explained, referring to the place where they had been held before Daniel met them.

'What did they do to you?' someone asked.

Silence fell in the Cigar Box. They didn't want to go into detail and Daniel imagined that the Brit had been their torturer, their Abu Hurraya.

'It will be a completely different daily routine if we are put under the control of the British,' said David and Federico.

They went through their advice for best behaviour. Look at the wall. Always respond succinctly to their questions. Be humble. Don't answer back. Be extremely grateful. Never ask for anything.

There was disquiet in the cell. What would this mean for their release? What would a negotiation be like under the control of the British jailers?

. * .

In mid-September 2013 Arthur received information that Daniel had been moved to a new location in Aleppo. There was no indication of where exactly or where the many other kidnapped journalists were – including James Foley, whom he had been trying to find for the last ten months.

There had been total silence since Susanne and Kjeld sent their personal appeal to Emir Abu Athir. They didn't know whether or not he had even received their letter. Every shred of information about Daniel gave them new hope, and with Anita they made regular trips from Jutland to Copenhagen to attend meetings at the Foreign Ministry, where they were served coffee, lemon moon cake and pastries. There was a definite culture clash when the couple from Hedegård, who were used to being in control of their lives, met the rather stiff and bureaucratic officials.

The Foreign Ministry's primary role was to host meetings at which the various actors who were dealing with the 'Daniel affair', as the Ministry called it, could exchange information and discuss strategy. Arthur was present every now and then, if he wasn't in Turkey.

Kjeld felt that the officials were friendly and welcoming, but it seemed to be part of their job to talk for hours without saying anything concrete. Decisions were often handed over to Kjeld, who felt totally unprepared. Neither he nor Susanne knew anything about kidnappings.

'We'll support you one hundred per cent in whatever you decide,' was the usual message.

It could, for example, be a question of whether the family should spend another 50,000 kroner (about £5,300) so that Arthur could send several local investigators into Syria.

There was also material that the Ministry held back for good reason, such as information that other states had shared with

Denmark and therefore couldn't be disclosed. It gave Kjeld an unfamiliar feeling of having lost control of the situation.

Another problem also weighed on the family: the insurance payment of 5 million kroner had run out. It had been used up during the last few months on Arthur and others who were working around the clock to get Daniel home. Kjeld and Susanne asked cautiously at the Ministry if there was any help to be had for certain expenses, such as Arthur's salary. But the bureaucrats were following the orders of the government, which insisted that they couldn't cover Arthur's work or any other costs in connection with the case. Luckily, they had some savings, and Arthur agreed to wait for payment.

The Ministry and the other authorities involved in Daniel's case kept a low profile and took on the role of informing the government, while Arthur was in charge of the search for Daniel and in close contact with the family.

Anita didn't experience culture shock with the Ministry in the same way as Susanne and Kjeld. She was used to going to meetings at ministries and other agencies as part of her work as a chemical engineer. She was able to keep some distance from the case and to understand it from several angles. However, she completely understood Kjeld's and Susanne's feeling of helplessness and their need for almost daily updates from Arthur. For them, no news quickly became bad news.

Every morning when Susanne dragged her body out of bed, she brewed herself a cup of coffee and sat down at the computer to check whether there were any important messages about Daniel. In addition to all the other new routines she had acquired to cope with the situation, she also listened every morning to the song 'Small Shocks' by the Danish band Panamah. For the three and a half minutes the track lasted, she let go, allowing herself to be in her grief, fear and longing, and cried from start to finish. Some mornings she played the song several times.

Although it was a love song, the lyrics expressed how she felt.

Will you come back home?
Here in the wee small hours, time goes by so slow
and when I think ahead
Knowing I have so much to do makes me feel so low

'Dawn's breaking soon, brothers'
'Dawn's breaking soon, brothers'

Promise me my love it's not over yet
It'll all work out
It'll all work out
When the time is right
I miss you so
It'll all work out
Now I pray with all my might
Hoping that the time is right

While I'm waiting here,
my lips go stiff and frozen without me knowing why
the small shocks that follow me no matter what
and why do I feel this longing
when all things pass away

'*Dawn's breaking soon, brothers*'
'*Dawn's breaking soon, brothers*'

. * .

The hostages were moved from the Cigar Box back to the basement. The guard took Daniel by the shoulders and removed his blindfold, so that he could see the surprise that awaited him.

'Toilet!' shouted the guard enthusiastically.

The workmen had built a toilet in the basement room. This must mean they were going to be there for a long time.

On the other side of the corridor in the basement, a number of one-person cells, which already contained prisoners, had also been built. Daniel had heard them screaming when they were being beaten late at night.

Their own cell received yet another prisoner. Spanish war correspondent Marc Marginedas became the cell's ninth foreign hostage. He was in his mid-forties and an experienced correspondent for the newspaper *El Periódico* in Barcelona. He had been in prison for a month in the basement of the children's hospital in Aleppo before he joined Daniel's group, but he still arrived with news from the outside world.

'Denmark won the Eurovision Song Contest,' he said, and told them about the Danish singer Emmelie de Forest performing in bare feet.

The more sombre news was that there had been a massive poison-gas attack at the end of August in the rebel-controlled areas on the outskirts of Damascus. Hundreds of people had lost their lives and the Americans had come close to intervening against the Assad regime, which they accused of being behind the atrocity. US involvement had been averted, however, because Russia put pressure on the regime and an agreement had been reached with the UN that Syria would allow its chemical weapons to be transported out of the country for destruction, including chemical warfare agents and the nerve gases sarin and mustard gas.

Daniel listened to the news from outside, which seemed strangely distant. Nothing other than the reality of captivity had existed for a long time. He had become accustomed to the days passing slowly and the now routine dramas of lice, faeces, blankets and food. After nearly five months in captivity, he had grown accustomed to being a hostage.

It was noon on 14 October. Daniel had just eaten a piece of bread with jam when they were asked to sit with their backs to the door.

He stole a glance under his armpit as more people entered the room and he saw a short man in a long camouflage tunic. Mattresses and pillows were dragged into the cell.

When the door was closed, Daniel turned round and instantly recognized James Foley and John Cantlie from the hospital prison. It was easy to remember James's underbite and striking brown eyes beneath wide eyebrows. He hadn't seen the man in the camouflage tunic before, but it turned out to be a German, Toni Neukirch. He was a trained chef and had travelled to Syria with a tent and sleeping bag to be a volunteer aid worker.

'Oh boy, it's just great to see you all!' exclaimed James. First he gave his compatriot Steven a hug, after which he greeted the rest of the prisoners. There were now twelve hostages in the same room.

James said that he, Toni and John had been moved from the basement under the children's hospital at the same time as Daniel and the others. They had been in the same prison, but in a different cell, until being moved together with the rest of the group. They rearranged their sleeping places, so now Daniel was in the corner furthest from the toilet beside Pierre. James took the spot by the door.

He was cool and collected and Daniel was extremely happy to see him, even though he didn't really know the man. He felt as if they had received guests in their cell and he took pains to eat in a civilized manner.

James arrived with his broad smile and some pages that the guards had copied from books on Islam and given to him and others in the cell, as well as a ballpoint pen and a chess game made out of cardboard, with black and white pieces. Daniel noticed James's long toes and that he also had a scar around one of his ankles. He couldn't help but smile when James's daydreaming and long limbs caused him to stumble or knock things over in the cell. When he reached for a water bottle, he was prone to tipping the other bottles over like dominoes. On the other hand, he took his conversion to Islam very seriously and prayed five times a day.

James and John had been kidnapped in Idlib province on 22 November 2012, during their last scheduled hours in Syria, where they had been for several weeks. They had been heading towards the Turkish border, when they stopped at an Internet café that they had used before. It was Thanksgiving and James chatted with friends in the United States, while sending off articles and photos.

As they were driving the last stretch towards the border, they were stopped by armed men and driven away.

While the US authorities and Arthur were still looking for James and trying to get information about him from the Syrian regime and other sources, he had been with Daniel and the others the whole time – now in a basement in Sheikh Najjar under ISIS control.

Despite the fact that James had been a hostage for nearly a year, he was spontaneous and easy to be around. He organized equal distribution of the food, of which there was never enough, and gave the impression that he was trying to survive by creating a good atmosphere. James had a strong sense of justice, willingly leading the way and taking it upon himself to ask the guards for more food.

'By the way, it's my fortieth birthday today,' he remarked late at night on 18 October.

'Congratulations,' said Daniel. 'I really hope that your birthday next year will be better.'

The atmosphere in the cell was lifted with James's arrival, which gave Daniel renewed energy and confidence. He resumed his exercise routine and persuaded the others to do some too.

'Put your forehead against the floor, not the top of your head.'

Daniel was trying to teach James to stand on his head. To no avail.

'Ouch, my neck,' winced James and sat back down.

Each morning from 8 to 10 Daniel did gymnastics with his fellow prisoners. On Mondays it was beginners or the older prisoners, on Wednesdays the youngsters, and on Fridays it was open to all. The number of participants varied, but most of them were keen to stay in shape.

James began his lessons on a Monday and when Daniel tried to cajole him to join in the following Friday, he shrank back into a corner.

'I think I'll skip it today,' said James.

'Come on now, be a man,' laughed Daniel.

'OK, I'll give it a go.'

When Daniel held his gymnastics lessons, the others provided their blankets, laying them folded on the floor, so that they could turn somersaults on their skinny backs without it sounding like a bunch of bones sliding over the concrete.

After a large chunk of bread and four olives, James came forwards and the others sat along the wall, cheering wildly.

'OK – I'm ready,' he said, encouraged by his fellow prisoners.

Daniel was euphoric. He was used to seeing himself as the weak idiot in the corner – the one who hated himself because he had been 'fucking kidnapped' and starved into an emaciated prisoner, who couldn't think of anything else than food and shitting in a bucket. Now he was contributing to the community with somersaults and balance exercises in ways that would strengthen their bodies and minds, and the other hostages applauded when someone mastered a move. On Tuesdays, Thursdays and Saturdays, Steven taught yoga. Sundays they kept free.

It was pitch black in the cell in the evenings, because the electricity cut out. They lay freezing and huddled together under their blankets. One day James asked Daniel if he would teach him how to do massage. He knew that Daniel had learned some techniques from his gymnastics, when he and his teammates eased each other's sore muscles.

Under cover of darkness at night, so the guards wouldn't see, they began the lessons. Daniel told James about the body's various fixed points, about how he should use the thumb or the elbow and how to do a scalp massage.

'You're too careful. I can't feel it,' said Daniel when James practised on him, but he still enjoyed the rare sense of being touched; for once, it wasn't a beating from a whip or a cane.

Even though James couldn't quite figure out how to do a massage, his gentle hands allowed Daniel to relax in a way he hadn't done since he had first been captured. They often talked quietly together during these times. James spoke about his experiences as a journalist in Afghanistan and his kidnapping in Libya, when he was imprisoned for forty days by Muammar Gaddafi's forces during the Libyan Civil War in 2011.

They also talked about women. James said that he had always felt clumsy with the opposite sex.

'Women,' Daniel said as he massaged James's muscles, 'they also like a good strong massage.'

James broke out in infectious laughter.

Can You See the Moon, Daniel?

During the day, when light reached the cell, the hostages tried to find creative ways of passing the time. Daniel got an idea from a white cardboard box which had contained dates and which the guards had left in a corner of the cell.

'Are you interested in making a game of Risk?' he asked.

The others thought it sounded like fun and Daniel began collecting material for the game. The side of the cardboard box measured approximately 16 by 24 inches, and on this they drew the world map from the Risk game, purely from memory.

When Daniel ate olives, he spat the pits into a metal tub, filled a bucket with water and scrubbed them clean. He then used a nail to scrape the fruit flesh off the pits and laid them out to dry on the wall that separated the room from the toilet. The others also gave him their date and olive pits, which he cleaned and categorized. The stones could be dark, light, large or small. A small olive pit symbolized a soldier, a large olive pit a horse, while a date pit symbolized a cannon with ten soldiers.

Daniel had saved a small yoghurt tub, which he used to construct a die. He pricked a circle in the bottom with a nail, then divided the circle into six equal parts and gave each section a number from one to six. When an olive stone was thrown into the tub, it landed on the number of dots that the player should move his piece.

They made mission cards and tore paper into strips to use as pieces. When everything was completed, Risk became a popular alternative to chess, the only game in the cell until then. Daniel had become a complete chess nerd and found a mental escape from his captivity by immersing himself in looking for gaps in his opponent's defence. There were a lot of them on James's half of the board, on the rare occasions when Daniel persuaded him to play.

The new game also helped him forget where he was, and between four and six of them would often play together. Daniel feared that the guards would mistake the Risk board for an escape plan, so they would sit in his corner with their backs to the door and play at conquering countries and territories around the world, ready to cover the pieces with a blanket if the guards should come in.

An independent judge would be appointed for each new round, although debates would quickly arise about how independent he was when he had to adjudicate how far a player could move if the olive pit lay on the dividing line between two numbers. The players would form alliances, which led to cynical power struggles and predictable intrigues. They took defeat so personally and seriously that they would fall out over it.

'I quit!' one of them would say suddenly. 'I don't want to play any more.'

'Come on now, it's just a game,' someone would say. It was as if it had become impossible to play for fun, because the fear of death, the longing and the pain, was all being channelled into a board game made of cardboard and olive pits.

Daniel stopped playing and thought back to his first shocking days in captivity, when he had imagined that it would be a matter of hours, days or weeks before he would be free again. Back then, it never crossed his mind to think in terms of months, and now six months had already gone by. Perhaps he would have to add 'number of years' to his internal accounting of his time as a hostage.

Around noon one day in November there was heavy hammering on the door and concerns greater than how many dots were in the tub arrived in the shape of the three British guards. Daniel was kneeling with his face against the wall, but he recognized their accent from the day when the Brit's unpleasant visit had turned Federico's and David's faces deathly pale.

Daniel stiffened, while the Brits went around the room selecting individual hostages, who were given a few blows on the torso. He could hear that they were being tough on Steven, accusing him of writing articles that were untrue. They also circled David for a long time.

One of the guards asked them, one by one, to say what they knew about Dawlah al-Islamiyah, the Arabic name for ISIS.

Daniel deliberately kept his answer very short.

'Your goal is to create an Islamic state where you implement sharia law,' he said.

The three Brits talked about the policies of western countries against Muslims and about the wars in Iraq and Afghanistan.

'Why are you sitting here? Because you support your stupid governments,' said one of them.

'Is there anyone who knows what democracy means?' continued the lesson. 'It comes from Latin. *Demos* means "people", *kratos* means "power". And who are the people? The people, that's you. So you are the sinners.'

After that day the hostages began to see the three hooded British guards more frequently. They nicknamed them the Beatles. That way, they could talk about John, Ringo and George, without the guards detecting that the prisoners were speaking about them.

The Beatles were always dressed in black hoods, desert boots and black or military green clothing, but several of the hostages in the cell noted that their hands were dark-skinned. They guessed that they came from Pakistan and had perhaps met each other in a mosque in London.

George was the most violent and unpredictable of the three and sometimes he held his nose while he walked around the cell, talking or telling bad jokes. According to David and Federico – and also James, who had encountered George earlier in his captivity – he had gone from being quiet to aggressive and domineering. Ringo, on the other hand, seemed to be reserved, while John was articulate.

Daniel hardly dared to listen when they were in the cell, so he often couldn't tell them apart. But it was immaterial – as a trio, they were frightening. Whether they came in together or separately, the forewarning was always a strong, bitter-sweet scent of male perfume that wafted into the room while they stood outside the door, waiting for the hostages to turn to face the wall before they entered. Sometimes Daniel thought he could smell when they were coming, but it usually turned out to be a false alarm. Every time the prisoners sensed a whiff of perfume, there was panic.

. * .

Towards the end of 2013, while Daniel and his fellow prisoners in Aleppo had fallen under the control of British jihadists, James Foley's family in the United States were approached by the father of a returned Syrian combatant. At the beginning of November Dimitri, Jejoen Bontinck's father, called James's brother Michael with the message that his son had apparently met James in a prison in Aleppo.

The family had been getting calls for several months from various people, each one more well-informed and well-intentioned than the next. Common to all of them was that they claimed to know where James was being held, without it ever leading to anything new. Even so, Michael thought that Dimitri's story was worth passing on to Arthur, who had been looking for James for about a year without success. Arthur listened to the long message that Jejoen's father had recorded. Dimitri spoke stridently, quickly and incoherently, but Arthur decided to contact him anyway to find out what it was really about.

Dimitri said his son had become radicalized and had gone to Syria to fight.

'I've been in Syria looking for him,' he continued, at which Arthur couldn't suppress a little smile. When Dimitri's son finally returned home, after more than six months, he had been imprisoned by the Belgian authorities on suspicion of committing terrorist acts in Syria and of being a member of ISIS, in the days when he wasn't under house arrest. Jejoen's testimony added to the public prosecutor's case against forty-seven members of Sharia4Belgium, including himself. According to Dimitri, Jejoen had told him that he had been held in the same cell as James for several weeks in the basement of a children's hospital in Aleppo.

When Arthur hung up, he sat back with a strange gut feeling. During the past few months he had spoken with hundreds of people who said they knew James's whereabouts. Their only motive had been money. But what in heaven's name would prompt a young Belgian jihadist to fabricate a story about having met James? he asked himself. The only motive Arthur could imagine was immunity, meaning that Jejoen hoped he might be released if he gave information about a well-known, kidnapped American in Syria. There were several details in Dimitri's story that aroused Arthur's curiosity, since much of his information about Daniel had also been obtained from released Syrians who had been held in the same prisons.

In the United States the FBI didn't think Arthur should spend even a second of his valuable time on the returned Belgian fighter. Even though the Syrian regime denied that James was in one of their prisons, this possibility was the only lead that Arthur had been asked to prioritize by the FBI. Prominent sources in the regime said that not even President Assad would necessarily know if there was an American in one of the secret prisons, because when prisoners were registered, their name was thrown away and the prisoner reduced to a number. It would be difficult to find the person without being able to match a name with a number. Moreover, it wasn't inconceivable that a general or a colonel somewhere in the system had 'stashed Foley away' as an insurance policy. If the regime fell, releasing him could be a ticket out.

'We have to use our scarce resources to follow the lead in Damascus,' was the message from the US. But Arthur, ignoring the FBI's view on the matter, followed his gut feeling and flew to Antwerp, Belgium.

Through Dimitri, Arthur obtained a permit to visit Jejoen under the guise of being a family member who had come from the United States to welcome him home.

The high-security prison couldn't deny the prisoner a family visit, but if he came for investigative purposes, the police had to be involved. Arthur wanted to avoid the latter at all costs. He could already imagine how authorization for the visit would evaporate in red tape and delays.

Before going through the prison security search, Arthur wrote a number of names on the broad palm of his hand that he wanted to check with the fighter. Abu Athir, Abu Ubaidah and Abu Suheib were among them; he wanted to know what they looked like and where they had been staying. He had also rolled up his shirt sleeves and hidden a mini ballpoint pen in the cuffs so the wardens didn't discover it when he went into the visiting room.

It looked like a classroom with small desks, and the visitors and inmates were only allowed to sit in specifically designated chairs. The prison wardens walked between the tables, keeping an eye on things; pen and paper were not allowed.

A few moments later Arthur was sitting opposite Jejoen, whose dark skin came from his Nigerian mother. Arthur spoke quietly and honestly from the beginning.

'I'm not a member of James's family. But I'm not from the intelligence services, either. I'm looking for James on behalf of his family. I'm also looking for a Dane called Daniel.'

'I've seen James and heard about the Dane,' said Jejoen.

In order to verify his statements, Arthur asked him to explain how he had ended up under the children's hospital in Aleppo.

When he finished recounting his story, there was no doubt. Jejoen told Arthur where James had gone to school and that he had been a teacher. He also gave information about John Cantlie that no one knew publicly, and John hadn't even been in the press. At that point in time the Brit's capture was still unknown to the public.

Arthur wrote everything on his forearm with his mini pen as unobtrusively as possible, while his cheeks burned. *This is the BREAKTHROUGH!* a voice said inside him. After searching for about a year, he finally had the first proof of life of James Foley. He was still alive.

The next breakthrough came a few minutes later when Arthur read out the list of prominent ISIS leaders that he had written on his palm. Jejoen nodded and described all of them in detail. Arthur suddenly understood the connection: James and Daniel had been taken prisoner by the same people.

With the knowledge that Arthur had about the other western hostages, it became clear to him that the same key characters among the kidnappers were popping up every time. Perhaps all of the hostages were being held at the same location.

As soon as Arthur came out of the maximum security prison he called the United States and Britain. As euphoric as he was to finally know where James had been staying, he was equally depressed at the thought that Daniel was sitting in the hands of the same Islamists who had made James disappear for a year without any sign of life.

It was no longer just one Dane who was imprisoned or one American. It was a multinational hostage-taking, since there was much to indicate that some Frenchmen, a Brit and a German were also hostages in the same place. Arthur knew from experience that when a case involved many nationalities, it would mean every government fighting against the other. But that wasn't the worst part.

When the kidnappers had several hostages in their custody, the risk increased that one of them would be killed. Not all of the captives would have the same value, and the captors were usually willing to sacrifice some more than others. Daniel might not be at the top of the list of those they wanted to keep.

Given these circumstances, Arthur realized that the appeal letter Daniel's parents had sent to Emir Abu Athir had been completely irrelevant. Now it was simply a matter of how long it would take before someone tried to get in touch with Susanne and Kjeld and what ISIS's grand plan was for Daniel, James and the others. Was it about money, politics, ideology or a combination of them all?

As Arthur saw it, Daniel and the other foreign hostages had become pawns in a dangerous political game in which the Islamists moved the pieces as and when it suited them. It was a game that could end up putting governments under pressure and presenting them with a dilemma: if they wanted their countrymen to be freed, they would be forced to indulge ISIS and pay ransoms to terrorists.

Arthur left Belgium with the feeling that anything could happen.

. * .

The family in Hedegård was living in the iron grip of uncertainty. It had been many weeks since they had received any sign of life and even longer since anyone had shown any interest in negotiating Daniel's release. Susanne was desperate to talk to her son, to see him and hear his voice as she remembered it. She and Kjeld went to the cinema more often than they had ever done; it was a place where they could forget reality for a while and where there was no one who asked about Daniel.

They wrote another letter, which Arthur's contacts would try to get delivered to Daniel. Susanne spent a whole morning writing it, crying and crossing out. The letter was to give her son information about what was happening. It was meant to inspire hope – and show that they loved him, in case they never saw him again:

Dear Daniel,

We, Signe and the rest of your family are thinking about you very much. How are you? Are they treating you well? We have seen pictures and videos of you; it was hard, but nice too. We hope and believe that you can use your always positive outlook and attitude in the difficult situation you're in, and your kind, friendly personality and maybe your gymnastics to benefit your body and soul.

Susanne and Kjeld wrote about how they were keeping his disappearance a secret, so that the press didn't get wind of the story:

We are doing everything in our power to get you safely home to Denmark, so just keep going and fight on. You should know that we are all ready to receive you with love; we will help and support you, and together we will no doubt move forwards, together we are strong.

Here in Denmark, it's the same old stuff. Christina has started her third year at high school. Signe is in school. Anita and her boyfriend both have new jobs, which are fortunately going really well. Dad is driving his truck and cycling a lot, and I'm working at Legoland, of course. Granddad and Grandma are worried, of course, like the rest of us, but they are holding out well.

We have had a fantastic, fine summer here in Denmark with a lot of sunshine and warm weather. We had three good days on Samsø, along with Anita and her boyfriend, who kayaked over and stayed at a campsite. Dad and I stayed in a boarding school, so now we have also tried that. We had our bikes with us, so we cycled all over Samsø. Christina went to Move Yourself in Viborg and has also worked at Legoland. Signe is a wonderful girl – she has been on holiday with her parents and her brothers and sisters. She misses you very much, but she is contributing enormously and fighting alongside us.

The harvest is now in and autumn is approaching; the leaves are falling from the trees and the dark time of year is approaching, the time with candles and cosiness. So we hope with all our hearts that you will come home soon and be able to enjoy yourself with us.

They ended the letter with a saying:

> A tree with strong roots can withstand even the fiercest
> storm.
> Many hugs and warm thoughts to you from your Mum
> and Dad.

. * .

After months with no proof of life or any signs of negotiations, Daniel was finally collected from the cell and taken up to an office that had windows all around, like a glass cage.

He cast a quick glance out of the windows and managed to get a sense of where he was – some old cars were parked in a yard, where there was also some building clutter and two dumbbells – before an English-speaking guard ordered him to sit down on a chair. The guard said some phrases that Daniel had to repeat in front of a video camera:

'My name is Daniel. I am a Danish citizen. I got caught by this group, because I had some pictures on my camera showing the houses of the mujahideen. This is a message to the prime minister of Denmark, Helle Thorning-Schmidt. Stop the support for groups like Liwa al-Tawheed and pay money in order for me to return home,' he said, referring to one of the larger, moderate rebel groups.

He was then taken back to the cell, without having the slightest idea whether or not any of the video appeals he had made were ever sent to Denmark.

James was holding a candle out towards the door. The electricity kept disappearing for increasingly longer periods in the evening. When it happened, the hostages called the guards, who lit the wick of the candle they had finally been given.

All thirteen of them were sitting covered by their blankets, staring into the flame, as they looked forward to a small meal – a little bread and olives. No one said anything. Daniel looked at the others' faces in the yellow gleam of the candlelight and for a moment he felt that it was actually quite cosy, especially when James distributed the food in equal portions.

The basement had become cold and damp. December was on its way. Daniel suggested a game he knew from when he taught at Bjerre Gymnastics and Sports School. During the Christmas month, the head of the boarding school had arranged a Secret Santa exchange that Daniel thought would work in the cell too. The rules were that everyone was secretly allocated someone who would be their Secret Santa and who would pamper them until Christmas. Then, on Christmas Eve, they all had to guess who was their Secret Santa.

Some were sceptical about playing Secret Santa in a Muslim prison and, except for James, who thought it was a good idea, those who had converted to Islam didn't want to join in. One of the Muslims who didn't want to be involved allocated Secret Santas to the hostages. He whispered in Daniel's ear that he should be Secret Santa for Steven and Daniel started thinking about how he could be pleasant towards him in the coming weeks.

The Christmas season also brought a new acquaintance. Daniel woke abruptly one night in early December when the door to the basement room opened and a new hostage came into the cell. It was a Russian called Sergei Gorbunov. He had a receding hairline and a bushy goatee beard on his chin and didn't speak any English, but Marc, the Spaniard, could communicate a little with him in Russian.

Sergei told them that he was a Muslim and a scientist and that he had been on his way to an area of Aleppo with some important papers when he was captured. The others couldn't figure out what he was really doing in Syria. He spoke incoherently and maybe he was a little crazy. But Sergei was good at being a prisoner. He settled in and quickly got into the rhythm. Apparently he had been imprisoned for several years in Russia, and Daniel thought that maybe there wasn't a lot of difference between an ISIS prison in Syria and a Russian state prison. The everyday routines were probably much the same.

Sergei was also good at chess, even though he cheated and moved his knight in a non-regulation manner. But not everyone was enthusiastic about the Russian. Pierre didn't like his energy and kept his distance. He thought that Sergei had come in with animalistic tendencies, where he attacked the weak and obeyed the strong. Most of all, Pierre's aversion was the result of his own efforts to maintain a civilized level of behaviour, a little dignity in the midst of a world in which they were controlled by the Beatles.

. * .

The hostages were dragged out of the cell one at a time. When it was Daniel's turn, he was thrown on to the floor of a room in which one of the Brits sat behind a table. On the table were a small computer and a sub-machine gun. Daniel was on his knees and

THE ISIS HOSTAGE 175

handcuffed, staring at the floor in front of him, while the hooded guard asked him his name and why he had come to Syria.

'Would you like to go home? Who can pay for you?' were the next questions.

'My family doesn't have any money, but they'll do everything they can to pay a ransom,' replied Daniel.

'If nobody pays, we'll shoot you,' said the guard, getting up and sticking a pistol barrel into Daniel's mouth.

'Do you want to die now or will you tell us what possibilities there are?'

Daniel calmly gave him a signal with his hand that he wanted to say something and, when the barrel was removed from his mouth, he told them how much he was insured for and reeled off email addresses for Susanne, Kjeld and his sisters.

'Have you heard of Guantánamo?'

Daniel nodded.

'What can you tell us about the place?'

He tried to say as little as possible about the US detention camp in Cuba, where there was evidence of widespread torture. The Brits were rough, uncompromising and unpleasant.

'I know they're holding Muslim prisoners who have been treated very badly,' said Daniel.

'It's your duty to know. You are part of the democracy that holds these people prisoner,' said the guard, emphasizing every word as he continued to outline how Daniel was complicit in the mistreatment of Muslims in western democracies.

'This is our response to how the West is treating our brothers.'

Daniel nodded again, knowing that the Beatles had previously subjected some of the hostages to a method of torture called waterboarding, which they had imported from Guantánamo. This involved putting a cloth over the prisoners' faces and pouring gallons of water over them so that they felt as if they were drowning.

The guard punched Daniel hard in the torso and led him back to the cell. His ribs were aching, but he was surprised that he hadn't reacted to having a pistol stuck in his mouth – as if he were indifferent to dying. Maybe his body had stopped feeling fear. Maybe he was just tired and had become immune to death threats.

The other hostages had also had email addresses demanded of them, which made the British and Americans happy. It was the first sign that contact might be made with their families. Until now, James had always been told that he would never be going home. Sergei was the only one who had no email address to give the Beatles. The prisoners talked a lot about what this demand for email addresses meant, while simultaneously getting involved in their Secret Santa roles.

Steven slept by Daniel's feet and some evenings Daniel would wrap him up in the blanket like a sausage, from his shoulders all the way down his body and around his feet. When Steven got up, Daniel would wish him good morning, and every time Steven suggested a game of chess, he would volunteer to be his opponent. He consistently took part in Steven's yoga classes three times a week and asked afterwards whether Steven would tell him about Israel and Palestine. The American was Jewish, something they never mentioned in front of the guards.

One day, beside his sleeping place, Daniel found a small boat shaped out of the wrapper from a packet of butter. In his universe, this gift from his Secret Santa symbolized freedom. The foil boat could drift wherever it wanted, depending on where Daniel's thoughts led it. The Secret Santa game was creating a larger mental space in the cell.

The daily guards who brought them food mainly spoke French. They called themselves Abu Idriss and Abu Mohammed and they acted professionally by keeping a distance and addressing the prisoners with the formal *vous* instead of the informal *tu* when they took them out to the toilet and brought them food.

Pierre also recognized a third French guard, Abu Omar, whom he had met when he first arrived at the hospital in Aleppo. He had evidently moved with them to the Dungeon, as the hostages called the prison. Sometimes, when Abu Omar was on duty, the prisoners didn't get any food, and the first time he came into the cell, his face wasn't covered.

Maybe it was the presence of Pierre and the other Frenchmen that got Abu Omar hanging out with them in their cell. He really enjoyed talking about the French police, the former Yugoslavia and the so-called Roubaix gang – a terrorist cell whose members had been in Bosnia during the war in 1992 and who had robbed and attacked several places in France throughout the 1990s. A large-scale attack against a police building in Lille in 1996 had failed, however, when their home-made bomb had destroyed only the Peugeot they had parked outside.

While other people had their favourite actors, Abu Omar had his favourite major criminals, which Pierre interpreted to mean that he personally wanted to become a famous felon. Little did Pierre know, but Abu Omar would later fulfil his wish. His name was in fact Mehdi Nemmouche. He had Algerian roots and, in 2014, he was accused of killing four people in an attack at the Jewish

Museum in Brussels. According to prosecutors, the twenty-nine-year-old French national from Roubaix admitted to carrying out the attack, which had been caught on the museum's security cameras. On 24 May he ran into the museum, took a Kalashnikov out of his bag and shot and killed two Israeli tourists.and a Frenchman, while a fourth victim, a Belgian employee of the museum, later died of his wounds. Mehdi Nemmouche managed to flee on foot and got as far as Marseille before being apprehended.

It was the first attack in Europe in which the perpetrator had a connection to ISIS.

Although Abu Omar probably beat the Syrian inmates in the prison – some of the hostages thought they heard it happening – it was still the British guards they feared the most. When the Beatles were in the room, no one knew what was going to happen.

One day in December Daniel immediately became apprehensive when they dragged him out to the toilet. He was told to take off his shirt and stand up against the end wall. Ringo was holding a video camera, while the other two coached Daniel to speak into the camera and appeal to all the important and rich people in Denmark to pay a ransom, so that he could go back home to his family. They handed him the front page of a Danish tabloid, which he had to hold up in front of him while asking for help.

'Pull yourself together!' shouted one of the Brits. 'Do it again!'

Daniel repeated the speech, while Ringo filmed.

'Stooooop! You sound like a tourist, like you don't mean it. Pull yourself together now. Do it again!'

Daniel tried to sound more frightened and after three or four takes the Brits deemed that the video was finally in the can. He put on his shirt and went back to the cell, where he and Pierre were getting ready for Christmas Eve.

They had been putting aside food from their meals for weeks. As a rule, they saved a chunk of bread, spread it with margarine and apricot jam and wrapped it in a plastic bag that lay between them while they slept. The feast grew every day as they added another piece of bread and jam. Pierre had convinced Daniel that the bread wouldn't go mouldy if it was smeared with jam and Daniel regarded the greasy jam roll in the bag almost like a baby that was growing between them – and which they had to guard with their lives, so that they could celebrate Christmas Eve.

. * .

In the days leading up to the first Sunday of Advent, Susanne strung Christmas lights up in the pots and bushes outside their house.

'We've got to carry on living as normal, so that we don't attract attention,' she thought to herself. She put on some Christmas music, while placing gnomes and spruce twigs in the windows. With tears rolling down her cheeks, she tidied up the Advent wreath that stood on the table, ready for the first candle to be lit.

Susanne and Kjeld went out and ate some delicious food at an Italian restaurant, and afterwards they laughed for a while at the Christmas show at Vejle Music Hall. One Saturday Kjeld went to a Christmas party with some truck driver friends, while Susanne went to a spa, then they ate steak and drank red wine together. They tried to honour their usual Christmas traditions, both outwardly and at home. As Susanne quoted in her diary:

'Our greatest glory is not in never falling, but in rising every time we fall.'

They ate traditional pastries and drank mulled wine, cut down a Christmas tree in the forest and sent a parcel to Daniel in Syria. It contained an old work sweatshirt from Bjerre Gymnastics and Sports School with greetings written on small slips of paper in the pocket. Christina enclosed a school photo of herself and wrote her own message on the back, along with an extract from the same song her mother had been listening to: 'I love you. I think about you every day and know that you can handle it. It'll all work out, when the time is right. I miss you so.' Despite this, every time Susanne stopped in the middle of the Christmas rush, she was overcome with grief.

'Tears are words the heart can't say,' she wrote in her diary on 16 December.

Two days later she read an article online about former Syrian prisoners of ISIS. A fieldworker from Amnesty International in northern Syria had collected eyewitness accounts by hostages released from ISIS prisons in the Raqqa and Aleppo provinces. The prisoners had been held between May and November 2013 and they told the fieldworker how they had been detained by masked, armed men who blindfolded them and drove them to a prison cell, where they were tortured. Susanne tried to forget what she had read and hurried outside to put out some firewood that her younger brother was coming to collect the following day.

Some evenings, when the sky was clear, she would gaze for a long time at the moon that shone over Hedegård's brown winter fields and empty roads.

'Can you see the moon, Daniel?' she asked quietly. 'I wonder if you can see the moon.'

It reassured her to think that they both found themselves under the same sky. Then her son didn't feel so far away after all.

. * .

Arthur spent December 2013 holding meetings with his network in the border region between Turkey and Syria. He was now receiving reports that Daniel, James and the other western hostages had apparently been moved from the children's hospital to what was thought to be a sawmill in the industrial area of Sheikh Najjar on the outskirts of Aleppo. The information didn't surprise him, since any negotiations or access to Daniel had ground to a halt after late August. Arthur was told that the guards had demanded email addresses for all the hostages' families. A Syrian prisoner who had since been released had overheard them being questioned. He had been sitting in a one-man cell just opposite the western hostages in the basement and heard the British guards question each of them.

In mid-December James Foley's family received an email with the kidnappers' demands. In return for James's release, they demanded that the family press the US government to release Muslim prisoners, or else they wanted the astronomical sum of €100 million. The email also contained an invitation to the family to send some proof of life questions for James.

Arthur interpreted the message as a serious opening. Even if the demand was sky high, the kidnappers couldn't be discounted as negotiators. He had seen before how kidnappers started out with enormous demands in order to suss out the families. The US authorities responded to the Foley family and rejected any question of a prisoner exchange or ransom negotiation. But that didn't mean that the dialogue should end.

'The starting point for all releases is dialogue,' Arthur told the Foleys.

He thought it might be a deliberate strategy to reach out first to a family in the one country where the payment of a ransom seemed the most impossible to achieve.

The Foley family quickly got an email back with James's answers to questions about where his brother got married, who had wept during his speech at the wedding and what position James played on the football team. But the communication stopped as suddenly as it had started. After only a few emails, before the family could begin any real negotiations, there was silence from the other end. The kidnappers wrote what they called a final message in which they insisted on €100 million in cash to release James.

Susanne and Kjeld in Hedegård were sharing a destiny with Diane and John Foley in Rochester. They too were waiting in vain for an email about their son.

. * .

On the morning of 23 December 2013 the guards came into the cell.

'You're going to be released now,' one said and declared that the rich Gulf state of Qatar had paid €260 million for all thirteen foreign hostages.

'You have ten minutes to get ready,' was the message.

'May we take anything with us?' asked one of the prisoners and got a no in reply. The hostages did some quick calculations based on Qatar's generous €260 million and laughed — they were worth more than 11 F-16 fighter aircraft. Deep down, everyone knew very well that they were probably just being taken to a new cell.

The prospect of a move created panic in Daniel and Pierre about what would become of their Christmas Eve treat, the bread and jam that they had been assembling for several weeks and was hidden between their sleeping places.

They decided to eat it straight away, so they split it into two equal pieces. Daniel feasted on the fatty, soft, sugary mass of old bread and lavish volumes of jam, margarine and butter. It was many more calories than he had taken in for several months. When the jam roll had been consumed, he pulled on a pair of Adidas trousers, Toni's military tunic, a pair of socks and the far-too-small turquoise sandals.

The guards tied the hostages' hands together with white plastic straps that cut into the skin. They were blindfolded and led out to a truck. Daniel lost his sandals on the way and felt a sugar rush rise up from his stomach, which was bubbling with a strange happiness. Tears ran down his cheeks, because he believed that he was going home – and minutes later because he thought he was going to die.

Suddenly, he felt an intense urge to go to the toilet, but it was too late. The truck had already started and the prisoners slid around each other in the cargo compartment. His stomach was gurgling, his mind racing, and he couldn't stop crying.

When the truck finally stopped, Daniel imagined that they had come to a refugee camp and would soon be released. Someone took him by the arm and he stepped out with his right leg first – the leg which had not had a knee injury – into the uncertain depths, without having any idea of how far down the ground was.

But he felt that there was a chair under him and he stepped onto it before he was in his stockinged feet on some gravel. A hand took his arm again and he felt someone run a finger along his neck in a sawing motion. So they probably weren't going home.

With their hands bound, the hostages were lifted up by the arms so they were forced to walk on their toes and led into a room.

After a short time, they were taken out individually.

Some guards with masks asked Daniel to take off all his clothes. 'My socks too?'

'Yes, everything.'

Daniel's stomach was rumbling as he stood naked on the chilly floor and was asked to bend forward and spread his buttocks. They apparently wanted to examine whether he had smuggled anything up his behind and he was terrified that he wouldn't be able to hold himself while they inspected him.

Afterwards, they threw into his arms a two-part orange prison uniform with loose trousers and a thin shirt and he pulled it over his naked body. The body lice were gone with his old trousers. On reflection, he dared not imagine what it could mean that all of them were now dressed in Guantánamo-coloured suits.

'It's their dream,' said James and related that, early in his captivity, the Beatles had told him that they were going to dress him in an orange prison uniform.

The hostages were divided into two groups. Daniel was relieved that he was put together with Pierre, James, Steven, John, Toni, Marc and Edouard in a large basement room with two small windows looking out on to a foyer, and with a proper toilet and shower.

The hostages were in the cell they soon dubbed the Five-Star Hotel.

· * ·

As usual at this time of year, Anita placed on the bookcase in the living room a small wooden church with an electric light. Her grandfather had made it back in the 1980s and, when she was a child, it had been on display at Hedegård every holiday season, lighting up a Christmas landscape of cotton wool. It had later become hers and it wasn't really Christmas until it had been unpacked along with the other decorations.

The Rye family alternated where they stayed for Christmas Eve, and this year Anita was waiting for Susanne, Kjeld and Christina to come and spend Christmas with her and her boyfriend at their house in Odense. They arrived in the early afternoon and enjoyed a glass of port around the coffee table before helping out in the kitchen. On the menu was goose with caramelized potatoes and red cabbage, followed by the traditional Danish Christmas dessert of creamy rice pudding with chopped almonds.

Anita thought back to last year when the family had Skyped with Daniel during dinner, because he was in Russia. This Christmas she had hoped so much that he would have returned from Syria that she had transferred some money into his bank account as a Christmas present.

While they ate, they talked about Daniel, who last year had been looking out at them from the computer on the windowsill. This year it was Kjeld's and Susanne's phones that lay on the windowsill. Kjeld checked his mobile regularly in the hope that Daniel would be allowed to call home. Maybe the kidnappers would show some mercy on Christmas Eve and let him wish them a Merry Christmas. But the only thing that came in was a text message from Arthur:

Dear Both, Merry Christmas. I hope you can find some peace with your family, even if it won't be the same this year. I've spoken to Alpha this evening. He hasn't heard anything from our contacts, but I've asked him to answer the Skype message I sent. All the best to you. Best wishes, Arthur.

Kjeld replied:

OK, thanks Arthur. Merry Christmas to you and your family too.

Anita thought that Daniel wouldn't have wanted them to just sink into a miserable heap, so they celebrated Christmas as they usually did. Kjeld got the whole almond in his rice pudding, so he won the special prize, which was a set of wooden salad utensils, and, after a relaxing walk round the neighbourhood to settle their stomachs, they danced around the Christmas tree. Susanne had not been looking forward to this Christmas tradition with such a significant person missing from the circle, but they ended as usual by singing 'Now It's Christmas Again' and dancing in a chain all around the house, both inside and outside.

Susanne and Christina fell asleep at each end of the sofa, while Kjeld slept on an air mattress.

. * .

On 24 December Daniel woke up early and washed himself under the ice-cold running water in the 'five-star' dungeon. He dressed in his lice-free orange prison uniform, which was too thin for the winter cold, and sat down on a mattress under a thick blanket.

A new prison guard, whom they called the Spanish Chef, soon brought some food into the cell. He got this nickname because he was responsible for their meals and he spoke a little Spanish. He was a tall, obliging man, even though he walked around in a suicide vest with a fuse hanging out in front. In addition to the vest, he wore what was, in the circumstances, a stylish jacket with matching trousers, and a waistcoat with pockets in which he placed rifle magazines.

When the Spanish Chef came into the cell, the hostages didn't have to turn against the wall. He was happy to let them see his face and the braces on his teeth. He wanted them to see that he was a human being. He said that he was from Tunisia and reassured them that their release was just a matter of money. He served two pieces of bread to each hostage and placed a metal tray in front of them with tuna, sardines, cheese, hummus and onions.

'Thank you,' they said.

It was a feast.

'You should thank God. It is He who gives,' said the Spanish Chef and left the room.

Daniel's thoughts went to his Christmas Eve the year before, when he had Skyped home from Russia. He missed his family and Signe, but wanted to have a good Christmas wherever he was.

Everyone in the cell seemed to be thinking along the same lines and they agreed that the best gift they could give each other was honesty. A circle of orange-clad hostages took shape and they began to tell stories about each other.

Edouard said that he was Daniel's Secret Santa and had put the tin foil boat by Daniel's sleeping space. He also told them that he had deliberately distanced himself from Daniel when they had met in the cell under the children's hospital, because Daniel had looked so damaged.

'You were an indication of the worst that could happen,' he admitted.

Daniel revealed that he was Steven's Secret Santa and he told James that he had read about him before they had met in captivity; that he had seen photographs of someone he believed to be tough war reporter. He also said that he had been amused when he discovered that James was a klutz who lurched around the cell knocking over water bottles. Daniel thanked James for the massages and all the chats about women and dreams of the future – and for sticking to his values when people behaved unfairly.

'You are quite simply a good human being, James,' he noted.

They laughed about their first meeting in the toilet. James teased Daniel about how he had looked – he had stood behind the others with his tousled hair sticking out every which way and stared at James with his sunken eyes.

'You looked like a frightened mouse,' laughed James.

'I noticed your underbite and thought you looked a little unintelligent,' teased Daniel back.

They talked about their first attempts at gymnastics and laughed about how weak and pathetic they had been when they turned somersaults on the blankets, and the time James nearly broke his neck when he tried to stand on his head.

That night, Daniel crept under his blanket on the soft mattress and fell into a deep, carefree sleep. When he woke up the next morning, it was without the usual pain in his hip bone.

In Orange with a View of the World

'**B**loody hell – that was Paul!'

The hostages looked at each other and laughed. Yet another British guard, whom none of them had met before, had just shown up in the Five-Star Hotel. He asked if they needed anything. They asked for extra blankets, after which he disappeared again. Even though he had nothing to do with the other three Brits, the hostages joked that he was the fourth and final member of the prison's Beatles.

It was also Paul who gave them Koran lessons.

'You can turn around and face me,' he announced to their great surprise. They sat in a circle, while he went through various verses from the Koran in Arabic and encouraged them to ask questions. He was dressed in a hoodie and gloves and wore thick socks in his sandals.

Paul made greater demands on the converts than on the others. He told them which verse the Emir wanted them to be able to recite by heart and ended all his sentences with *inshallah*, God willing. His speech was neither political nor inflammatory, unlike the atmosphere that was created when the rest of the Beatles were there. They would suddenly enter the cell shouting '*Takbir!*' to which the prisoners had to answer '*Allahu akhbar!*' as loud as they could.

The Brits had also composed a verse to the melody of The Eagles's 1977 hit 'Hotel California' and ordered the hostages to learn the verses by heart, so that they could sing the chorus:

Welcome to Osama's lovely hotel,
Such a lovely place,
Such a lovely place.
You will never leave Osama's lovely hotel,
And if you try, you will die, Mr Bigley-style.

Daniel sang along as best he could and James said he had sung it earlier in his captivity. But the reference to Mr Bigley was anything but funny. Kenneth John Bigley was a British civil engineer. In the autumn of 2004 he had been kidnapped in Baghdad, while working for a Kuwaiti construction company. The group that took him and two American colleagues was led by Abu Musab al-Zarqawi, who later became the leader of al-Qaeda in Iraq – the group that preceded ISIS.

A video put online on Islamist forums in 2004 showed the Islamists' murder of Bigley. He sat in an orange prison uniform and was forced to read a manifesto out loud – after which his throat was cut. As a finale to the execution, the executioners placed his severed head on top of his body.

The video of the murder was so gory that it backfired among some of al-Qaeda's supporters, who felt it went too far. Bigley's body was never found.

Daniel was slowly regaining his strength. The Spanish Chef brought the prisoners food three times a day and Daniel was feeling full for once, and he was training more often. In true five-star-hotel-style, he was also given a toothbrush, toothpaste and lotion. It was the first time in more than six months that he had brushed his teeth and he let the Spanish Chef cut his hair with a shaver. Thin wisps that looked like wool lay on the floor afterwards and his scalp was nothing but dead skin that sprinkled down on to his shoulders when he touched the top of his head.

During the day on New Year's Eve, the guards switched two hostages around, so Edouard and Sergei swapped cells. The Russian had new information for the prisoners in Daniel's group. In the cell where he had been sitting, three more hostages had been brought in: two Spanish reporters, journalist Javier Espinosa and photographer Ricardo Vilanova, and an American aid worker, Peter Kassig. This meant that there were now a total of sixteen foreign hostages divided between the two rooms.

When New Year's Eve arrived Daniel could hear what sounded like Syrian fireworks in the form of bombardments in the distance. They all went to bed early.

. * .

On 27 December welcome news came to the Rye family. In the midst of the winter darkness, Daniel's cousin had given birth to a little miracle – almost 9 lbs in weight and 20 inches long.

'We're still waiting,' wrote Susanne in her diary about the absence of any sign of life from Daniel. 'We find the waiting long and difficult, but when we think of how you must be experiencing the waiting, we realize we shouldn't be complaining.'

Three days into the New Year, Susanne and Kjeld were sitting on the sofa watching television. Kjeld's finger slid around on his iPad, when he suddenly exclaimed, 'A Dane has been kidnapped in northern Syria, one from Médecins Sans Frontières, along with four of his colleagues!'

They switched over to the news channel, which was broadcasting a long report on the kidnapping. The names of the captives were not mentioned and it was unclear – at least publicly – who had taken the five representatives from Médecins Sans Frontières (known as MSF).

The organization, which was made up of doctors and nurses who treated people in the most dangerous places in the world, was a highly experienced one. No matter where they worked, MSF always cooperated with the local population, regardless of tribe, ethnicity or community. It was part of the job that anyone sent into the field had to be able to work in difficult areas, and something must have gone seriously wrong if, after several years' presence throughout Syria, MSF had now had five employees kidnapped. It was a testament to the fact that no foreigners in Syria could feel assured of their safety, not even emissaries from a charitable organization that gave medical assistance to everyone.

Kjeld and Susanne feared what the media's focus on the capture of a Danish aid worker in Syria might mean for the secrecy surrounding Daniel's kidnapping. Kidnapping cases involving westerners were generally kept out of the news through a so-called media blackout. Most of the Danish newspapers and television stations knew about the kidnapping, but had agreed not to write about the case in the interest of Daniel's safety.

Now and then, the international press published stories about ISIS keeping at least ten western hostages, and James Foley's family had been running a public campaign to rescue him since January 2013, while the rest of the hostages remained anonymous.

It was usually up to the individual families if they wanted to break the silence. The media blackout didn't necessarily help the situation, but it was often seen as a sensible precaution, since no one knew how the kidnappers would respond to international publicity. It allowed those trying to get the hostages released to work in peace, and ensured that news articles didn't motivate the kidnappers to raise the ransom money or make the hostages' conditions worse.

Kjeld and Susanne were divided about the right thing to do. Susanne felt some relief at the thought that she would no longer have to tell lies to keep it a secret. If she spotted someone she knew out of the corner of her eye while shopping in the supermarket, she often had to flee in order to avoid a conversation.

Conversely, she and Kjeld were waiting for the kidnappers to contact them by email and they didn't dare take the risk that Daniel's possible release might be thwarted by the Danish and international media writing about the case, so together with Arthur, they decided to wait and see. To be on the safe side, Susanne drafted an email to be sent out to family, friends and neighbours in case the media chose to write about Daniel.

'We don't know what the newspapers will come out with,' she wrote in her diary, 'so it's important they get the true story.'

That same day in Syria, a large-scale offensive began against ISIS.

. * .

Daniel was sitting in the cell, listening to the enormous blasts from the falling bombs. The building shook and exchanges of gunfire echoed in the air. The prisoners were also feeling the physical effects of the attacks coming closer. Meals were sporadic and one morning they didn't get any bread.

'The fighting is too fierce,' the guards explained. 'We can't get out to pick up food.'

Daniel wondered if ISIS was on the defensive. If so, he had no idea who was doing the attacking and what the situation was on the ground above his head. But it turned out he was right: other Syrian rebel groups had launched an offensive against ISIS around Aleppo, Deir ez-Zor and Raqqa. Fighters of the Free Syrian Army, the Islamic Front and Jabhat al-Nusra were all launching a war against ISIS.

According to several reports, the Islamic Front, a gathering of various more or less moderate Syrian rebels, had so many fighters that they were rapidly advancing, especially in some districts of Aleppo and in areas around the town, where they took over control. At the same time, Assad regime troops were taking advantage of the internal struggle between the Syrian rebels and ISIS. Other reports described how the regime's forces were advancing and trying to recapture parts of Aleppo's industrial district, Sheikh Najjar, where the hostages were imprisoned.

The moderate insurgents had for a long time regarded ISIS as an enemy of their original revolution, which first and foremost was about overthrowing the Assad regime and stopping its oppression of the Sunni majority in Syria.

When ISIS made gains, they captured areas from other rebels, partly with the help of the Assad regime, which mainly attacked the moderate rebel positions rather than ISIS, and partly with help from the rebels' own ranks, as some fighters joined the more powerful ISIS.

But patience was running out among the moderates and Daniel sensed some panic among their kidnappers when, one morning just one and a half weeks into January 2014, the hostages were blindfolded, handcuffed, thrown into the back of a truck and driven away.

There could no longer be any doubt that ISIS was facing pressure in the area where the hostages were being held, so they were hurriedly moving them.

They rumbled along some gravel roads for about fifteen minutes. When they arrived, they were allowed to take off their blindfolds and found themselves in an urban area none of them recogized. For once the cell wasn't in a basement. There were windows out to a corridor and to the outside world, but the panes were covered. The hostages could see a tower on the horizon through a small hole in the cardboard.

Eighteen hostages were now assembled, among them the newly arrived Spanish journalists, the American aid worker and two others that Daniel hadn't heard of or met before. A voice suddenly spoke Danish to him.

'Hi, I'm Dan. I'm from Denmark.'

'Hi Dan, I'm also from Denmark,' said Daniel in English, caught off-guard after so many months and unable to find the Danish words.

'You can just speak Danish,' laughed Dan with his deep voice.

He had been kidnapped a few days earlier, along with four

colleagues from MSF. Daniel stared in amazement at the Dane, who looked like a big teddy bear with his round cheeks, his bushy beard and long hair. He and his Belgian colleague were dressed in orange jumpsuits like the other hostages and Daniel felt that Dan, who was both broad and tall, was twice as big as him.

Dan told him that three of his female colleagues had been captured with them and were in the cell next door.

'What's happening in Denmark?' asked Daniel.

'Nothing in particular,' said Dan.

Daniel had previously experienced how a new hostage could be in a state of shock, so he held back until Dan was ready to talk. But it wasn't long before he and Dan were having long conversations together in Danish about both of them having been Scouts in the same Christian organization and how much fun it was to go out in Aarhus. Dan had been a volunteer at an annual music festival and they agreed that when they got out, they would go to the festival together.

Having an extra Dane in the group expanded Daniel's mental space. They could speak freely about the other hostages and air their frustrations. Daniel had been listening to the French for months, while they spoke confidentially in their mother tongue about their fellow prisoners.

Oh boy, this is great, he thought, feeling closer to Denmark when chatting with Dan.

The cell looked like an office: it had a desk, shelves and parts of the floor were carpeted. Posters for household appliances were stuck up on the walls – one showed a picture of a piece of roast meat in an oven, while a woman stood to one side, smiling. The guards had tried to cover her face with a piece of cardboard, but it constantly fell down, so her smile came into view.

The Beatles were still part of their everyday life and eternal constant reminder that anything could happen. One day Daniel was sitting on the windowsill, while the others were arranging the blankets in the limited space. A guard saw him sitting by the covered window and thundered, 'Why are you sitting on the windowsill? Are you about to escape? You've tried that before.'

The following evening the Beatles came in, led by John.

'Squat in the middle of the floor,' he ordered Daniel.

John had brought a sabre with him, of the type that Muslim armies had used in the Middle Ages. It was almost three foot long and had a silver handle. Daniel felt its sharp edge when the sabre was placed against his neck.

'Have you tried to escape?' shouted John threateningly.

Daniel explained that he had simply been sitting on the windowsill.

'Do you want to lose your head?'

'No,' answered Daniel clearly.

'You were lucky,' said John, after the Beatles turned their attention to two other hostages, John and Peter.

They accused the two hostages of planning an escape, even though they had just been playing a quiz in which they had to name films that began with different letters. They were instructed to sit at opposite ends of the room.

The psychological torture was beginning to lose its effect. Mentally, Daniel had donned an iron vest, which tightened his emotions into an unwavering line. If he didn't get too happy when the food came, too scared when a sabre was put to his neck and too sad when the proof-of-life pictures came to nothing, the whole situation became endurable. His mind had turned into a comfortable, grey mass, even when Paul was cramming verses from the Koran and the shahada (the Islamic declaration of faith) into the hostages to – as he put it – prepare them for death. Daniel numbly repeated the short phrases that formed the shahada: 'I bear witness that there is no other god than Allah. He has no partners. And I bear witness that Muhammad is His slave and messenger.'

On 19 January 2014 the cell received its nineteenth hostage, the British taxi driver Alan Henning from Manchester. Just after Christmas he had been taken by masked and armed men in the Syrian city of Adana outside Aleppo, when he was working as a voluntary aid worker.

It was the third time he had travelled in Syria as a volunteer for Aid for Syria and he had worked hard in his taxi to save enough money and earn time off to drive a relief convoy all the way down through Europe to Syria. His commitment to the war-torn country was kindled after he had held a Syrian baby in his arms in a refugee camp.

'The way she looked at me. I felt terrible,' explained Alan, who had 'Aid for Syria' tattooed on the inside of his wrist, while a carp graced one of his shoulders. He told Daniel that he loved to fish for carp and had taken his wife on a fishing trip on their honeymoon.

'If we continue sitting here, it'll become a bloody goldfish,' he joked about the tattoo.

Alan had barely arrived before the hostages were chained together in groups. Daniel was tied together with the Belgian from MSF and the Russian Sergei. They collected all the blankets they could carry and Daniel dragged a small mattress up on to the back of a pickup, where the hostages were covered by the blankets, so that no one could see them. After a short drive, they were separated into two trucks and began a journey of several days to the ISIS stronghold.

Daniel crawled over some boxes and further into the back of the truck. With his blindfold on, he arranged the blankets and the mattress so that he sat fairly softly against the metal skeleton of the cargo hold.

When the truck set off, he pulled the blindfold down around his neck. Beside him sat Pierre and in the light that penetrated through the cracks in the tarpaulin over the hold, Daniel and Pierre could see the Spanish Chef wearing a suicide vest. Pierre was annoyed that the guard was sitting with the prisoners. It precluded an escape attempt and Pierre left the piece of aluminium from a can of hummus, which he often used to unlock his handcuffs, in his pocket.

Then Pierre noticed that the cartons which surrounded them in the cargo hold resembled those the prisoners had previously been served dates from. Pierre leaned towards Daniel.

'Look in the boxes,' he urged.

They were indeed sat among boxes of dates and, when it was dark and the Spanish Chef was sleeping, Pierre took out a bag from one of the boxes. Should they open it? If they were caught eating the dates, the guards would regard it as theft, which in the caliphate's book was punishable by chopping off a hand. Their hunger won and they sneakily ate from the bag, which they afterwards hid at the bottom of the box.

There weren't only dates in the cargo hold. There were also some wooden boxes with the word 'explosives' printed along the sides. Daniel could feel his insides contracting as it dawned on him what this meant: he was being transported next to explosives, probably roadside bombs, which were one of ISIS's trademark weapons. When enemy forces advanced into ISIS territories, they were often met by mines that ISIS buried in roads, in gardens and in doorways.

After their meal of dates Daniel lay down to sleep, while Pierre made use of the silence of the night to look out from under the tarpaulin to get an idea of where they were going. Far into the night, the truck stopped and, after several requests, the prisoners were finally allowed to get out and pee. Daniel walked a few metres off into the roadside to urinate. It was the first time in over eight months that he had been able look around outside.

There was a frosty mist, but an otherwise clear sky. The moonlight penetrated the greyish-white, dusty air, which was illuminated by the headlights of a long convoy of trucks waiting in queues in both directions. He could see vehicles for as far his poor eyesight could stretch. Pierre noticed a huge truck loaded with military vehicles, while on the back of a small pickup sat women and children. Other vehicles were loaded with goods and cargo that were apparently being transported to and from the ISIS areas.

When the convoy set off again, a whispered rumour spread in the back of the truck. Pierre and the Spanish hostages wanted to try and escape. They would cut a hole in the tarpaulin and jump out when they reached a desert landscape like the one in which they had just stopped. Pierre imagined that it would be impossible to see them if they quickly got away from the road. They would run in the direction of the border and avoid towns along the way.

Daniel shuddered at the thought. His own failed escape attempt fresh in his mind, he thought the plan being drawn up by Pierre and the other prisoners would be impossible to execute. There were at least ten of them in the back of the truck, all dressed in orange prison suits and barefoot. They had no idea where they were or what lay hidden in the surrounding area. Their orange clothing would shine like spotlights in the dark and they would be dependent on meeting someone willing to help them. Moreover, those who were left in the truck would probably be punished when the guards discovered that some of the hostages had escaped. Those hostages who had experienced torture didn't want to try to escape, including Daniel. He would rather die than escape, then be captured and tortured again. It was different for Pierre. He hadn't experienced the worst of the torture.

It was still dark when the truck stopped at a farm along a country lane. They were thrown into a concrete shed with frosted windows, where the hostages from the other truck were already waiting for them. None of them had been given any food.

There was a washing machine and an iron bed in the shed. Blankets and mattresses were scattered over the floor. Pierre and one of the Spaniards found a pair of scissors, which they could use to cut a hole in the tarpaulin. Someone put the scissors in his pocket, after which they went searching in a pile of clothes that were scattered about. There were used trousers and shirts for men, which they could wrap around their feet and use as shoes. Pierre told Daniel about the escape plan in detail and

he briefly considered escaping with them, because he couldn't
handle being left alone.

Just before dawn all nineteen hostages were pushed into the
back of the truck. One of them asked if they might eat the dates.

'As many as you want,' came the reply.

It became a date feast. Daniel opened different bags. Some
were dry and tough, others juicy and soft. As they assuaged their
hunger with the dates, their thirst increased; and then there was
the next challenge: a toilet visit. Some of them got diarrhoea
from the dates. They found a plastic bag, which they stuffed
into a cardboard box to form a makeshift toilet. But it wasn't
an easy target to hit in the twilight, while in a moving vehicle.
When one of them tried to use the box, he didn't aim straight.
The others got angry and asked where they were supposed to
sit in the cramped space when people were crapping all over the
place. Some of them howled with laughter and tried to cover the
faeces with a blanket. It stank. It was a madhouse, with nineteen
hostages in a few square metres.

Meanwhile, Pierre sat preoccupied, looking out through the
tarpaulin. They had stopped in a convoy, as if permission wasn't
being given to drive any further. Besides that, it was beginning
to get light out and he saw for himself how the grand escape
plan was crumbling.

The truck made several stopovers during the journey, when
the hostages were temporarily stored in rooms and cellars. After
they had been travelling for several days, Pierre observed through
the tarpaulin how the desert landscape was coming closer and
they sensed they were heading northwards.

They drove past some ancient Roman walls in what looked

like Sergiopolis, south-west of Raqqa. Between the old ruins, Pierre caught sight of oil that was flowing out into the sand and the warriors raised their guns and shouted 'Allahu akhbar!' while firing into the air. It made Daniel jump, because he was sitting next to a box of explosives.

Later they drove past some green fields, which could indicate they were close to the Euphrates River, which runs through Raqqa province. When they stopped in a small town, the Spanish Chef got off. Before he left them, he stuck his head into the cargo hold and gave the hostages a final piece of advice:

'Find another job; stop being journalists.'

It was a relief when the truck finally reached its destination and they were led into a room with uncovered windows. They weren't allowed to bring their blankets, but were given new ones and some pizza, which they shared among themselves.

Daniel could hear the three women from MSF complaining loudly in the room next door.

After only a couple of hours' break, they were fetched again and led back to the pickups.

'Look down between your legs,' they were ordered.

After a short drive, they entered a courtyard, and when Daniel raised his head, he saw a large mansion in front of them. In the doorway stood the three women from MSF, wearing headscarves and arranged like a welcoming committee.

The hostages were led up a flight of stairs to the top floor and into a small bedroom. There were mattresses spread out ready on the floor and there was a toilet with a bathtub. A door led out to an enclosed terrace, where there were sofas and tables. A couple of young, clean-shaven, well-dressed guys in jeans and leather jackets asked what they would like to eat. Daniel thought he had misheard. He didn't know what he wanted. He had forgotten what it was like to decide for himself.

'Just chicken and fries,' said someone.

To everyone's surprise, their hosts brought them barbecued chicken and French fries.

The next morning, the obliging, clean-shaven hosts from the night before invited the hostages to breakfast on the terrace. The sun was still low and the morning mist lay across the Euphrates. Daniel shaped some binoculars with his forefinger and thumb and could just make out a small boat on the river. In the distance, he could see fields and the city of Raqqa, and on the other side of the river was a water treatment facility. On the neighbouring property, a satellite dish pointed east.

He drank a cup of tea, while quietly enjoying the view of the world and the Euphrates. They were between the Tigris and the Euphrates rivers, where some of the greatest civilizations in the history of the world first flourished: Babylon and Assyria. According to the Bible, the Euphrates sprang out of the river of Eden, along with three other streams. Daniel thought more than six months back to the time when he had tried to hang himself. He was still a hostage, yet it felt as if that had happened in a completely different world to the one he was in now.

'This is the Islamic State,' said their host. Daniel nodded.

The latest civilization to be found here was known for darkness and violence, except for their host who fussed over them and seemed interested in treating his western 'guests' well.

Breakfast consisted of tinned tuna and sardines, hummus and plenty of bread.

The first four days in the mansion-prison, which the hostages called Riverside, proceeded quietly. During the day, when the guards were present, they could walk around freely. In the evening, they sat chained together in pairs, while the women were made to cook dinner. Fully covered, they rummaged around in the kitchen, but one evening no food arrived. One of the prisoners knocked impatiently on the door to get an explanation and a female hostage came into the cell and said that there was apparently no more money for food.

Daniel tried to distract his hunger by playing games. He had hidden some cardboard in his trousers, which he took out from its hiding place. On one side he drew a chessboard and on the other, a backgammon game. Although he was still chained to the Belgian, they found a lighter in a drawer and made two chunks from a piece of candle, which they melted into cubes. They shaped the eyes on the dice with a warmed up nail and then filled them with ink.

The Belgian and Daniel also made two sets of playing cards from the bottoms of some cardboard boxes that had contained Laughing Cow cheese and some flyers with Arabic script, which they had found somewhere in the room. They didn't think for a moment about what was on the flyers until a guard spotted the cards.

'What's that?' he asked.

'It's a card game we made,' Daniel replied.

The guard took the cards from them. They had committed a great sin, because they had made playing cards out of what were apparently Jabhat al-Nusra's recruitment flyers. They had thoughtlessly torn into pieces the Prophet's words and verses from the Koran and turned the holy scriptures into a game with infidel kings and queens.

Daniel expected they would be punished, but life as a hostage with ISIS was unpredictable. To his great relief, nothing more happened.

Card games, tea and sardines couldn't numb Daniel's longing to escape. This was further encouraged by the large windows in their cell. Right out there on the other side of the glass stretched freedom. The hostages began to conduct a sort of public hearing on the topic of 'golf', a code name for their escape attempt. Everyone had something to say. Would it actually be possible to 'play golf'?

Daniel shared his own experiences. He showed the scars on his wrists and throat. That was why he had tried to escape, but there was a high risk of failure – also, they were in the middle of ISIS's stronghold in winter, when it would be possible to see them for miles in their orange jumpsuits.

'It isn't enough just to be out on the other side of the window,' he said.

Some of the hostages argued that it was better to die free than to rot in captivity. Pierre would rather flee than allow ISIS to get money for him, if indeed that ever became an issue.

David, who had experience from the British military, strongly advised that they reflect on the matter, because statistically the vast majority of hostages are released through successful negotiations. An escape would have to be arranged and planned down to the smallest detail, he said, because escape attempts often ended in death. It might well have been an escape attempt that had cost Kenneth Bigley his life. According to the *Sunday Times*, Bigley had managed to escape from his captors with the help of a Syrian and an Iraqi, who had infiltrated the group. But after a short time on the run, Bigley had been recognized at a checkpoint, even though he had been disguised. This example was one of several that supported the notion that escape attempts often ended up going wrong – even if one had outside help.

'I know the odds,' David insisted. 'I'm betting on coming out through negotiations.'

Even so, Daniel whispered in Pierre's ear that he would join him if he planned to escape.

Despite the grim statistics, there was agreement among the hostages that they could at least explore the possibilities. They delegated tasks to each other. Some of them had to keep an eye on what was happening outside the windows, so that they could understand when the guards came and went, what weapons they carried, who replaced whom, how many guards were in and around the mansion, and how to attack a guard and steal his car.

The hostages created a document in which they noted what they had seen. They were cautious and wrote in code, as if it were player rankings from a card tournament. They were always ready to swallow the most dangerous notes.

David was the voice of pragmatism.

'You have to convince me it's possible,' he said and asked the others to find patterns in the guards' activities that could be exploited. For example, did the guards sleep before dinner at a certain time or was there a period during the day when there were fewer of them?

They took notes as they watched through the windows and saw cars driving to and from the mansion; when the guards checked the cell and brought food; and where and how many lookouts there were.

The Americans thought that they had to work fast, because it was perhaps the last chance they would get before they were again moved to a basement cell without windows.

They watched the guards for four days, but there was no regularity in their activities. There didn't seem to be any regular routines.

There is no damn pattern at all! Try finding a pattern in the Middle East, thought Daniel.

Their escape plans were given the final death knell when the Beatles moved into the closed terrace next to their cell. Only a thin curtain and a window pane separated the hostages from their worst guards. At any moment, John or George could pull aside the curtain and monitor every movement the nineteen men were making. It gave Daniel the chills. It was as if the curtain and the side of the room where it hung had become toxic. Now it was just about survival, because the British guards seemed more unpredictable than ever.

'Peter Kassig!' shouted George one day to the American.

'Yes, sir.'

'Do you like to be in the army, Peter?'

'Yes, sir.'

'Do you like to kill Muslims, Peter?'

'No, sir.'

'Don't lie to us.'

Peter was ordered to stand up for several hours on the spot. Another time it was James who had to stand for a whole night.

When this happened, the other hostages took turns staying awake and giving them water or bread if they needed it, but the Beatles even put a stop to that outbreak of solidarity. They installed a camera on top of a cupboard in the cell and hooked it up through the door and out to the terrace where they lived.

'Now we can see every move you make,' announced John.

Daniel stopped doing his daily sit-ups and the hostages held back from playing and talking together out of fear that it could give the British guards an excuse to punish them. The Beatles watched them through the camera, which Daniel felt pointed straight at him. They could come in at any second. He felt as if he was chained to the radiator again.

'You're sitting looking out the window!' shouted John to Daniel one day.

He had just leaned his head against the cold pane. 'No, I wasn't.'

'Yes, you were. I could see you.'

The mental torture also consisted of Ringo and John standing in the doorway, demanding specific answers to political questions.

'Do you know Blackwater?' one asked, to which the hostages would answer that it was the US security company that, among other things, was guilty of killing seventeen civilians during the Iraq War.

At other times they demanded that the hostages ask them questions to which they responded with long, preaching answers. It was a game of 'ask a question or get beaten up'.

'Why are you so opposed to women being educated?' asked one hostage.

'We don't say that. Women should be educated in the Koran, because it is they who must raise our children. The more they learn about the Koran, the purer and better the children will be,' one of the Brits replied and went on to talk about 'the true path'.

Ringo said that, while living in Britain, he had phoned in to a debate on the radio and said that the western forces would lose in Afghanistan and Iraq, because God was on the Islamists' side. The host of the show had claimed there was a problem with the connection and had hung up.

'That is proof that there is no culture of debate in western countries,' he said.

James asked what was the point of converting to Islam if other Muslims still considered a convert an infidel? The response from the Brits was that only God could cast doubt on the sincerity of one's belief.

The Beatles also played the hostages off against each other. One day they gave Toni, who had converted to Islam, a whole chicken at one of the meals.

'Toni is a good Muslim,' they said.

'May I share the chicken with two others?' asked Toni.

'Who?'

Toni suggested giving a little of his chicken to two of the other prisoners who had also converted, James and John.

'James may not have any,' they answered. 'He is evil.'

Daniel tried to make himself as invisible and insignificant to the Beatles as possible; to merge into the wall and hide himself among the others as if he didn't exist. He didn't dare to even look at them, unlike Pierre, who was on alert whenever they were in the cell.

One day George, for the first and only time, entered without covering his face. While he stood in front of James and put a plastic cable tie around his tongue, several of the hostages paid close attention to his appearance. He was quite young, maybe in his early twenties, with shoulder-length, wavy hair, a thin beard and full lips. Terror had finally been given a face.

Daniel mostly succeeded in staying under the British guards' radar – until one day in early February 2014, when they again asked for email addresses for Daniel's immediate family members.

'If you give me your girlfriend's email address again, I'll beat you to a pulp!' shouted John.

Daniel gave him his mother's email address. But he wasn't sure if he had remembered it correctly.

Emails from the Dark

On Saturday, 8 February 2014 Susanne and Kjeld were at a birthday party at the Hedegård Community Hall. Their relative and neighbour Sven Olaf was celebrating his seventieth birthday and the room was buzzing with talkative friends and neighbours dressed up for the occasion. Under normal circumstances, Kjeld and Susanne would have enjoyed being part of this festive gathering, but not on this particular day, because, as usual, the conversation veered towards the subject of how the children were.

'Where's Daniel?' their friends asked.

'He's off somewhere taking photos. He lives in Copenhagen,' lied Susanne, stifling the anguish of betraying her desire to tell the truth.

Susanne and Kjeld were on tenterhooks all evening and took turns going into the bathroom to check their mobiles for any new messages. They thought it would be rude to have their phones sitting out next to the birthday cakes. Later in the evening, they went home exhausted. Kjeld went to bed and Susanne switched on the computer in the office to check her email one last time.

At 9.26 p.m. an email had arrived. She didn't recognize the sender, loo2tomc@Safe-mail.net, but opened it anyway; it was written in English and used a lot of capital letters, making it look at first glance like spam. It began:

This message is to inform you that we have taken the Denmark citizen Daniel Rye Ottosen PRISONER. It's very simple, a CASH PAYMENT will secure his release.

Susanne held her breath as she read on.

If you want to confirm we are really the ones holding Daniel, then we will except [*sic*] three questions from his family of a personal nature that only Daniel could possibly be able to answer correctly.

The CONDITIONS OF DANIEL'S SAFE RETURN IS, NO MEDIA INVOLVEMENT, WHATSOEVER, AND A CASH PAYMENT!

Reply FAST, with clearly written email messages, to this email address and NO ATTACHMENTS! Act FAST, so as not to endanger the safety of Daniel.

Susanne flew out of the office and ran to the bedroom. Kjeld was still awake.

'There's an email from Syria!' she shouted.

Finally, after almost nine months, the kidnappers were interested in making contact.

They're ready to negotiate, thought Kjeld, as they forwarded the email to Arthur and called him. Arthur was on holiday with his family, travelling on some Norwegian road in the middle of nowhere. Since he had started working to find James Foley – and later Daniel – he had hardly stepped foot in Denmark. Having spent more than 275 days travelling in 2013, he had finally taken a couple of days off to spend time with his family.

'I'll have a look at it and send you my thoughts as soon as we get to our cabin,' he said.

When he read the message from the kidnappers, he could see the wording and the use of capital letters were similar to the email that James's family had received in December 2013.

Susanne and Kjeld couldn't sleep that night. The words from the email swirled around Susanne's head, especially the sentence about not speaking to the media. She couldn't help but worry about what would happen if journalists wrote about Daniel anyway.

The following day they discussed their next move with Arthur and at noon they sent their reply to the kidnappers. They made sure that the proof-of-life questions would make Daniel think of something positive.

'*Assalamu alaikum*, greetings,' they began their message. They went on to explain that for nine months they had been trying to negotiate a 'practical' solution that could bring Daniel home, and that they had managed so far to keep the story out of the press.

Then they listed their three carefully selected questions for Daniel: 'At which family event did Daniel give a speech shortly before his departure to Syria, and where did it take place? Where did Daniel and Signe first meet? With whom did he travel to Nepal?'

The email ended with a heartfelt request: 'Would you please pass on our best wishes to Daniel from Signe, Anita, Christina, Dad and Mum. Best regards, Susanne and Kjeld Rye Ottosen.'

. * .

The day after the family had replied to the kidnappers' email, the hostages were moved to a new location. Had Daniel been able to look at a satellite photograph, he would have seen a square, fenced-in area. It lay south-east of Raqqa in the middle of the deserted, sand-coloured expanse, a short distance from the verdant areas surrounding the Euphrates. The vegetation alongside the building indicated that it was being watered and trees had been planted in long, straight rows. Two iron towers stood high above and the large containers standing close to the building indicated that this could be an oil refinery.

The new cell, where Daniel was to spend the remainder of his captivity, was named the Quarry by the other prisoners.

When the captives' handcuffs and blindfolds were removed, Peter blurted out: 'I've been here before!'

He reassured the other men, telling them that the last time there had been a nice guard and that he had been given plenty to eat, even though he was served only one meal a day. It was also in this prison that Peter had converted to Islam and taken the Muslim name Abdul Rahman. Pierre recognized the room as being the first one he had stayed in when he was originally captured in June 2013.

The cell was dark and measured about 170 square feet. The only sunlight there was filtered in through a ventilator in a corner of the room. They used the daylight to help them count the days and the guards' calls to prayer to work out what time it was.

There were storage boxes for clothes and medicine, so they could keep things tidy. They were given a couple of blankets each and, as the weather was becoming milder, they had no difficulty staying warm in the overcrowded cell. New prison suits were also handed out, as the orange ones had become infested with lice. Daniel wore dark-green trousers and a jacket.

They had been in the Quarry only a couple of days when the Beatles banged hard on the cell door. Daniel sat with his hands against the wall, as one of the Brits kicked him in the side.

'Danish boy . . . we've got some questions for you. Make sure you answer them right. Don't screw this up!'

The first proof-of-life question was put to him: at which family event had he given a speech just before he travelled to Syria?

He felt a surge of energy rushing through his body. His captors had taken images and videos of him at random, and he had no idea if any of them had ever reached home. Suddenly, he felt as if his family were speaking directly to him.

'My maternal grandfather's birthday,' answered Daniel.

'Where did you meet your girlfriend, Signe?' the Brit continued.

'I met her at Vesterlund Ungdomsskole.'

The Brit burst out laughing.

'Vester-what? You'll have to spell that for us!'

Daniel started laughing too, and a warm feeling spread throughout his entire body at the thought that Signe was still waiting for him. She had to be, otherwise he wouldn't have been given that question.

The Brit ordered him to spell out 'Vesterlund Ungdomsskole'

using the phonetic alphabet, but he could remember only Alpha, Bravo, Charlie. Instead he found random words that began with the respective letters to dictate the rest.

The answer to the last question was easier: who had he travelled with in Nepal?

'My friend, Ebbe,' answered Daniel, who could no longer conceal his enthusiasm and answered a bit too cheerfully. A punishment was promptly issued: one of the Beatles whacked him in the side. His instinct was to contract and draw his body in on itself, but he remained sitting upright. Then kicks began coming at him from all angles, landing on his legs, shoulders, ribs, until he could no longer sit up. He ended up in a foetal position on the floor to protect his stomach and internal organs. He felt a desert boot using his face as a doormat, wiping the sole against his ear, while other boots continued relentlessly kicking his lower back and thighs.

Petrified, Pierre sat in the mandatory position, with his face and hands against the wall, and listened to the merciless beating of his screaming friend. When the Beatles left the cell, everyone looked at Daniel, who was crying. Pierre asked in a concerned voice if he was OK and Dan asked where it hurt most. After a while in captivity, they had learned to protect their internal organs from the beatings; bruising would disappear, but permanent internal injuries would not. Despite the pain, Daniel laughed and cried with relief that he hadn't been seriously hurt.

'Signe is waiting for me! Signe is waiting for me!' he exclaimed.

During this period, the prisoners held proof-of-life parties whenever one of them was asked questions like the ones the guards had asked Daniel. Emails had been sent to the hostages' families or employers, who hastily sent back questions. The only people who had nothing to celebrate were the six British and American hostages. Nobody asked them proof-of-life questions. The other captives had various theories as to why. Perhaps the silence was part of a political game, perhaps the US and UK were playing hard to get, or maybe the Beatles could manage only a certain number of negotiations at one time.

With impatience and a deep sense of foreboding, the six hostages nevertheless waited for a sign that negotiations for their release would begin soon.

. * .

Five days passed before Daniel's family in Hedegård received answers to the questions they had sent the kidnappers; the responses confirmed that they were indeed in contact with those holding Daniel captive.

'The family event was his maternal grandfather's 75th birthday that took place in Ribe,' stated the kidnappers' email. 'Daniel met Signe at Vesterlund Ungdomsskole. He travelled to Nepal with his best friend, Ebbe.'

Susanne began to cry. She was communicating with her son for the first time in nine months. It was as if, through his answers, he was speaking directly to her.

A few lines further down in the email came the long-awaited demand for a ransom.

For his release we are demanding a CASH PAYMENT of TWO MILLION EUROS NOW!! You've been contacted a while ago, yet you've responded very late . . . We hope for

his sake you care about him, because time is now against
him. The longer you take the less likely Daniel will live!!

The amount requested by the kidnappers was exorbitant – the
equivalent of 15 million Danish kroner (about £1,500,000) – but
Kjeld thought that now they had a negotiating position, they would
be sure to get Daniel home for much less.

Communicating with kidnappers is a special skill, requiring a
thorough knowledge of who the captors are; every single word
has to be carefully weighed. Arthur knew that negotiating with
ISIS would require a different strategy to dealing with criminal
gangs in Nigeria or pirates in Somalia. Moreover, this was the
first time ISIS had initiated any actual communication for a
ransom for male hostages from Denmark, France, Spain, Italy,
Germany or Belgium.

The captors swore allegiance to an uncompromising Islamist
ideology and had a clear political agenda, which was far more
important to them than money, the usual motivation behind pirate
kidnappings. But the ISIS captors were also extremely strategic.
Some months earlier, they had demanded a staggering ransom from
James Foley's family. The United States had categorically refused
to negotiate and if the family collected the money itself, it would
be in breach of US law against funding terrorism. Now ISIS was
negotiating the release of hostages from the European countries
that often did pay a ransom (with the exception of Denmark),
which demonstrated a clear difference between American and
European approaches to hostage situations. Arthur assumed the
kidnappers intended to play off the different governments against
one another. Undoubtedly this strategy would only increase the

pressure on the families of the American and British hostages, whose governments refused to negotiate with terrorists.

Advised by Arthur of the latest details of the proposal from ISIS concerning Daniel's case, the Danish authorities offered to take over all of the correspondence between the captors and Susanne and Kjeld in order to protect them. But Susanne and Kjeld didn't want to give up control. They preferred to handle the situation personally in close collaboration with Arthur, whom they trusted – even if no one could predict the kidnappers' next move. Arthur decided they should continue to communicate as 'the family' and not let the correspondence seem too 'professional'. They must not under any circumstances give the impression that the government was behind their emails, especially since this was not the case. It was important that they separated themselves from the other negotiations that Arthur knew had already been initiated by European authorities for some of Daniel's fellow prisoners. The captors should understand that in Daniel's case, they were negotiating directly with an ordinary Danish family who had no way of paying such a high ransom.

They also needed to realize that, unlike Spain, France and some other European nations, the Danish government didn't generally pay ransoms. Arthur and the family concluded that the best approach would be to try and appeal to the kidnappers with the truth and to speak to them from their emotional and exhausted hearts.

The crucial next step would be to buy time in order to scrape together the money, without putting off the kidnappers, while simultaneously trying to lower the exorbitant ransom of 15 million kroner.

The family were unwilling participants in a race against time, as the captors never failed to remind them. 'The longer it takes, the less likelihood Daniel has of survival,' they threatened.

Arthur had no doubt that the captors were capable of murdering Daniel if they didn't get what they wanted. He wrote to them from the family's email account, explaining that they hadn't heard from the captors until this point and that they had repeatedly tried to communicate to find a solution.

'We are a simple, hard-working family [. . .] The amount you are requesting for Daniel's release is unrealistic for us to put together,' he wrote. He stressed that at the beginning of the coming week, they would go to the bank to ascertain how large a sum they could manage to raise towards the ransom. To keep the email personal, he signed off with: 'We would very much like you to tell Daniel that we are thinking of him and praying for him.'

The following week, Kjeld and Susanne went to the bank to find out exactly how much they could borrow against their house. Kjeld couldn't stand the thought of going and begging for money from other people and he was confident they could raise the entire amount with a loan from the bank.

On 17 February they requested the maximum sum they could borrow, which came to just over 1,350,000 kroner. They stated their offer to the kidnappers in American dollars, because they thought the sum sounded more impressive than in euros. Once their offer of $251,000 had been dispatched, Kjeld sent Anita a text message: 'Let's just hope they're feeling generous.'

· * ·

'You have to write some letters,' ordered the Beatles as they handed out sheets of paper to the hostages in the cell in Raqqa. It was at the end of February and they were told to write home to their families in English. The letters were to contain specific wording and Daniel added no personal feelings to it, as he was ordered to write:

Dear Mum and Dad, I'm so sorry to put you all through this. Please follow the instructions of the group that is holding me. This is all about money. Collect as much money as possible and I will be released. I love you all very much and hope with all my heart to see you all again. Yours, Daniel.

A few days later the Beatles came back to record a video with the Spanish hostage Marc Marginedas. It came as no surprise that Marc was the first to be filmed, since a ransom had already been paid for his release. They knew this, because when the hostages had been kept in the house overlooking the Euphrates, George had told them, 'It's looking good for you Spaniards.'

The hostages had cautiously anticipated that the Spaniards would be the first to be released. Daniel felt dismay spread throughout his body that he wasn't the one on his way home. When Marc had finished thanking them all, the Beatles turned towards Daniel and ordered him to take off his shirt. With open palms, they slapped his chest and rubbed him with the sole of a shoe until his skin looked red and raw. Then he remained bare-chested as they positioned him against the white walls of the cell and ordered him to look directly into the camera. With the marks across his chest clearly visible, he said in staccato sentences: 'Hi

Mum. I heard that you're going to the bank next week. Please collect all the money that you can get. It's just about money, so I can get released. Please help me.'

. * .

On the day Marc was meant to be released, the Beatles banged hard on the door and stood in the doorway calling for him as he stood there with the hand-written letters that he had been told to take away with him.

'You're going home now,' announced the Brits.

'The rest of you can also get ready. You're being moved.'

Marc stood in the middle of the room and said nothing. The Beatles went up to James.

'Look at him closely. It's the closest you'll ever get to freedom.'

Marc was told to take a shower and he was allowed to go to the toilet. The electricity had gone out and it was dark in the cell. The Beatles put a flashlight in the corner, while the hostages were allowed to go to the toilet one at a time.

'Make sure you empty your bladders. You're going to be travelling a long way. You're going to Iraq,' the Beatles told them loudly, stomping around among the hostages, stepping on their arms and legs whenever possible. Then they split them up into smaller groups.

'Denmark, sit together,' came the order. 'France, you too.'

Daniel and Dan moved close together and put their arms round each other's shoulders.

'Right then, boys, it's taking a long time to go to the toilet . . . We can sing our little song, do you remember it?' asked George as he held his nose.

One of the Brits found an empty pot, which he put on James's head.

'Can you balance it . . . ?'

When the pot fell off, they turned it over and put it on James' head like a hat.

'Have you been practising "Osama's Lovely Hotel"? America, start singing!' ordered the Beatles, who walked among the small groups in the dim light from the flashlight and conducted the singing.

While some of them took turns to go to the toilet, the remaining hostages had to sing in rounds about Osama's lovely hotel, where you would die if you tried to escape.

'Come on, Denmark!' shouted the Beatles, randomly pushing and kicking the prisoners. When it was Daniel's turn to urinate, he was given a light and hurried out to the toilet. As he washed his hands he could hear the hellish singing, a din that wailed in the background like a broken record. Then he returned to the room, sat down, put his arm around Dan and started singing too.

When the song was over, nothing more happened. They weren't moved, even though the Beatles had made sure they had said it loud enough for Marc to hear. This was presumably so that on Marc's release he could convey false information to his government's intelligence service by telling them that the hostages were no longer being held captive at the Quarry in Raqqa.

They never saw Marc again. At some point the Beatles must have sneaked him out. Later that day, Daniel saw Marc's old clothes in a tub in the bathroom. The first prisoner had left the cell, negotiations were under way for the others, and Daniel prayed that he would be next to leave.

But the threat the Beatles had issued to James just before Marc left the prison hung heavily in the air.

. * .

There was no news from Syria. Susanne and Kjeld checked their email inbox almost every minute. Susanne even set her mobile phone to beep when an email arrived. On 25 February, eight days after they had sent their ransom offer to the kidnappers, Arthur decided they would follow up. They didn't receive an answer from the kidnappers until the evening of 3 March. Daniel's captors maintained their demands for a ransom of €2 million. The tone in the long email was angry.

> We also remind you of the millions spent by your country's newspaper companies to print insults of our beloved messenger and Prophet Muhammad (peace and blessings of ALLAH be upon him) and the millions more spent by your government to protect these companies and ensure the continuation of their blasphemy. Surely they can pay 2,000,000 Euro for the safety of one of their citizens, or is it that your wretched people value attacking Islam more than they value protecting their citizens? Curse be upon you, this will never be forgotten.

The captors described how easily it could be arranged, referring to Marc, the Spanish hostage whose freedom had been bought, and explaining that he would contact them and bring them a personal greeting and a video appeal from Daniel.

We remind you of our conditions: NO MEDIA + QUICK CASH PAYMENT = his safe return home.

The family hurried to reply that they were doing everything within their power to raise the money and that they looked forward to hearing from Marc. However, Arthur wasn't making any headway in reaching Marc or the Spanish government to obtain the video and the letter. Arthur feared this might mean they were missing some vital information. He therefore proposed on 8 March that Susanne and Kjeld should write to the captors, explaining that they had desperately been trying to make contact with Marc for five days without success, and to ask if they could possibly have any contact details for the Spaniard.

The email ended: 'In two days, it is Daniel's 25th birthday. Will you please tell him that we are all thinking of him on this special day and we are praying that he comes home to us soon.'

On Daniel's twenty-fifth birthday, 10 March 2014, Susanne, Kjeld and Anita were once again invited to have coffee and cake at the Ministry of Foreign Affairs. Arthur also attended the meeting.

Kjeld was boiling with anger and had difficulty controlling himself in front of the officials. The captors were still sticking to the €2 million ransom, and the family was far from being able to pay that amount. Kjeld was frustrated that the government wasn't even willing to at least help pay Arthur's salary. From Kjeld's point of view, Arthur's knowledge of the situation in Syria was a huge benefit to other hostages and countries – and to the Danish government as well. But the family was left to pay for Arthur's work, Daniel's insurance having long since been depleted. Kjeld felt that more was being done to take care of Danes who had joined ISIS and were now returning home from the war and receiving social security benefits, than for a young, law-abiding citizen from Hedegård.

The Danish authorities held firm in their refusal to help with any kind of expense. Yet the fact remained that everyone at the meeting at the Foreign Ministry agreed that there was no time to lose. The family decided to throw all their energy into a comprehensive fundraising initiative. The risk that this could turn Daniel's case into a front-page story in the media was a risk they would have to take.

Anita took two weeks' leave from her job to coordinate the fundraising, which was initially directed at the large network of schools and associations that Daniel had had contact with during his gymnastics career.

The family was busier than ever.

. * .

Daniel was finally getting plenty to eat. Once a day, outside the cell, a huge flame was lit, which the hostages named Hellfire. Either a huge bowl of lentil soup was carried in for sharing or they were given some potatoes and bread. Daniel gradually increased his training routine by adding jumping squats, regular and oblique sit-ups, and weightlifting. He used jam jars or plastic buckets filled with water as his weights.

The prisoners were also given books and pamphlets to read. They were all about Islam. One of the books was titled *The Life, Teachings and Influence of Muhammad ibn Abdul-Wahhab* and was published by the Ministry of Islamic Affairs in Saudi Arabia.

Abdul-Wahhab had founded Wahhabism, the fundamentalist sect within Sunni Islam that was embraced by the Kingdom of Saudi Arabia and became the country's state religion. Followers of Wahhabism are known as Salafis and they believe in the ultra-conservative interpretation of the Koran that inspired ISIS.

Another small pamphlet from the Ministry was about *Useful Ways of Leading a Happy Life*. They were also given an English version of the Koran with a dark-blue cover and gold-coloured writing. Daniel threw himself into reading and used the texts to expand his English vocabulary. The only thing he had read until then had been the penicillin label.

The hostages gradually fell into a tolerable everyday routine, until the Beatles once again disrupted it with fear. They had just had their food brought in and Steven was dividing the tomatoes between them. Sergei got angry and made a scene, because he thought he was always given the worst and smallest tomatoes. An argument flared up about tomato distribution, which stopped abruptly when one of the Beatles shouted: 'Where's the Russian?'

Sergei stood up on the floor of the cell. One of the Frenchmen stepped in to act as interpreter. In broken Russian, he translated the message to Sergei that he was going to be released, because the Russian authorities had paid a staggering ransom. Then the Beatles took Sergei away.

A feeling of emptiness lingered in the cell. There hadn't been any proof-of-life questions for Sergei, who hadn't even been able to give an email address for somebody the kidnappers could write to. Everything indicated that the Russian had no family, no one who would miss him, and his fellow prisoners barely knew who he was. Nobody believed for a minute that he was really going to be released.

The next time George entered the cell, he pinched his nose tightly with his fingers and said in a nasal voice, 'I have good news and bad news. Which do you want first?'

The good news was that Marc had been released and was probably at home with his family. The bad news was that he had gone back on his agreement and spoken to the press. This was why, George announced, they had shot Sergei as a punishment for Marc's sins.

The hostages sat cross-legged, facing the middle of the cell, as the British handed around a laptop.

One by one they were asked to describe what they saw on the screen.

George, John and Ringo stood in the centre of the room. Daniel didn't dare look above their sand-coloured desert boots.

'It's a picture of Sergei,' said one of the captives.

'Yes, but what do you see?'

'He's dead,' answered another.

'Can you see where the bullet has hit him?'

They were forced to explain in minute detail how the bullet had gone through his eye, about the blood in his beard and the wrinkles in his forehead.

George gave them a technical speech about the type of ammunition used: the bullet was a dumdum bullet, which explodes when it hits the victim and thus creates more damage.

'It gives a much better effect,' explained George, holding the computer in front of Daniel's face.

THE ISIS HOSTAGE 231

'Daniel, what do the colours symbolize?'

Daniel looked at the picture of Sergei's head. It looked like he was lying in some sand.

'His face has a blueish tinge to it, which shows that he's cold . . . and that he's dead,' explained Daniel.

George made it very clear that if any of the other released prisoners spoke to the press when they got home, they would shoot or torture one of the remaining prisoners.

None of them believed that Marc had said too much, which was indeed confirmed later. It seemed more likely that the Beatles had disposed of a prisoner for whom they knew they couldn't get any money.

On his twenty-fifth birthday Daniel made a makeshift roulade for his fellow prisoners out of bread and jam, which he rolled together. He cut it into seventeen equal slices, which he shared around the cell. The others wished him a happy birthday and Pierre and James gave him an extra-long hug.

The Beatles also thought his birthday should be celebrated.

'We have a present for you from your parents,' said Ringo, going over to Daniel, who was sitting with his head facing the wall. A searing pain rose from the pit of his stomach as Ringo slammed his boot into Daniel's ribs.

'Your parents think this is some kind of gymnastics camp you're at, so they've asked us to wish you a happy birthday!' he shouted.

Twenty-five birthday kicks ensued, with short intervals between each one.

Daniel swallowed his screams as he shifted about to protect himself from the blows.

When his hands instinctively moved to protect his torso, Ringo shouted at him to lift his hands up again.

Some hours later something bulged out from Daniel's ribs that looked like a blue tennis ball.

. * .

Late at night on 11 March Anita's mobile rang. Susanne and Kjeld sounded extremely upset at the other end. They had just received an email with an attachment.

'It's a dead man's face,' said Kjeld.

The man lay with his head in the desert sand and blood in his beard; it looked as if he had been shot in his right eye. They didn't know who the man was, but the kidnappers wrote that he had 'shared a cold cell with your son'.

> DO NOT WASTE OUR TIME with useless messages that will not benefit you or your son the slightest way! You mention nothing about our 2,000,000 EURO demand and yet you're asking about written messages/videos and sending birthday wishes!! You are digging your son's shallow grave with your STUPIDITY!

They also mentioned Marc's email address, together with a warning that Daniel could come home in a body bag, because 'our lions are hungry to let Danish blood flow in revenge for the Mohammed cartoons'.

Kjeld tried to reassure himself with the thought that so many people were killed in Syria that it could be a picture of anyone. But he still stayed home from work the next day and Susanne agreed to give Arthur her password so that in the future the family wouldn't open any attachments before Arthur had checked them.

Anita drove to Hedegård the next morning to kick off the fundraising.

It was time for the family to make a higher ransom offer.

The Experiment

The dining table in the living room in Hedegård was littered with small notes with names, phone numbers and email addresses of people in Daniel's and the family's networks. Kjeld and Susanne noted down all the contacts that they could possibly think of.

Anita sat at the computer, editing the draft of a letter that Arthur had sent her. She had experience from her job with seeking funding for environmental projects and, even though this was something quite different, she knew a lot about raising money.

The letter was to be sent to wider, but still controlled, circles of people they knew and trusted, for example, via the Listserv at Vesterlund School and the gymnastics clubs. It was crucial that the wording struck the right tone and that she didn't reveal too much, and she hoped that those who knew Daniel would be willing to help.

'This request is about a human life in danger,' began the letter.

After this, there was information about why Daniel had travelled to Syria and why the case was very sensitive:

The papers you are holding are marked 'confidential', which doesn't restrict you in a legal sense, but we hope that you will treat this request confidentially as, in a worst-case scenario, it could cost Daniel his life if the information is made public.

If recipients wished to offer their support, they should go through the family's lawyer, Oluf Engell, from the law firm Bruun & Hjejle, which was helping to manage the account where donors could anonymously deposit an amount.

There is a professional and competent team behind this fundraising and everything is being done properly and in accordance with all laws and regulations. The money goes into a trust account that only the lawyer can manage. We as a family and the public will never know who has contributed to the cause.

According to the Danish Penal Code, section 114b, it is an offence to give, collect or otherwise disseminate money to terrorist organizations. This law was passed in order to prevent people in Denmark from helping to finance terrorism. Denmark hadn't yet put ISIS on its list of terrorist organizations, even though judicially it would take only a couple of videos of some of ISIS's crimes to prove the claim.

But neither in the law nor the extensive background material of the Act was there any reference to whether the law applied to paying ransoms for hostages held by terrorist organizations. Since no Danish court had yet dealt with such a case and thereby settled the question, it was unclear whether it was legal or illegal.

A ransom payment still ends up in the terrorists' pockets. At the same time, it could be argued that the aim of collecting money for a ransom was not to finance terrorism, but to save a human life.

Because the family's fundraising was operating in a legal grey area, it was carried out under the supervision of the relevant Danish authorities to ensure that neither the contributors nor the family would be prosecuted for giving money to terrorists.

Even though ISIS would receive the ransom, for Anita and the rest of the family it was purely a matter of getting Daniel home alive. Anita's boyfriend had been a soldier and he thought that paying a ransom to ISIS was highly problematic, but they had no choice if they wanted to get Daniel released. Anita was aware of the dilemma when she asked people for a contribution and could easily understand if they didn't want to donate.

The motto for the fundraising was 'many small streams make a big river'. In addition to people from associations and schools in the gymnastics world who knew Daniel, the letter was sent to friends and acquaintances in the local community. The whole family helped. Daniel's paternal grandmother wrote the account number on the bulletin board where she went to choir and told her friends about the situation, while Daniel's maternal grandfather collected contributions from neighbours and friends in the retirement home where he lived.

Although the family had reached out to only a relatively small number of recipients, they had just sent off the letter when representatives from the Danish Security and Intelligence Service (PET) rang the doorbell in Hedegård.

Susanne welcomed the visitors, turned on the coffee machine and asked the PET agents to sit in the living room, so they could talk about the case over a cup of coffee. Anita was in the office receiving constant phone calls. The line to Hedegård was ringing off the hook at the same time as the agents from PET were expressing their concern about the fundraiser. They felt it was almost impossible to ensure that the news of Daniel's capture wasn't shared on social media and made public.

In a break between phone calls, Anita recognized that the fundraiser was an experiment and that she couldn't control whether or not someone might write about Daniel on Facebook.

'We have a choice between the plague and cholera and we have chosen cholera, because we simply can't live with the plague,' explained Anita.

A short time afterwards, the fundraiser was out of their control. The magazine *The Gymnast* sent out an email about Daniel to everyone who received the magazine's newsletter. Anita almost had a heart attack. But donations poured in and no one said a word about Daniel on Facebook.

The family now truly believed that it might be feasible to keep Daniel's case out of the public eye, even though they had told some people. Anita therefore reached out to the athletics BGI Academy and other organizations that would help to spread the word. But as the circle grew, several challenges presented themselves. It turned out that private institutions, associations and schools were not allowed to give money for a ransom, so BGI suggested making copies of Daniel's photographs of young gymnasts from his trip to Russia, which associations and schools could then buy. In this way, Daniel's alma mater Vesterlund School and others could contribute indirectly.

The collection was extended to principals, gymnasts, directors, management committees, bridge clubs, Rotary clubs, grandparents, friends and colleagues. During the first twenty-four hours they collected 145,000 kroner (about £15,000) and after two days the amount had reached half a million (£52,000).

Anita got a buzz when receiving updates from the lawyer about how much had been raised, although there was still a long way to go. The family was counting on taking 5 to 6 million kroner (about £521,000 to £ 625,000) to buy Daniel's freedom.

Arthur didn't know what to expect from the negotiations. ISIS could be an organization that wasn't willing to negotiate. He had been involved in more than twenty cases as a security consultant around the world and he had never witnessed a hostage case as spectacular as the one that Daniel and the other hostages were involved in.

The Danish government hadn't either. The Foreign Policy Committee discussed it behind closed doors on several occasions. Most are, but because Denmark had published the Muhammad cartoons, there was a far more immediate risk that the kidnappers would use a hostage to put pressure on the Danish government. It was therefore important for the government and parliament to keep the Daniel affair completely at arm's length in terms of negotiations, ransom and everything else.

Kjeld also experienced the extent to which parliament – across parties and behind closed doors – had decided to distance itself from the Daniel affair. In desperation over the growing expenses, Kjeld sent an appeal to, among others, Kristian Thulesen Dahl, the leader of the Danish People's Party and a prominent MP, who lived in the village of Thyregod, less than six miles away.

'This is a cry for help,' began Kjeld's email. 'Can it be true that we aren't entitled to any financial support or assistance? I know only too well that the Danish government will never negotiate with kidnappers, but what about support to pay for the people that are working for us?'

The party leader replied succinctly that he couldn't do anything to help.

So it was the family's good fortune to have a daughter like Anita, who had professional experience in fundraising. It was not least thanks to her that, on 14 March 2014, the family could send a new offer to the kidnappers of $512,000 (£350,700), equivalent to more than 3 million kroner.

A week passed with no response from ISIS. On 22 March Susanne and Kjeld re-sent the email with the offer of $512,000 in the hope of getting a reply.

With help from large and small donations, they had now collected a total of about 5 million kroner, and there were several initiatives under way. Among other things, an Easter gala was going to be held in April, organized by several of Daniel's old gymnastics acquaintances and the editor of *The Gymnast* magazine. Daniel's former teammates and many of the country's most talented gymnasts had agreed to come and perform. All of the profits from the event would be donated to the fund. A text message service was also set up, so that people could easily and quickly contribute 150 kroner (about £15).

At the same time, the family had finally received the letter and the video of Daniel that the Spanish hostage Marc Marginedas had brought with him out of captivity.

In the video, Susanne and Kjeld saw their son sitting shirtless against a white wall. His chest was covered in red marks and he had lost so much weight that his collar bone was sticking out. Maybe it was the way the video had been recorded, but it made him look as if he had shrunk.

Nevertheless, both the letter and the video offered a welcome reassurance that he was alive and that they just had to be persistent with the fundraising, so that he could come home as soon as possible.

The kidnappers were silent. They still hadn't replied by 7 April, so the family decided to send a new email; this time with an increased offer. For the first time, and at Arthur's request, they dared to name the amount in euros and offered to buy Daniel's freedom for €845,000 (£654,100) or just over 6 million kroner.

The reason the kidnappers hadn't replied was probably because they were busy finishing deals on some of the other hostages. Two more Spaniards, the journalist Javier Espinosa and the photographer Ricardo Vilanova, had been released from ISIS captivity towards the end of March.

. * .

When Javier and Ricardo were about to be released and to leave the cell, the Beatles did the same thing they had done with Marc's release. The Spaniards were made to believe that their fellow prisoners were going to be moved.

A truck backed up to the door at the end of the corridor outside the cell. The hostages were divided by nationality and Daniel climbed into the truck first, along with Dan and the Belgian, blindfolded and handcuffed. Then came the French, the Spaniards, the Americans and the British.

Although they knew that the Spaniards had been given proof-of-life questions a couple of days earlier, there was nevertheless a quivering uncertainty over what the Beatles might do next. After ten minutes, the truck stopped. Daniel could hear that a four-wheel-drive vehicle with a diesel engine was idling next to the truck and the British prisoners were asked to jump out.

'Say goodbye to your friends!' shouted the Beatles.

Daniel's heart was pounding in his chest when the rear door slammed shut again and the truck continued on its way. He counted himself lucky to be at the very back of the cargo hold with Dan and the Belgian, who appeared to be valuable to the kidnappers. There was a difference between being a Danish prisoner from the little village of Hedegård and a Danish prisoner sent out by a major French organization.

When the truck stopped again, the Americans were separated from the rest and at the third stop the Spaniards disappeared.

Daniel breathed a sigh of relief when the truck drove back to the Quarry, where the British and the Americans were already waiting for him and the other hostages. The Spaniards were on their way to the border to be released.

It became harder for the hostages to discuss negotiations and ransoms, because there was still nothing happening for the British and the Americans. On the contrary, James got increasingly hard treatment.

'Do you like being in the army, James . . . just like your brother?' asked a Beatle one day.

Daniel sat facing the wall and could hear that they had put James in a stranglehold and he was struggling to breathe. Afterwards, there was a thump on the floor as James fainted and knocked his head against the concrete. When he came to, he had a big black eye. But this time they had crossed a line. Other guards, whom the hostages had never seen before, came into the cell and asked with concern about James's head. As the hostages didn't dare to speak ill of the Beatles, they lied and said that James had fallen over. The guards took photographs and disappeared. When the Beatles returned, they laughed at James's black eye, but Daniel had a sense that they also came to check whether they had gone too far.

They asked James, 'What did you say to the other guards?'

'That I had fallen over,' he replied.

'Well, you did.'

Negotiations were ongoing for Pierre and the other three Frenchmen. Although it didn't officially admit it, the French government usually did not hesitate to pay for the release of French hostages, using funds from state-owned companies, which in turn received benefits. According to a survey conducted by the *New York Times*, from 2008 to 2013 France topped the list of countries that had paid ransoms to groups linked to al-Qaeda. France had paid a total of $58 million (£39 million) in ransoms, while for Spain, the equivalent amount was $5.9 million (£4 million). The United States accused these European governments of financing terrorism and of ensuring that the kidnapping industry remained a lucrative business. At the same time, America's strict non-negotiation policy left their countrymen and their families in the worst possible situation.

While the European hostages in the Quarry waited for the negotiations to result in their releases, Pierre drew a pencil sketch of Daniel. He took his time sketching on the small piece of cardboard from a Laughing Cow cheese carton.

They had spent more than eight months together and only needed to look at each other to know what the other was thinking. Daniel could be completely himself in Pierre's company and he loved Pierre's ability to talk for hours about fish and other subjects that interested him, while at the same time admitting that he had never experienced being drunk.

'It looks like me,' said an impressed Daniel when Pierre had finished the sketch. The Frenchman nodded.

'I'll see if I can take it out with me.'

Pierre broke a tooth off a plastic comb and pulled a piece of thread out of a random piece of clothing. Then he unstitched a small piece of Velcro on the right sleeve of his jacket. He put the sketch under the Velcro and sewed it back on with the home-made plastic needle. He said he would put on his jacket when he left the prison and that Daniel would get the sketch when he, too, was one day released.

'Look, Daniel,' laughed Pierre, holding his right arm. 'You're right here.'

. * .

It was early April and the three women from Médecins Sans Frontières had been freed through negotiations. Daniel and the others hadn't seen them, but the Beatles had ordered the hostages to be quiet, as if they didn't want the women and the men to hear each other. Even so, Daniel could hear the women in the corridor when they were being taken from their cell to the toilet.

With the previous three releases, there had been a pattern.

First, the hostages were given proof-of-life questions, then there was silence until another question came, and then the final release a few days later.

On the day Pierre and the other Frenchmen received their second question, Pierre couldn't sleep. He lay awake all night, scratching his long beard. He hated the idea that someone should pay the Islamists so that he could live, and he hated himself for accepting that he was just a white foreigner who could be sold as an object. The activist and the super-idealist within him had surrendered to darker forces, and he was disgusted. Pierre seemed so indignant about the situation that Daniel was worried he would take his own life to avoid being bought.

Everything indicated that Pierre would be released before Daniel. The Beatles had told Daniel that his family had collected only €845,000.

'They're still over 1.3 million euros short,' said George disdainfully.

So Daniel made a plan for what Pierre should tell his family. The stories had to be from the good times – that they had sat together by candlelight and played chess and had long conversations.

'Don't tell them I was tortured,' Daniel asked.

Inspired by the Spaniards and the Frenchmen, they also got another idea. So that Daniel could get a hint of how the negotiations about his release were going, they agreed that some secret codes should be inserted into the last proof-of-life questions which the family would be asked to send to Daniel.

If things were looking bad for his release, they would send a question about Kjeld's red truck. In that case, Daniel could make up his own mind whether or not he wanted to try to escape if the opportunity arose. If a release seemed possible, but they weren't absolutely there yet, the question should be about his old motorcycle. Although the motorcycle wasn't amber, he would remember the question as amber. And if they had collected all the money, the question should deal with the apple-green car he had sold to his parents.

Red, amber, green. He would be able to remember the colours of blood and hope, even if they beat the life out of him.

Pierre and Daniel gave each other a long hug. When the moment came for Pierre to leave, they had already said their goodbyes.

'We'll see each other when we go to Scotland,' said Pierre, referring to an earlier promise they'd made to each other.

Before the Frenchmen were released, the Beatles brought a guest to the cell one day in mid-April 2014. When the hostages were given the order to turn around again, a woman in a black veil stood by the far wall. She pulled the veil to one side and introduced herself as Kayla Mueller from the United States. She said she had a message for the US government that the Frenchmen should deliver.

She said that she was well and the demand for her release was €5 million – or a woman prisoner for a woman prisoner. If the latter, ISIS was demanding the release of Aafia Siddiqui, a Pakistani neuroscientist who had been sentenced to eighty-six years in prison in the US for an attack on US agents and military personnel in Afghanistan. Kayla said that she had been held hostage since August 2013. The young aid worker had been kept in many of the same prisons as Daniel.

When she and the Beatles again disappeared out of the cell, the hostages talked about how they could help Kayla, who was probably locked up in a cell alone.

The day after Kayla's visit, the Beatles told the Frenchmen they would be released, but that among the many euros that had been delivered as ransom were 4,000 damaged banknotes.

'But we aren't Jews, so we will free you in a few days,' said one of them and ordered the Frenchmen to tell the authorities about the worthless notes they had received. At the same time George demanded that the other hostages should write letters home.

The Beatles came back the next morning and George was furious because nobody had finished their letters. One of the hostages objected gently that he had told them they had two days.

'Did I say two days . . .?' mumbled George.

Daniel scribbled down a few sentences to say that his family should hurry and pay the ransom.

Pierre sat waiting with his hands and face against the wall, while the guards came and went through the open door to the corridor, where there was intense activity. Pierre and his countrymen were led out of the cell for the last time.

On his way out, Pierre quickly laid a hand on Daniel's shoulder.

'Goodbye, see you later,' he said, and Daniel watched him disappear, wearing the jacket that had the drawing of Daniel sewn into one sleeve.

. * .

The kidnappers' response to Susanne and Kjeld's offer of €845,000 wasn't exactly encouraging. Using exclamation marks and capital letters, they emphasized in their reply that they wouldn't accept less than €2 million. They once again urged Daniel's family to contact the freed hostages, including the three women from MSF, who had been released in the meantime.

'You may also take the opportunity to ask these families and representatives how they managed to raise the sum demanded for their release, so that you may do the same,' was the message.

The daily updates on the fundraising weren't encouraging either. The flood of contributions had slowed. As a result Anita extended the circle of contributors to include people who didn't necessarily know Daniel. A letter was circulated to the principals of Denmark's schools and colleges which had been signed by several principals of the schools where Daniel had been a student and taught, as well as by the bishop of Ribe Diocese, where Susanne was originally from. Because they hadn't yet been able to collect the whole ransom money, the letter called on each recipient to 'share it by email with people you trust in your own network'. They explained:

A lot of money has been collected for the family and they now have more than half of what is expected to be needed to free Daniel. There are a number of private companies and business people who have chosen to support the collection. But it has also to a large degree been the breadth of support from the community, where the 'many small streams' have made such a difference.

While the family in Hedegård was in a race against time, in mid-April happy pictures of the four released Frenchmen made news around the world. Because France had the exact opposite approach to hostage negotiations as Denmark, when they landed on French soil in front of rolling cameras the released hostages were greeted by a welcome committee consisting of President

François Hollande and Foreign Minister Laurent Fabius.

'France is proud to have been able to secure their release,' said Hollande as he stood beside the four men.

Pierre tried to blend in with the asphalt and stood furthest away from the president and Didier François, who gave a speech, saying how great it was to be free and back 'out in the open'. Pierre felt uncomfortable about being seen with the president and about the state making such a big deal out of his release. Moreover, this was what the Beatles had warned against: talking to the press while negotiations about other hostages were still ongoing.

. * .

When the Frenchmen left the Quarry in Raqqa, the remaining prisoners were divided into Muslims and non-Muslims. James, John, Peter and Toni were escorted into another room diagonally opposite. Daniel, Dan and his colleague Federico, Alan, Steven and David stayed in the cell where they had always been and where there was suddenly so much space they could turn around without getting someone else's foot in their crotch.

Daniel used the space to train himself to run a marathon in a circle on the floor. As he ran round and round on a blanket, so that he didn't make a noise, he updated Dan about how it was going. He was in poor shape, so he started out gently with a daily distance of what he loosely calculated had to be about two kilometres, when the running circle was about nine metres and he ran 220 laps.

His training programme was interrupted when a new hostage was thrown into the cell.

'Get to know him well – he's going to be here a long time,' said one of the Beatles, slamming the door behind him.

The man was of dark complexion and seemed to be in his mid-fifties. What little hair he had left was grey and he wore a long, grey tunic. He had a frightened look in his eyes and asked in poor English who these people were that had taken him. The hostages offered him food and water, but he declined and prayed to Allah. A few hours later, George came into the cell with a marker pen and some sheets of A4 paper and ordered the remaining hostages who weren't from Britain or the United States to write exactly the words he dictated. With the marker, Daniel wrote:

I don't want to end like him. Pay 2 M. Go to Danish Government.

Daniel accidentally wrote the 'G' in 'Government' backwards and George kicked him in the side, screwed up the paper and gave Daniel a new sheet to start again. Maybe it was fear, but Daniel wrote the 'G' backwards again. George gave up and made Federico write Daniel's message instead.

Daniel's brain was running at full speed. 'I don't want to end like him.' What the hell did that mean? And why weren't Alan, Steven and David, who were sitting in the same room, writing a similar message? Daniel, Federico, Dan and the Belgian were asked to follow, while Toni, who had also written a note, was dragged out from the other room, where the Muslim converts were sitting. For the first time, they didn't have their hands tied behind their backs, only blindfolds. Daniel, Federico and Toni were pushed into the back seat of a car, while Dan and the Belgian were in another car.

'Do you know what you're going to do?' asked George cheerfully from the driver's seat.

No one answered.

'You're going to watch someone be executed,' he said. He told them that the man who was to be executed was a North African spy who worked for the West, which was why the ISIS sharia court had sentenced him to death for espionage.

'And you're going to watch. Don't worry, you're OK.'

The Brit began playing music in the car, a *nasheed*, an ISIS Islamic hymn, and he chanted along as they drove.

'Stay in your seats,' ordered George when the car stopped.

The door opened and a hand gripped Daniel's arm. He got out of the car and could feel through his thin sandals that he was walking through sand and scattered pebbles. George pushed the blindfold down around Daniel's neck so that he could see a desert landscape with scattered tufts of grass – and a bulldozer. He led Daniel and the other four hostages in front of a hole, the size of which was similar to what an excavator could take with a shovelful.

The middle-aged man from the cell was on his knees next to the hole, in his grey tunic and a reddish-yellow blindfold. His hands were tied together with a strip of fabric and it struck Daniel that the Beatles weren't going to waste a pair of handcuffs on a dead man.

The hostages were asked to hold their A4 sheets up in front of them. The wind was gusting strongly and Daniel held his paper tight, so it wouldn't blow out of his hands.

The man's lips were moving in a final prayer. John was standing behind him with his Glock pistol; Ringo was filming from the other side of the grave, and George was choreographing the entire scene.

'Look into the camera and hold your pages towards the camera!' shouted Ringo.

'Don't fuck up, Daniel, or we'll shoot you!' George chimed in, picking on Daniel even more.

The wind threw the warm desert air into Daniel's face as he gazed at the praying, condemned man and gripped his page.

John took a few steps back and shot the man in the back of the head, so that he toppled over, head first, then landed on his back with his legs against the wall of the grave. The sound of the shot from the pistol cut through the wind and blasted through Daniel's eardrums with such force that it felt as if they were exploding.

John went over to the grave, targeted his pistol at the already dead man and sent eight more shots into his chest. Blood was pouring through the victim's reddish-yellow blindfold and out on to the cracked desert floor at the bottom of the pit. Ringo panned with his camera from the executed man and up to the five hostages who were kneeling like sand sculptures by the edge of the hole with their messages in front of them. Daniel stared at the man's lifeless body and felt a sense of relief that death happened so quickly when it finally came. The Beatles had talked so much about beheadings that it was a relief to see that they could also use a firearm.

The hostages were ordered to climb down into the grave, after which Ringo took photographs of the hostages with his SLR camera. Daniel was between Dan and Toni, and while they held up their papers to the camera, Ringo took a series of photos with at least two hostages in each.

'Look into the camera!' shouted Ringo to Daniel, who was staring down at the corpse by his feet.

When Daniel raised his head and looked towards the camera, which Ringo was holding in front of his face, the Brit shouted, 'Noooooo, stop staring at me!'

On their way back to the cell, Ringo leaned towards Daniel and whispered in his ear, 'Want to hear a secret? You're next.'

Daniel's heart was pounding. Ringo was right. If his family didn't collect the money fast enough, they could use him as blackmail in the other cases. They probably wouldn't kill an MSF worker, Italy would pay for Federico, and the Americans and British were worth more politically than a man from a small country.

When they returned to the cell, Steven, Alan and David asked what had happened. While Daniel and the four others had been forced to watch the execution for the proof-of-life video, the Americans and the British had been left in uncertainty. Daniel didn't want to express his fears in front of others who had been given no sign that negotiations for their release were taking place. Instead, he went over to Dan, who, thanks to his employer paying the ransom, would soon be on his way out. Still afraid that Ringo was right, Daniel began desperately writing down names of people his family could contact in order to help raise the ransom. He used a green ballpoint to draft a list that Dan could take home to his family: names of business and media people, politicians, trade unions, 'the Queen and more'.

'If I'm going to get out, then it fucking well needs to be now,' Daniel said despondently.

'Calm down, everything will be OK,' reassured Dan.

'If I don't get out of here alive, and you get out, will you do me a favour?' Daniel asked.

Dan nodded.

'Buy a bouquet of roses for Signe, and one for Christina when she finishes high school.'

. * .

On 19 April an email landed in Susanne's inbox. It was the sort of email the family had agreed with Arthur they wouldn't open. It contained a compressed file that came with instructions on how to download it, as well as a password which included '9-11'.

Arthur was the first to download the file. It was Ringo's video from the grave in the desert. There were also several photographs of Daniel, who was holding the paper with the demand for €2 million. He stood in a white shirt, and his blindfold, a piece of grey cloth, was wrapped around his neck. The captors wrote in the email:

Stop wasting valuable time and come up with our demand for cash before it's too late.

The Easter gala for Daniel's benefit was held in Svendborg. Volunteers had been working hard to get the arrangements off the ground. A number of gymnasts were going to perform; some people had organized a bake sale; and Anita had made sure the audience

THE ISIS HOSTAGE 255

could further contribute to the fund by buying photographs that Daniel had taken of the World Team in Denmark.

Anita gave a welcome speech and she took a deep breath as she stood alone in the spotlight on the floor in front of 1,100 paying spectators, who had crowded into the hall. She stuck closely to her script.

'First, on behalf of the family, I'd like to thank you all for coming here today – not only those of you who knew the purpose of the show in advance, but also those of you who have just found out. For obvious reasons, it has been necessary to exercise great discretion about the show being a support show for my brother,' she began.

'Unfortunately, we haven't reached our target yet and that is why we still need your help. But we also know that many of you who are here today have already supported us financially and that the possibilities you have of giving us further support are limited. So the greatest help you can give is if all of you go home and pass on the message to your networks and anyone you think will support us.'

The sea of people in front of her applauded and the show began.

Even though the Easter gala brought in 175,000 kroner (€23,500/£18,200), Anita was running out of ideas about where next to turn to reach the target. Daniel's pictures hadn't exactly been bestsellers. It was only thanks to some slightly larger contributions, and because they took a chance and offered about 2 million kroner more than they actually had, that, on 24 April, the family could email Syria with an offer of 9.7 million kroner (about €1.3 million or £1,009,300).

The agreement was that the kidnappers would send a picture of Daniel when the family had collected €1.3 million, which they did the same day. Susanne thought that Daniel had put on weight. His face looked almost plump or swollen as he sat there, holding a sign with the message: 'We appreciate your quick reply and the fact that four more have been united' – a reference to the release of the French.

Pierre also reached out to Daniel's family. He called Susanne's mobile while she was sitting on the sofa with a blanket over her legs. She had difficulty understanding the French-English accent, but managed to interpret that, according to Pierre, Daniel was well. They agreed that the family would call Pierre over Skype, so that Arthur could also be present and act as interpreter.

They all gathered in front of the computer, listening to Pierre as he recounted how he and Daniel had played games, done gymnastics and spent time together in the evening.

'The kidnappers would like to release Daniel,' said Pierre.

Anita asked about the pearl-shaped marks around Daniel's neck, which were there on the first images the family had received during the summer of 2013.

'What happened to him?' she asked.

'I don't know,' replied Pierre. 'Daniel got those before I got to know him.' He went on to address Anita, saying that he knew she had won the World Championship in bodybuilding.

The most important message he had to pass on, however, was the wording of the questions that Arthur and the family had to formulate the next time the kidnappers asked them to send some. Pierre passed on the codes that he and Daniel had agreed about the red truck, the amber motorcycle and the apple-green car.

'Daniel wants to know the truth,' concluded Pierre. 'Even if you send a question to which the answer is Kjeld's red truck.'

. * .

'Where's the Danish boy?'

The question echoed around the cell, where all the hostages were now together again. The converts, James, John, Peter and Toni, had been moved back.

John was standing with a camera in his hands.

'Are you ready to have your picture taken?' he asked. Daniel felt that the British guard was staring at his body. 'Have you been exercising?'

'A little,' said Daniel.

'Then we can box with you,' suggested John and began hitting and slapping Daniel's body.

'I'm not so good at boxing,' Daniel said, trying to avoid being drawn in to the fight.

John and Ringo threw punches at his shoulders and ribs until Daniel lay on the floor in the foetal position.

'You're bad at boxing . . . Would you rather dance?' John took hold of Daniel's clothes and pulled him to his feet. 'Come on, let's dance!' he shouted.

Daniel felt John's hand on the upper part of his back. He stood face to face with the hooded Brit who was holding Daniel's outstretched arm and forcing him over the floor in a stiff tango pose. Daniel didn't dare look at John and instead stared down at his desert boots and his own bare feet, which were moving in tandem, back and forth in a fierce tango, while the rest of the Beatles laughed.

John's back felt broad and muscular under Daniel's hand. Each time they turned, the Brit exaggerated the movements before again flinging Daniel across the floor.

Stop, stop, stop! he screamed inside. Suddenly John stopped.

'Look into the camera,' he said and gave Daniel a few slaps. 'Look unhappy,' he continued, while he took pictures of his Danish prisoner.

'Perfect, Daniel. That was well done.'

Suddenly, one of the Brits tackled Daniel from behind while another pushed him forwards, so he toppled to the floor.

'Do you like my boot?' said John, sticking the toe end of his boot into Daniel's mouth. 'Taste the earth.'

One of the other guards found a pair of pliers and, while holding his arms and legs against the floor, they put the pliers on Daniel's nose, to their own great amusement. Then they clamped it on his fingers.

'What do you think? Should we cut off his nose or his fingers?' they teased.

When the Beatles were finally done beating him up, Daniel sat back bruised and bewildered.

'Is there anyone who can cut hair?' asked one of the British guards.

Daniel raised his hand.

'Then come with me.'

They let him walk out of the cell into the corridor without a blindfold or handcuffs. With his face to the wall, he sat cross-legged on a carpet with a trimmer, scissors and a comb and a bucket for the tufts of hair. John stood in the doorway and called James out from his place in the cell. James came out and sat down opposite Daniel with a document in his hands on which there were a series of statements he had to practise saying.

The haircut was an attempt to get the three American and the three British hostages to look good on the video recordings the Beatles were preparing. Daniel trimmed James's sideburns, cut back the length of his hair a little and trimmed his moustache, while James practised reciting a demand of €100 million in ransom – or the extradition of six Muslim prisoners from the United States. James had to talk about his brother, who was in the Air Force, and about his own trips as a reporter, when he had been with the US forces in Afghanistan. Daniel got a chill down his spine. The message sounded more like a death sentence than a real demand.

'I'd like to keep it a bit long,' said James about his hair and, while Daniel concentrated on fulfilling his wish, Ringo stood staring at them.

'Is that OK?' asked Daniel.

It obviously was, because Ringo ordered James back to the cell to get ready to be filmed. Daniel subsequently gave a trim to the five other Americans and Brits, all of whom had also received a piece of paper with a message they had to recite. In the cell next door to theirs, George was rummaging around, preparing to film the hostages. But it turned out that it was too dark in the room and the Beatles postponed the video production until they had found some lamps.

When Daniel's fellow prisoners came back from the unsuccessful recording in the other cell, they said that Kayla Mueller was there with another western woman they hadn't seen before. They decided to try to smuggle a message to the women when they had to go back and make the videos. The Beatles didn't take long to get hold of lamps, cables and a Nikon camera, and talked elatedly about what they called their 'new media centre', where the two women were apparently staying. Six new orange jumpsuits were delivered to the British and American hostages, who disappeared into the room to be filmed.

When they returned, they were told that they should put on their normal clothes and save the orange suits for later. While they had been away, they had managed to deliver a note to Kayla. It said that they could communicate through a small hatch in the toilet, which all the hostages shared.

There was silence. Peter was in a panic and afraid. James tried to take care of his countrymen.

'I know it doesn't look good, but we just have to keep hoping until the end,' he said to Steven and Peter. They were no longer united in hope. It was clear to everyone that the remaining prisoners held by ISIS were now in two different categories: those who made videos in front of a grave carrying messages about ransoms, to be used in negotiations, and those who, wearing orange jumpsuits, had to recite unrealistic demands to countries that didn't pay ransoms or allow the families of hostages to raise money.

Daniel had been told that a ransom of €1.3 million had now been offered for him, yet he feared that his family would never be able to collect the amount demanded, despite the list of potential sources of money he had given Dan when he and his MSF colleague left the prison in mid-May. Something suggested, however, that the two released hostages were still waiting somewhere in Syria to cross the border with Turkey, because suddenly the Beatles demanded that Daniel write a letter to his family. He felt that time was running out. Apart from the British and Americans, there were only Federico, Toni and himself left. Since the Beatles didn't demand a specific wording in the letter, he wrote something more personal.

'It's hard to see people who have been here a much shorter time than me go home to their families,' he wrote, and made suggestions about whom they could ask for help.

I pray every day that this nightmare will soon have a happy ending [. . .] I pray that Christina stays strong and will soon be finished with high school. Thinking of you makes me strong. Signe, I love you more than you can imagine and I am so sorry that I put what we have together at stake [. . .] I pray that one day I can come home and see you all again.

. * .

Arthur was in Lebanon when he received Daniel's letter. If it had been possible, he would like to have delivered it to the family personally when he was back in Denmark, but he thought it would take too long. He wasn't planning to go back soon. So he decided to call Susanne and read it aloud to her. The aim of the letter was to put pressure on the family, but the tone of it was different from the letters they had previously received from Daniel. This time Daniel had put his feelings into it – and written it in his own words. In Arthur's view, Daniel being able to write and express himself was a positive sign. Susanne was at work in Legoland when the phone rang. Since she couldn't stand in the shop and talk, she took it with her outside to a courtyard.

As Arthur read her son's words, she hid behind some containers, because she couldn't hold back the tears. Daniel was asking her to be strong and to fight. He missed her and was thinking of her.

Hidden from her colleagues behind the container's iron surface, she could no longer observe the proprieties of being an unworried mother and employee. She hung up, but sat there for a long time afterwards until her tears had dried.

Hi Mum, It's Daniel

Anita had to think creatively. Even though she was grateful and proud that the family had been able to collect many millions of kroner, it still wasn't enough and donations had dropped so much that she feared the family wouldn't be able to pay to free Daniel. She had to get more people to take an interest in her brother.

In the middle of May an anniversary celebration was held for Vesterlund Youth School's former pupils and Anita set up a stand where she sold Daniel's pictures and gave a speech, in which she quoted his recent more personal letter from Syria.

But Anita had to admit that Daniel's plight wasn't attracting the attention it once had. Their network of contributors had given all they could, and the event only brought in a modest amount. The family had raised about 80 per cent of the ransom and Anita felt that the time was ripe to contact large companies and business people. Since they had already collected most of the amount, it seemed less presumptuous to ask wealthy people who didn't know the family, whether it be individuals or companies, if they could help.

She took the chance and went all-in with a new letter that described the details of Daniel's situation, which she urged them not to bring to public attention while the case was unresolved. In the document, she included the first proof-of-life image of Daniel and she revealed the ransom amount, as well as how much the family had collected – and she described the video from the grave with the threat that Daniel could be killed if they didn't pay.

Within days, the donations began coming in. There were apparently some people in Denmark who were prepared to go to great lengths to help a person in need and, on 22 May, the family submitted a new offer to the kidnappers.

'We really hope that you will consider this offer and respond,' wrote Arthur and the family in the email. They offered €1,710,000 (£1,300,100), equivalent to more than 12.8 million kroner.

Three days later the kidnappers responded, briefly and unmistakably: 'Only 300,000 Euros left to go.'

They enclosed an audio file in which Daniel said 'Hurry up' – and added that they would more than double the demand to €5 million. The negotiations, which in fact were not negotiations but an absolute demand, were going in the wrong direction.

Anita checked her mobile every fifteen minutes for messages and answered calls, day and night. She couldn't even sit and have dinner with her boyfriend for half an hour without being interrupted.

In late May she took a day off from fundraising and went to the cultural festival in Odense Harbour. There were stalls with organic honey, folk dancing and a climbing wall, and Anita played a game of kayak polo. During the hour she was in the water, her mobile was in her bag in the judge's tent. She let go of the battle between life and death for a moment and felt only her body moving around in the kayak.

When she came ashore, her bag had gone. Thieves had zipped open the tent and snatched the bag containing her mobile – her lifeline to people who were trying to help the family. The latest letters she had sent out contained only her and their lawyer's contact information, so as to spare Susanne and Kjeld.

Anita took the situation with her usual stoic calm and did everything to get back up and running, but it wasn't without obstacles, especially when it turned out that her email account had been hacked. She couldn't get her Gmail account to recognize that it was she who was logging in and there was no customer service department to call. She got hold of someone who sold advertising for Google and berated him with her story of a younger brother who was being held hostage in Syria and would be killed unless they collected enough money. The employee put her in touch with the right people. When she was finally able to log on to her email account, everything was in Arabic and emails to her had been deleted or automatically forwarded to the thieves' email address. The worst thing was that the thieves had sent an email out to all her contacts, including those she had emailed in recent months about the fundraiser, stating that Anita was in distress and needed the money.

In the midst of this chaos, the family received a new email from Syria filled with threatening capitals.

We hope for your sake that you're checking this email frequently because AS OF THIS POINT ON you have 24 hours to have the FULL 2 Million EUROS CASH READY!!

If the family didn't pay the full ransom by the deadline, the kidnappers would add on another €5,000 for each day they had to wait. According to them, this punishment had been meted out by a sharia court and the daily penalty wasn't negotiable.

. * .

Daniel and his fellow prisoners had succeeded in exchanging brief messages with Kayla and the other woman who were in the cell next door. They developed a system where they hid small pieces of paper in the toilet. When the messages had been read, they tore them into pieces and ate them.

Sometimes they were serious messages; other times they played Trivial Pursuit. The women would leave a piece of paper with a question such as 'Who played the role of Aragon in *Lord of the Rings*?' The men would hide the answer and a counter-question when they were next allowed to go to the toilet.

Daniel considered these communications to be extremely dangerous, but it also felt right to try to keep everyone's spirits up. He mostly just concentrated on his training, which was easier to do now, because there was more space in the cell. The Italian Federico had been the latest to leave the prison. Apart from the women the only ones left were Daniel, German Toni and the six Brits and Americans.

On 2 June the Beatles launched a new cycle of violence. At four in the morning they came storming in without the usual warning and ordered the hostages to sit with their backs to them and their hands four inches from the wall. They had to go to the toilet one at a time. When it was Daniel's turn, he put on his sandals and grabbed a piss bucket, but as soon as he came out into the corridor, he was struck several times with a truncheon. He ran into the toilet, emptied the bucket, peed, washed his hands and ran back towards the cell, the Brit with the truncheon close behind him. Daniel threw off his sandals and walked onto the blankets with the piss bucket in his hand.

'Why are you doing that?' cried the guard and hit him hard four more times with the truncheon as punishment.

The Beatles introduced this new routine around toilet visits four times a day. The hostages woke up in a panic early in the morning, ready for the Beatles flinging the door open and beating them on their way to the toilet. It was worse still when the violence struck randomly and unpredictably outside the toilet visits.

'Who is the Danish boy?' shouted one of the Beatles. Daniel didn't dare answer.

'WHO is the Danish boy?'

'Me,' he whispered.

'You're from the country with the Muhammad cartoons!' they shouted and hit him three times.

This sort of thing happened at all times of day and night and the violence befell everyone. The Americans, James, Steven and Peter, sat in the corner of the cell and clung to each other. Everyone was beside themselves.

And suddenly the Beatles were there again.

'Who wrote these letters?' shouted Ringo.

He didn't wait for an answer, but began clubbing everyone on the back of the head. They must have found the small pieces of paper with the messages to the women in the toilet.

Only a brief moment passed before they stomped into the cell again and gave Daniel and James thirty dead legs each. The dead legs weren't like those Daniel and his friends had given each other in school. They came with such violent force that he feared they would break a bone. He lay on his blanket and wept, and neither James nor he could walk the following two days.

The hostages moved their sleeping places as far away from the door as possible, and to overcome the fear that hung in the air Daniel told stories about the European Championships in gymnastics. He also invented a method of relaxation that he used on the others. He squeezed his fellow prisoners' skin so hard between their thumb and forefinger that the pain was excruciating. He held on for one minute. When he let go, they relaxed. The Beatles were becoming more officious, searching the room regularly and forbidding the prisoners to do just about everything. Daniel wasn't allowed to exercise any more.

'You've gotten bigger!' they shouted, and took away food and the card games from the prisoners.

The daily routines that the hostages had built up and cherished despite everything were being irrevocably ripped to shreds by the Beatles.

. * .

For the family, every hour – even every minute – counted. In the past week they had collected an additional €156,000. They now only needed €134,000 to reach €2 million, plus the daily fines. Even in a situation like this, when there was just a small amount of the required ransom missing, the authorities would do nothing. They wouldn't step in and lend the family the balance.

Fortunately, three individuals offered to cover the rest by lending the family the remaining money and on 4 June Susanne, Kjeld and Anita could finally send an email to the kidnappers, with Arthur's help, explaining that they expected to be in possession of the full ransom sum the following week. They outlined the reason for the delay:

> Unfortunately, the banks here in Denmark are closed for the next few days – Friday, Saturday, Sunday and Monday – due to public holidays (Constitution Day and Whitsun). We give you herewith our guarantee that we have the required amount, but the money will not be available to us before next Tuesday (10 June).

They emphasized that they had no control over the final practical arrangements or the delay, and that they didn't want to extend the process any further. Finally, they asked for instructions on how the money should be handed over.

The ransom sum was to be exchanged for euros by the National Bank, at a cost of 20,000 kroner, and thereafter taken to Turkey in cash. The Danish state wasn't allowed to transport ransoms, so the family – and, therefore, Arthur – would be responsible for taking the money to Turkey. Just two hours later, the kidnappers wrote back. The family had to verify when 'the full amount' in euros arrived in Turkey, and there was one further demand:

> THE CASH MUST ALL BE IN 500 EURO NOTES that are not torn, misprinted or damaged in any way!

Arthur was beginning to prepare for Daniel's release bit by bit, while the crisis psychologist acquainted the family with how such a process normally took place. No one could know the mental and physical state Daniel would be in when, as Arthur hoped, he came across the border into Turkey. There was still the possibility that Arthur would have to arrange for Daniel to be picked up in Syria and brought to Turkey.

However the exchange was going to take place, it was essential there was a crisis team around Daniel which, as a rule, didn't include members of his family. Experience showed that it could be initially difficult for the person who had been released to relate to an unhappy mother, an overexcited friend or a delighted sister.

Even so, the crisis psychologist and Arthur suggested that Anita come to Turkey with them. She was capable of putting aside her emotions and could therefore be of assistance to Daniel, because she would be a familiar face among a lot of strangers.

A representative from the Danish Foreign Ministry was also part of the crisis team. The Ministry's emissary was going to Turkey with them to provide so-called consular assistance, such as the issuance of an emergency passport and to sort out any hassles with the Turkish authorities. One scenario might be that Turkey would want to hold Daniel in order to get information from him or because they suspected him of complicity with ISIS. As Arthur explained to the family: 'I'm your fixer, but I'm not the authorities.'

How Daniel was going to fly from Turkey to Denmark was also a subject of discussion. Since no one knew what state he would be in, Arthur suggested that it would be better if Daniel didn't have to fly commercially, such as on Turkish Airlines. The Danish Air Force had an aircraft available which Peter Bartram, the Danish Chief of Defence, thought could do the job. If Daniel was in a poor physical or mental condition, he wouldn't have to wait for weeks to come home to Denmark.

In addition, a doctor and an operative from the intelligence services would be part of the team in Turkey. Since a criminal offence had been committed against a Danish citizen, PET's responsibility was to ensure that the procedures were followed and all the evidence was collected if there was a possibility of filing a case.

Arthur prepared himself for what he both hoped and feared was just around the corner: the money transfer to ISIS that would set Daniel free.

. * .

The Beatles dished out thirty more dead legs. Daniel no longer screamed in silence. He resisted for the first time.

'If you don't stop, you'll ruin my legs!' he shouted, beside himself with pain.

It worked, but not as intended, as the Beatles then began beating up one of his fellow prisoners instead. He waited apprehensively for a proof-of-life question, but none came. Meanwhile, he talked with James about taking a letter out to his family in New Hampshire if Daniel was released. Perhaps it would be James's last chance to communicate with them.

'I don't know if I'm strong enough to do it,' said Daniel, looking at James's three-page handwritten letter. He was frightened of carrying a physical letter from an American whom the Beatles were denying any channel of communication. He and James talked about whether Daniel should stick the letter up his rear end, or if it would be OK just to hide it in his underpants. They had no idea what would happen to Daniel when he left the cell. Perhaps he would be body-searched.

'You shouldn't take the risk,' said James.

They decided that the safest method was for Daniel to learn the letter by heart. They sat next to each other, cross-legged with their backs against the wall. When Daniel read the first line, he ground to a halt. James's i's looked like z's and his handwriting was almost illegible. James took the letter and read out one line at a time, which Daniel repeated. He also asked detailed questions about James's family in order to remember the words better. James talked about his cycling trip with his mother and the shopping centre he visited with his father; about his sister, who was going to get married; and he repeated the names of his brothers, Michael, John and Mark, whom he missed every single day.

James started talking about the lack of any negotiations. He wanted Daniel to say to his family that he believed his captors had another plan for the British and American hostages, and that he had written this letter as a last farewell, because he was afraid that he would never come home.

'Don't ask me to deliver your own death certificate,' pleaded Daniel and asked for more specific greetings to the family.

They reviewed the letter over and over again, until Daniel knew it by heart, so that they could finally tear it up and eat it.

In the following days, Daniel memorized the words and would sometimes ask, 'Repeat that sentence again.'

James sent greetings to his brothers, his sister Katie, his mother Diane and father John and his maternal grandmother. Daniel promised that he would call them and pass on James's message as soon as he was free.

. * .

The tenth of June was a day of relief. When Susanne and Kjeld pressed 'send' on their email to ISIS, it carried a message that the ransom had arrived in Turkey. They also sent an apple-green question to Daniel.

Who bought his old car?

'Susanne and I guarantee that we will keep our part of the agreement. It is extremely important that nothing goes wrong at the last moment. We hope to hear from you soon.'

After an hour and fifty-five minutes, the answer was in their inbox.

We are pleased to hear that you have our CASH ready.

For once, there were fewer capital letters, but before the kidnappers would give proof of life, the family had to confirm that the money was in €500 banknotes and that they had included the daily penalties.

This confirmation MUST be within 24 hours. Also you MUST be ready to follow any instructions given IMMEDIATELY.

Susanne and Kjeld confirmed straight away. Arthur was waiting in Turkey, ready to hand over the €2,040,000 as soon as they had a proof of life from Daniel and instructions on where and how to deliver the money.

The payment of the ransom took place at a critical moment. On the same day, ISIS launched an offensive in Iraq that could have put Daniel's life in danger if he remained in captivity.

Thousands were fleeing Mosul, Iraq's second largest city, with whatever they could carry, while clouds of smoke rose into the air over the metropolis and the nearby military camps. ISIS fighters quickly seized control. The Iraqi security forces, who had been trained in the 2000s by the United States and Denmark, among others, fled from their positions faster than the civilians. Widespread corruption and lack of loyalty in the Iraqi army led to the soldiers discarding their uniforms as soon as they sensed an attack was on its way.

'The city fell like a plane without engines,' a businessman from Mosul told the *Guardian*.

It was no coincidence that Mosul fell to ISIS so easily. After the American invasion of Iraq and the overthrow of Saddam Hussein, the Iraqi army had been dissolved; an action that stripped away the livelihood of hundreds of thousands of soldiers. Moreover, the Americans introduced a policy of 'de-Ba'athification', the purpose of which was to remove the influence of Saddam's Ba'ath Party on any new political system. This meant that all civil servants affiliated with the Ba'ath Party were banned from future employment in the public sector. In short, many Iraqis were excluded from participating in building the new Iraq. This strategy contributed to an uprising among Sunni Muslims, whose role in Iraq had diminished due to their affiliation with Saddam's Ba'ath Party.

After US forces withdrew from Iraq in late 2011, the now heavily Shiite-dominated government further excluded the country's Sunni Muslims. Despite what President Barack Obama proclaimed, it wasn't a 'sovereign, stable and independent Iraq with a representative government' when the Americans left, but a cauldron of sectarian tension and a corrupt power apparatus.

ISIS was born in the shadow of the western invasion, nurtured in the chaos of the Syrian Civil War and matured into a fully fledged army and political presence in Iraq when its warriors captured Mosul, where many Sunnis welcomed them as an alternative to the Shiite government in Baghdad.

ISIS looted hundreds of millions of dollars from the city's banks and took over military equipment that had been given to the Iraqi army by the Americans. Within a few days ISIS troops were driving around in American Humvees in their capital of Raqqa. They had successfully abolished the borders between Iraq and Syria with their self-proclaimed caliphate.

It was only a matter of time before the United States would return to Iraq with bombs.

. * .

On 11 June the Beatles pounded heavily on the wooden door and the hostages turned towards the wall. The British guards went round, hammering their fists into the hostages' ribs, before George stopped at Daniel. While holding his nose, he asked, 'Are you the Danish boy?'

'Yes, I am.'

'We have a question for you,' continued George.

Daniel tensed. He was about to know for certain whether he was on his way home.

'Who bought your old car?'

There was no question in the world he would rather answer, because his old car was, of course, apple-green. Green. Freedom.

'My parents bought it.'

'Write about the car on this piece of paper. How much did they pay for it?'

'Thirty-five thousand kroner, about five thousand euros,' said Daniel.

'You stupid boy. Did you really sell your car to your own family?'

He wrote it all down: that he had bought it new in 2007 for 110,000 kroner; that it was a Chevrolet Matiz with a 0.8 litre engine; that a medal from the Danish national championships hung from the rear-view mirror; and that the car was apple-green.

'OK,' said George. 'Daniel, you are going home.'

They hadn't said it so directly when any of the other hostages had been freed and the relief that Daniel felt for a moment was replaced by anxiety. What if they knew the code with green, red and amber? What if they had tortured Pierre and he had told them everything?

The Beatles disappeared and Daniel turned to the others, who knew the code with the apple-green car. Fear showed on their faces. They couldn't hide the fact that they had only one hope: that they would soon be released too.

Yet they all gave Daniel a hug.

'You've earned it,' one said, but Daniel couldn't take it in. The idea that he might be the last man to leave the prison alive was unbearable.

'If you have something I should say once I'm out, tell me,' he urged.

James stood up and gave Daniel a warm embrace and then he sat on his blanket between his countrymen. There was silence.

. * .

Just before 3 p.m. on the afternoon of the same day, 11 June 2014, the family received answers to the proof-of-life question.

'His parents bought the 2007 apple-green Chevrolet 0.8 from him for 35,000 DKK,' wrote the kidnappers, who also wanted clarification of where the money was in southern Turkey.

Susanne was happily surprised by all the details about the car that Daniel sent back.

'He's understood the message with the green car!' she said excitedly to Kjeld and wrote in her diary, addressed to Daniel, 'You responded nicely to our question.'

From then on, Arthur took over the email correspondence. It was now up to him to bring Daniel home.

. * .

Late at night on 11 June, the first instructions about the handover of the money arrived.

You will make your way to Kilis ASAP.

The kidnappers ordered Arthur to be in Kilis by 4 p.m. at the latest the following afternoon. He was told to constantly keep an eye on his email – 'BY THE MINUTE' – and have a yellow taxi waiting on standby until the last instructions were sent.

There were also demands about how the money would be transported: a strong, matte-black rucksack with a padlock on the zipper.

Hostage cases and handovers of ransoms were inherently volatile, but Arthur had never experienced anything like this. The terms came exclusively from ISIS. He felt extremely vulnerable and the exchange had so many risks at play that he stopped counting them.

Arthur lit his pipe. Although it could have consequences, after long consideration he chose to depart from the kidnappers' instructions on one point.

He rented a white four-wheel-drive vehicle rather than be transported by an unsuspecting taxi driver who couldn't speak English. He didn't want to expose other people to the risk associated with handing over €2 million to ISIS.

Furthermore, he could imagine a scenario in which a nervous taxi driver called the police, because he was sitting on an abandoned road along the border with a strange, chain-smoking foreigner in the back seat, who was perhaps about to blow himself up or kidnap him. Arthur couldn't confide in a random person about his intentions. He at least wanted to be the master of his own means of transport if the terrorists were dictating everything else.

On 12 June at 4.50 p.m. he received further instructions about driving east from Kilis to the town of Elbeyli.

At the beginning of this town there will be a welcome sign that reads 'Hosgeldin' and will possibly be worn out and unreadable. Nevertheless, this sign will be your meeting place, WHERE YOU WILL STAY, WAIT AND HAND OVER OUR CASH.

He should arrive at 8.30 p.m and wait until 10.30 p.m. at the latest. Someone would meet him and say the password 'Turkcell', to which he would respond 'Vodafone'.

Arthur waited a little over an hour before answering with a meticulous repetition of the instructions and adding: 'I have had difficulty finding a taxi driver who I can communicate with and provide detailed instructions to. I would therefore like to ask for your permission for me to come alone in my white 4x4 rental car.' He added the number plate.

Arthur checked the rucksack with the cash one last time, as well as the satellite tracker that was his only lifeline. It would send a signal every minute to an operations room in the city of Aalborg in Denmark, which was in contact with his backup team, who were on standby two miles from the meeting point. The team included a doctor, who could handle a sudden emergency and would sound the alarm if they received coordinates that indicated Arthur was about to cross the border into Syria.

Arthur drove about six miles to Elbeyli, found his way through the small town and reached the sign that stood near the border. There were no street lights. The only light he could see came from a town some way off.

He parked the car so that it pointed in the direction of Kilis, turned off the engine and wound down the windows so that he could hear if anyone was approaching on foot in the dark. He could just make out a border fence and some vegetation in the rear-view mirror.

Arthur lit his pipe and thought about possible escape routes. At the side of the road heading into town there was a ditch, which he could jump into, but the nearest house was quite far away if he needed to take cover. He had previously studied the area on satellite photos and knew the terrain in his sleep.

The silence was broken only by the cicadas. Arthur waited and stuffed more tobacco into his pipe. The first vehicle he heard rumbling in the darkness was a tractor that was being driven without lights.

It's probably just a Turkish peasant on his way home, thought Arthur. The next vehicle had its lights on. It was an armoured personnel carrier containing Turkish soldiers coming from the border. If they asked him to move on, Arthur had several explanations ready, about needing a pee and an engine that had stalled. Personally, he thought it looked strange that he had parked right there. The soldiers slowed down and gaped at him, but drove on.

Then he saw a motorcycle tearing up from the border towards Elbeyli at high speed with its headlights off. That drove by, too. A bunch of refugees then appeared out of the dark and stared into the car as they slowly walked past.

Suddenly he heard the motorcycle again. This time it stopped about ten feet from the car. There were two men sitting on it. They were both dressed in black from head to toe, including black ski masks, and Arthur could see they were armed. The engine was idling, while the man sitting behind the driver stepped down. Arthur opened the car door and got out. He had rolled up his shirt sleeves and clearly revealed his palms and arms as proof that he was unarmed as he walked a few steps towards them.

'*Assalamu alaikum,*' Arthur greeted them.

'*Wa alaikum assalaam,*' replied the man who had got off the motorcycle. He was about six feet tall and broad-chested under the black tunic.

'Turkcell,' continued the hooded man.

'Vodafone,' said Arthur.

Moving slowly, Arthur stuck his arm through the car window and lifted the rucksack off the floor behind the passenger seat. With the ransom money in his hand, Arthur went over to the ISIS fighter and gave him the rucksack. For a moment, the man lifted it, as if to check its weight was equivalent to €2 million.

Arthur put a hand out to signal that the deal was over and received a firm, almost hard, handshake. They nodded in agreement and held eye contact. Arthur felt they were both sizing each other up, looking for confirmation that they had a deal.

Then the man put the rucksack over his shoulders and sat on the back of the motorcycle, which revved its engine and headed towards the border.

Arthur stood for a minute and watched them disappear, before calmly getting into his car and driving towards Elbeyli. He sent a text message to his team: 'All done.'

He then wrote a message via Susanne's email to the captors, reporting that the money had been handed over to the men on the motorcycle.

'We exchanged the passwords that you sent and I shook hands to seal a successful transaction with your representative, who had a very impressive grip,' he wrote and asked for instructions on where and when Daniel would cross the border.

. * .

Anita packed a large bag. After conversations with the crisis psychologist, she had gathered various things that Daniel would want when he came out; first and foremost, a pair of glasses so that he could see properly again. She had already sent them with Arthur to Turkey.

She filled Daniel's old toiletry bag with luxury body scrub and a scrubbing glove, shampoo, lotion, a razor and shaving cream, nail clippers, a face mask and pills for diarrhoea.

She and Susanne found some of Daniel's old, worn Birkenstock sandals and trainers in a cupboard. She had been told that people store a lot of their memories in the feet and Daniel should therefore have something pleasant and recognizable to wear. She also packed some clothes. Susanne had bought a pair of boxer shorts with hearts on them. In addition, Anita packed a new mobile, Daniel's favourite kind of liquorice, and some notes and photos that she had collected from Daniel's friends and immediate family.

On 15 June, three days after the money had been delivered, Anita flew to the Turkish town of Gaziantep with the crisis psychologist. As they prepared to land, she stared into Syria and wondered if she could see the building in which Daniel was being held.

They settled into the hotel, where the representative from the Danish Foreign Ministry had already arrived. The hotel was situated in a beautiful old castle, but, as the psychologist pointed out, the otherwise romantic setting might present some challenges for a recently released hostage. By the entrance, old bullet holes adorned the wall, while the rooms were small and dark with bars on the windows. Anita's room had bare stone walls and only a small window that made it feel like a cave. The psychologist didn't think it would be a good idea for Daniel to sleep there.

They checked the bridal suite, which had gold painted walls and furniture, but that wasn't appropriate either. Daniel shouldn't be spending his first night of freedom in a bridal bed with his sister. They finally found a corner room with large windows and more air. It would just about do, so Anita set herself up there.

Everything was planned down to the last detail. The emissary from the Danish Foreign Ministry would receive him, while Anita waited in the adjoining room. The psychologist and Anita had already discussed what they would say if Daniel asked about Signe. It seemed to Anita that Signe had become more distant recently, and she rarely answered the phone when Anita called. Perhaps Signe was no longer waiting for Daniel to come home. Perhaps she needed to move on with her life.

The border police along the Turkish–Syrian border were informed that they should call Arthur if they came across a blond Dane. Arthur kept a lookout for him, too, and drove back and forth along the border for several days, but nothing happened.

Time passed. Anita sat in the sun at the hotel, managing the fundraising, crocheting and, during the first days, waiting patiently for her brother to cross the border. Then a nervousness began to spread. All the evidence suggested that Daniel would be the last hostage to be released for the time being. It had occurred to them more than once that ISIS might refuse to release him if this was going to be their final deal.

Arthur sent messages to the kidnappers and asked about Daniel, but there was no reply.

. * .

Daniel woke up every morning with a heavy head and body from disturbed sleep and nightmares. Hostages were usually released in the morning, but the Beatles kept Daniel in suspense.

You think you're going home and then you don't, said his inner voice.

Most of the other released hostages had been freed two, three or four days after the last proof-of-life question. One had had to wait for eight days, but that didn't make Daniel feel any easier, even though he had been waiting for only three days.

He went and sat with Alan and David.

'If I get out, I'll tell your children how great you've been,' he said.

'You've also been great, Daniel. You helped us to work out.' They told him that they couldn't understand how he had managed to recover from the torture he had been subjected to in the beginning.

They hugged each other. Daniel never knew whether he would suddenly be fetched, so he wanted to make sure that he had said goodbye to the remaining seven hostages.

Four days after Daniel had been given his question about the apple-green car, the Beatles asked Toni a question. It only made Daniel even more uncertain and despondent, because it could mean that the German was first in line to be released.

The days crawled by and so did the nights. Daniel lay sleepless, staring out into the darkness and got up before dawn.

On the morning of 17 June, James was also awake. He went over and sat with Daniel and put his hand on his knee.

'You need to be strong,' said James softly. 'Don't worry, everything will be OK. They'll probably come in a minute and then you'll be on your way.'

Daniel didn't understand where James got his extraordinary reserves of inner strength. He wished so much for all of them to be on their way home, not just himself and Toni.

James went back to sleep in his place in the corner. Shortly after, the Beatles banged on the cell door. They all knelt and turned to face the wall, their hands over their heads a few inches from the concrete. It was now, thought Daniel, that he would either die or go home.

The Beatles asked Daniel and Toni to turn around. In front of them stood a woman whom Daniel hadn't seen before, but who had to be the other woman who was locked up with Kayla. When she removed her veil, he saw that she was quite a bit older than him.

'Can you confirm that she's alive?' asked the Beatles.

'Yes,' answered Daniel.

The Beatles ordered the woman to pass on a message.

'Just say they should hurry up and pay the money and do what they're being told to do,' she said.

Then she had to write the ransom sum on a piece of paper. She seemed nervous and Daniel tried to calm her by asking whether there was anything else he should tell her family.

'Yes,' she replied. 'Tell them I love them.'

'Is there anything else you want to say?' asked one of the Beatles irritably.

'No.'

Then she was taken from the cell.

Daniel ended up leaving the cell without another word. He and Toni suddenly had blankets thrown over their heads; their hands were handcuffed behind their backs and, with a heavy shove, they were led away.

They were put into the back seat of a car. All three Beatles were going with them and George started the car. The hostages were told to duck down so that no one could see them.

'Tell us what you know about us,' ordered George from the front seat.

'I know you're from Great Britain and that you're here to perform jihad,' said Daniel.

'Who are the Beatles?' they asked.

'That's you,' said Daniel.

George told him they had found a note that said something about the Beatles. He was probably referring to one of the notes that Daniel and his fellow prisoners had exchanged with the female hostages in the toilet.

'What do you know about the Beatles?' they asked, and Toni and Daniel told them that they called them John, George and Ringo, because they didn't know their real names.

The interrogation stopped there and, after an hour, they pulled off the road and switched cars. That was the last time Daniel saw the Beatles – until one of them appeared in a video he would see two months later.

The driver of the car made Daniel and Toni put on blindfolds while he drove along small bumpy roads, before turning on to a larger, asphalted road.

After a few hours they were led into a house. They were allowed to move freely between two rooms, a toilet and a corridor, where there was an open window. Daniel recognized an orange floral blanket that one of the other hostages had had with him in the cell. It was a good sign.

A muscular warrior and a little boy came in with hummus,

sardines and butter. Toni only ate the butter, while Daniel tucked into the rest, before falling, exhausted, into a deep sleep.

Late in the afternoon they were woken up with yoghurt and twelve pancakes, and, in the middle of the night, bread, tuna and cream cheese were served. After yet another night, on the morning of 19 June, they were hurriedly given hoods and handcuffed and herded a few hundred yards across a gravel yard to a new room, where Daniel did his usual training exercises to keep a cool head.

He was interrupted by a friendly man, who asked, 'Is there anything you need?'

Daniel and Toni said, 'No, thanks.'

They had no idea how they were supposed to reply to a question they hadn't been asked for months. They just said, 'We're fine.'

'Do you have shampoo and toothbrushes?' asked the man and continued without waiting for an answer, 'You need some new clothes. What size are you? Large?'

The man wrote a shopping list and came back with toothbrushes, shampoo, towels, cream, hair gel, soap, cotton buds, toothpicks, nail clippers and some lotion for the scars on Daniel's wrists.

They were promised a bath later in the day, so they waited to change their clothes.

Then another man appeared in the doorway and motioned for them to follow him. Daniel bent down to pick up his blindfold and handcuffs from the floor.

'No, no, you're free now,' the man said. 'Just take your things and come with me.'

Daniel lifted the plastic bags containing toiletries and clothes and stepped out into the light. His fear disappeared immediately. The soft afternoon sun streamed out to meet him and he could

see the outside world, the sand-coloured buildings, a gate, a street
with two men on a motorcycle, a checkpoint with armed men.
He suddenly felt that he had forgotten something – his keys or
his wallet, which he always double-checked before he left home.
Then he laughed at himself.

A young and slightly fat man asked Daniel to get into his
four-wheel drive, while Toni was shown a place where he could
take a bath. Daniel looked around him from the back seat. A
few older men in tunics were drinking tea on the other side of
the street and a man with a long beard was talking to the driver.
They laughed and the man looked at Daniel, who looked down.
Toni soon came back and the scent of soap permeated the car.

'The water isn't very good here. You'll get a bath later,' they
promised Daniel.

As they drove off, Daniel looked at the small shops along the
road, at the people out shopping, and at the dry, brown fields that
stretched to the Turkish border. Life had obviously been going
on as usual during the thirteen months he had been in captivity.
It was only inside him that everything had changed.

The driver said he had also driven an Italian with a full beard
and two aid workers from Médecins Sans Frontières.

'Cool guys,' he remarked, before continuing, 'You will always
be welcome to come back to the Islamic State. You just need a
press permit. We have nothing against journalists as long as we
know who you are. If you don't have one, we have to arrest you.'

They had reached the outskirts of the Syrian border town of
Tel Abyad, where small farms lay spread out over green fields.
A shepherd was crossing the road with his animals.

'Dawlah has taken control here,' said the driver, meaning ISIS.

'We're much bigger than you think. You'll get a shock when you see how powerful we are.'

They arrived at a building on the border; there were bullet holes in the walls and it was in the process of being renovated; some men were outside watering the plants. Once inside, Daniel signed what appeared to be informal exit papers, before being shown upstairs, where he took a short bath and rubbed lotion on the scars on his wrists.

Although the clothes in the bag had been bought in large sizes, the tight green shirt didn't cover his stomach and the underpants were too small, so his penis hung out under the heavy, olive-coloured trousers he'd been given.

Toni and Daniel sat for a few hours in a waiting room with a fridge and some heavy furniture. While they were waiting, the driver showed them a BBC graphic on his mobile, showing how far the caliphate had spread in the past year. Daniel could see that ISIS had increased its territory from Raqqa and northern Syria across the border into Iraq, where they now held Mosul.

'The caliphate is a well-functioning society under the rule of law,' the driver said. 'We aren't as bad as people think. Send an email next time you want to come to Syria.' He followed them out into the foyer, where another young man with glasses received them.

The man asked about James Foley, about whether or not he was still alive, because he had heard rumours that he was dead. Daniel was then asked to write down the names of those hostages who he knew were still in captivity, before he and Toni were taken outside.

It was pitch-black along the border. Daniel could hear the cicadas as he walked over to a large car park near the border fence. The only thing he could see ahead was a military truck with some Turkish soldiers. The yellow glow from the border lights illuminated the soldiers, who jumped into a car as soon as they had let Daniel through a gate. He had thought a million times about this moment, where each step took him a few more inches away from all the horrible things he had been subjected to during his captivity.

In this instant, his mind was empty. He was caught in a void between what had recently been the constant fear of death, and now, life and the ordinary thoughts that he could look forward to. The transition happened during the few hundred yards it took to reach the Turkish border police. Then he was struck by a practical thought: would he have to try to find a flight home or would there be someone to meet him?

The Turkish guards invited Daniel, Toni and the Syrian who had accompanied them across the border into the border post, where police officers were busy watching a World Cup match between Colombia and the Ivory Coast. They sat down on a sofa and joined them. At one point an advertising banner rolled across the screen. For the first time in more than a year Daniel heard music with drums and guitar, while a sexy woman ran along a beach.

'Daniel, would you like to borrow my mobile?' asked the Syrian thoughtfully.

Daniel hadn't given a single thought to being able to call home. He hurried outside and stood under a canopy beneath the starry Turkish sky. On 19 June at 8.37 p.m. he dialled his mother's mobile number and heard her pick up the phone.

'Hi Mum, it's Daniel.'

Return to Freedom

Susanne came home from work, took a long bath and put on an old sweatsuit and thick socks. Kjeld was away at a gymnastics meet, so she crawled under the blanket on the sofa and turned on the television. She watched a news report about some people in a nearby park who shot rook chicks, which they then prepared and invited the townspeople to come and taste. The owner of a local wine shop was asked which wine would go best with the meal.

In the middle of the news item, Susanne's mobile rang. She could see a long number from abroad on the display, so she made her voice sound hard, just in case it was the kidnappers.

'This is Susanne.'

'Hi Mum, it's Daniel. I'm free.'

'What . . . is that Daniel?' repeated Susanne, although she immediately recognized his voice.

They were both weeping so much that they could hardly hear what the other was saying.

'I'm fine, Mum,' sobbed Daniel. 'Everything's OK.' Then

he asked the three questions he had been thinking about for a long time.

'Is Signe still there?'

'Yes, she's been so sweet.'

'Have you sold everything you own to free me?'

'No, we haven't.'

'Has Christina finished high school or has she dropped out?'

'No, she's working hard to finish her final exams.'

Susanne told him how good everyone had been and that no one had paid more than they could afford for the ransom.

'Say hello to everyone,' said Daniel.

'Arthur's coming to get you,' said Susanne.

'Who's Arthur?'

'The man you talked to before you went to Syria. Anita's also in Turkey waiting for you.'

'Mum, I have to go. Toni also wants to call home.'

Susanne immediately sent a message to Arthur that Daniel was at the border. Then she called Kjeld, who didn't answer. Christina didn't pick up her phone either. Signe answered and was given the news, and then Susanne managed to get hold of Kjeld. He swallowed a quick celebratory beer with his gymnastics friends and hurried home to Susanne, who had already opened a bottle of red wine, while the phone rang off the hook and friends and neighbours came by with champagne.

They were both fairly tipsy and very relieved when they fell asleep that night.

. * .

Daniel wiped his eyes and went back into the guard room. He sat down on the sofa and tried to follow the World Cup match. But the players looked blurry on the little television, because he didn't have his glasses. He looked at Toni, who was totally absorbed in the game.

'Do you want to borrow the phone, Toni?' he asked, but the German shook his head and took a bite of the kebab he had been given.

Daniel was restless and wanted to call home again. This time he got his father on the other end.

'It's good to hear you're back,' said Kjeld quietly and with relief.

The Internet didn't work in Anita's hotel room in Kilis, so she didn't get the message from Susanne about Daniel's release. It wasn't until half an hour after Daniel's call that the crisis psychologist and the representative from the Danish Foreign Ministry knocked on her door and told her that something was happening.

They also said that Arthur was speeding towards the border at 120 miles an hour.

Anita took a bath. Her stomach was so jumpy that she had to take some of the diarrhoea pills she had brought for Daniel. Then she sat on the bed and waited.

A white car drove up and pulled into the covered car park in front of the Turkish border control. A tall man stepped out from the driver's seat. Daniel squinted and recognized Arthur, who rushed towards him with a broad smile. When he reached Daniel, he stretched out his arms and embraced him.

'My, am I glad to see you, man! You idiot,' said Arthur, with the emphasis on 'man' and 'idiot'.

'I didn't know it was you who was looking for me!' exclaimed Daniel.

'Yes, it's been me ever since your father called when you didn't come back,' said Arthur, fishing out a pair of glasses from his pocket and handing them to Daniel.

Suddenly, Daniel could clearly see the faces staring at him. Arthur wasn't alone. Beside him stood a doctor, a man from Danish Intelligence (PET) and some Germans with gelled hair and polished shoes who had come for Toni.

The doctor immediately shone a light in Daniel's eyes and took his pulse.

'Are you hungry or thirsty?' asked the doctor.

Daniel shook his head. Arthur was keeping his distance and had lit his pipe. As everyone was preparing to leave, Daniel and Toni shook hands and gave each other a pat on the back as a farewell.

'Have a good trip home,' said Daniel and went and sat with the doctor in Arthur's car.

They drove to the first stop on their way, the local police station, where Daniel had to make a report. The local officers didn't bat an eye.

'Do you want to make a complaint against those who have been detaining you?'

'No,' replied Daniel, signing the report that declared he had been released.

Daniel glanced over at Arthur, who was leaning against a wall, looking pleased.

The PET agent had to gather evidence. He took pictures of the bruises on Daniel's torso and the scars on his ankle and wrists. Daniel's clothes were placed in sealed bags for later DNA testing and Daniel helped by setting up the camera, so that the marks from his torture became clearer under the dim lighting.

He was handed a pair of board shorts and a loose T-shirt to replace the tiny shirt and olive-coloured trousers he had been given. Then they proceeded to a local hospital, where a senior doctor examined him rather superficially before writing a report.

The rumour had clearly already spread among Turkish journalists that ISIS had released two hostages. Local film crews turned up outside the hospital's main entrance and Daniel wore a cap and sunglasses as he was taken straight to a car, which had pulled up in front of the entrance, and away from the glare of the lights.

When they were finally able to head towards the hotel in Gaziantep, Daniel remembered that he had talked with his fellow prisoners about what music each of them wanted to listen to when they were sitting safely in a car on their way out of Syria.

'Do you have any music, Arthur? *Dark Side of the Moon* by Pink Floyd, for example?' he asked.

Arthur looked for Pink Floyd on his iPhone.

'No, unfortunately, I don't,' he said.

However, he had saved Signe's mobile number and gave the phone to Daniel, who had spent so much time thinking about her. After the ringing tone had sounded a few times, he heard her voice in his ear. She was out for a walk alone and began crying. She told him that she had bought an apartment.

'Is there room for one more in that apartment?'

'No, well, I don't know . . . I heard that you've put on weight.'

It didn't sound like a joke. Daniel could feel the distance between them.

'I've been exercising a lot in there, so I'm not at all fat any more.' He ended the conversation by saying, 'See you when I get home.'

He sat quietly for a moment. It had been the most awkward conversation of his entire life.

The representative from the Foreign Ministry and the crisis psychologist met Daniel at the hotel entrance. They introduced themselves and followed him up to his room, while Anita waited in the adjoining room.

'May I see her soon or what?' asked Daniel eagerly.

He felt that they were all trying to size him up and that there was an unknown plan that they were following to the letter, but the only thing he wanted was to see his sister. Finally, the door to Anita's room opened.

They stood in a long embrace, surrounded by the others.

'I've talked to Signe – it didn't go too well,' said Daniel.

Anita didn't comment, but just looked at her brother, who had a beard, was as white as a ghost and had visible scars snaking around his wrists and one ankle.

When Arthur also gave Anita a long hug of relief, Daniel said, 'That's a bit strange, you two. How come you know each other?' and laughter broke out.

It was around midnight when the Foreign Ministry issued the press release that the family and Arthur had helped to write.

The 25-year-old Danish photographer Daniel Rye Ottosen from Give has been released after having been detained in Syria since 17 May last year, when he travelled to Syria to photo-document the conflict and the living conditions of the civilians – especially the children.

Under the circumstances, Daniel Rye Ottosen is well and is now being reunited with his family.

The Rye Ottosen family would like to take this opportunity to extend heartfelt thanks to everyone who has assisted them in getting Daniel home.

Daniel's case has been known to the Danish press for a long time, but out of consideration for Daniel's safety, everyone has refrained from covering the story. The press is requested to continue to show consideration and discretion.

The family does not wish to comment further. The Rye Ottosen family does not wish to have contact with the media or other outsiders and would like to thank you for your understanding.

Despite the timing, Danish Intelligence wanted to ask Daniel some questions straight away about his capture in order to gather evidence about ISIS.

'I can't cope with that right now,' said Daniel.

'No, I quite understand,' replied the PET man and he remained seated.

Daniel wondered why there seemed to be such a rush. Couldn't it wait until the day after, the week after? What if he had been released and had to stay in hospital for a week?

Eventually, the PET agent left Daniel and Anita alone, while the crisis psychologist went into the room next door so that he was close by if they needed him.

Daniel went into the bathroom and closed the door. His time was his own and there was no guard outside waiting with a stick. He sat down on the clean toilet and stayed there a long time. It was so wonderful to be able to shit in peace that he began to cry. Then he turned on the shower. The water gushed out of the huge shower head above him, while he filled the scrubbing glove with gel and scrubbed the dirt off his body. The foam slid down over his skin. He made the shower warmer and shaved off the beard on his cheeks and his moustache. He stood under the warm, clean water for a long time and washed off thirteen months of captivity.

He threw all his clothes out of the bag Anita had brought with her and put on an old, washed-out T-shirt that the boys from his boarding school had made. There was a picture on the chest of them all together with his apple-green car. He took a beer out of the fridge for himself and one for Anita too.

'I bring greetings with me,' she told him and went through the gifts, photographs and letters in the order that the crisis psychologist had suggested.

Daniel was given a picture of some boys he had gone to Free School with. One of them had become a father and was sitting with his daughter on his lap. There were pictures of Christina with their grandparents and one of Anita's boyfriend sitting in a kayak. Susanne and Kjeld had also written a letter, and Susanne had sent a Lego set of *The Simpsons* to Daniel, with the mini-figures of Homer, Bart, Lisa, Maggie and Marge that were the new hit at Legoland. Daniel and Anita looked at each other and laughed when Daniel unpacked them.

'It's good that she's still herself,' said Daniel, looking at the figures. 'It's just like Mum.'

In one picture, Signe was sitting on a beach. But she wasn't there for him any more, he thought, and the proof-of-life question about how they had met now felt hollow and misleading.

Daniel and Anita lay under their blankets as he told her everything that had happened to him without censoring anything. She finally found out how he got the marks on his neck. The story of how he had tried to commit suicide to escape the torture was the worst. Anita's and the family's darkest fears had been correct.

Anita noticed that her brother was constantly eating. When they left the room so that Daniel could smoke a cigarette outside, there was a used plate with some French fries still on it, which he picked at in passing.

He asked for an Internet connection to see what the Danish media were writing about him, but Anita refused. Now wasn't the time for him to be relating to other people's opinions of him.

They didn't sleep all night, but lay under the blankets, talking until first light.

The next morning brunch was laid out on long tables in the hotel restaurant. Daniel filled his plate, while watching a couple sitting across from each other at one of the tables. The man had his newspaper and iPad in front of him, as well as a mobile alongside. Daniel was surprised that someone could sit opposite his wife in such a nice place, so deeply buried in electronic gizmos.

When he had eaten his fill, he had conversations with the psychologist and the PET agent, before he had a chance to call Christina, who was on her way to an exam, with the mobile he had finally been given.

'They're going completely berserk in the media,' said Christina.

'Really, what're they saying?' asked Daniel, who knew that no one in the family had said anything about his situation.

There were already several articles about Daniel on Danish newspaper websites. His former mentor, the photographer Jan Grarup, had said that Daniel 'was aware that Syria is a dangerous place, but he may not have been completely updated on how dangerous it really is'.

One newspaper also wrote that they had information that he 'had primarily been held in an area around the town of Raqqa', which wasn't true.

In another article from the news agency Ritzau, the headline said, 'Leading Psychologist: Danish hostage will never be the same.' The article described how traumatic an experience it is to be a hostage.

On another website an article began with the phrase 'In May, two days after Daniel Rye Ottosen ignored Foreign Ministry warnings and travelled to Syria for the first time, everything went wrong' – this ignored the fact that journalists and photographers often don't follow the Ministry's travel advice, because it would make it impossible for them to report from the world's conflict and disaster areas.

Generally, the media contained a lot of discussion about how defensible it was for a young photographer to have gone into Syria when the security risk was so great. But several articles were erroneously comparing the situation now with that which existed more than a year ago. When Daniel was captured in May 2013 very few journalists in Denmark had even heard of ISIS. It was very different in June 2014, because ISIS had grown and had taken control of large areas of northern Syria and captured Mosul in Iraq. One newspaper conveniently failed to mention that its own young reporter was in northern Syria at that very moment.

Journalists sitting comfortably at home in Denmark, ignorant of the details surrounding his capture, were now analysing everything that Daniel had been blaming himself for during the last thirteen months. He had often regretted that he went into Syria with Aya and that he hadn't insisted on travelling with his original fixer, Mahmoud. He had often asked himself whether he had been too unprepared, and whether it had been naive of him to travel to Syria when he had never been to the Middle East before. But the guilt had faded gradually as the prison cells he sat in were filled with hostages, several of whom had far more experience than him.

The articles in the media revived all his old guilt. Anita noticed that his face had turned as white as a sheet and suggested that he call Pierre, who had also been through the experience of coming home after being held captive by ISIS.

Daniel sat on the orange sofa in the foyer and ate half a chocolate bar, while talking to Pierre over Skype. Pierre had hated his own homecoming, because, unlike Daniel's, it had been a hero's welcome. President Hollande had spoken about how proud he was that the nation had Frenchmen like Pierre, who went to Syria to report on the situation.

Pierre reassured Daniel that no matter what the media in Denmark wrote – or what the president of France had to say – about everything they had experienced in Syria, none of them knew what had really happened.

302   PUK DAMSGÅRD

'They know nothing about you or what you have done or experienced, so don't worry about it,' said Pierre in his usual calm manner.

Daniel told Pierre about his last violent weeks in captivity and his fear of what would happen to the remaining hostages.

They agreed to meet again sometime soon.

That afternoon Daniel, Arthur and Anita drove to the airport to take a flight to a safe house at Aalborg Air Base in Denmark. They were transported home in one of the Armed Forces' aircraft, and Arthur had made arrangements for them to stay at the air base for a few days. Daniel could get the peace and quiet that would enable him to recuperate and avoid media attention. It was a move designed to help him with his first fragile steps back to his old life.

Daniel was sitting in the white leather seat, staring out of the window at the flat landscape, when finally, on 20 June 2014, he landed on Danish soil.

. * .

Kjeld, Susanne and Christina stood waiting for Daniel at Aalborg Air Base. They were in high spirits. They were going to see their long-lost son and brother – and they had come directly from Rosborg High School, where Christina had just got top marks in her penultimate exam.

The family was greeted at the barracks by a psychologist, who made it clear that Daniel should come to them, not vice versa. It was important that he had a choice after so long in captivity. Christina was only half-listening, while intensely watching the sky for her big brother. The family was led out into a small corridor with glass doors, so they could watch as the plane hit the runway – and then Daniel got out. As soon as Christina saw him, she raced out and threw herself, weeping, into his arms.

Susanne and Kjeld followed at a more modest pace. Daniel and Susanne both wept as they embraced each other.

'How lovely you look, Mum,' said Daniel.

Kjeld was more calm and collected. He gave Daniel a hug and a firm pat on the back and Daniel noticed that his hair had become greyer.

'You're so lucky . . .,' sniffled Susanne, '. . . that you're loved by so many people.'

At the barracks Daniel was assigned a room where they all sat down to listen to his story. He skated lightly over the torture centre and his suicide attempt. He slowed down when he came to the moment when he tried to escape, which he related with a modicum of humour. He dwelt on tales of the hostages exercising and playing home-made games.

They had never imagined that he would try to take his own life. As his mother, Susanne knew instinctively that the captors must have been very hard on him for him to choose that path.

'I'm well,' said Daniel. 'I've been broken down, but I've also rediscovered myself. Please don't feel bad for me.'

But he had changed. When the barracks served sandwiches as a snack before bedtime, he chose the most boring one, with rolled meat sausage, and ate it with some potato crisps from his room. If food dropped on the floor, he picked it up and put it in his mouth. He also ate what the others left on their plates, because he didn't want to let any food go to waste.

They thought he was eating oddly and Susanne noticed he'd developed a lazy eye. She suspected that it was probably because he hadn't been wearing his glasses for a long time. Anita stayed at the barracks, but the rest of the family left to go home to Hedegård. At which point the conversation that Daniel was dreading awaited him.

'Come with me,' said Arthur and Daniel followed him out into the kitchenette. 'I've made an appointment with Diane Foley. You can call her now.'

Daniel knew that the time had come to contact James's parents, and he was glad that Arthur had taken the initiative. It was going to be a difficult conversation.

Diane answered the phone in New Hampshire.

'Hi, dearest Daniel, so wonderful to hear your voice,' Diane said in a soft voice. 'How are you? We hope you're doing OK under the circumstances.'

Daniel said he felt fine.

'That's good to hear. How nice. We just wanted to hear if you had talked to Jim. Did he say anything to you?' she asked gently and put the phone on the speaker, so that James's father John could listen in.

Daniel walked in circles around the kitchenette, while he delivered James's greetings from memory: his thoughts about his grandmother, whom James hoped would carry on dancing; the message that he could feel the family when he prayed in the dark and that he hoped and knew that everyone was staying strong. Daniel told them that James had put on weight and was getting better food. He could hear that Diane was writing everything down.

'How has it been for all of you? How did they treat you?' asked Diane afterwards.

The longing for just a tiny bit of information burned down the wire. They had been living in the dark for months.

'James is better than he was in the beginning,' said Daniel. He refrained from talking about the last two weeks, when the Beatles had been behaving violently and unpredictably. Instead, he told them about the Risk game and the chessboard and the Secret Santa scheme and how much strength their son had shown.

'What do you think is going to happen, Daniel?' asked Diane.

He took a deep breath and paused.

'I don't know, Diane. I don't know any more than you do. It's as if there's a different plan for the British and the Americans.'

He told them about the video that had been recorded with James in which he had been forced to demand €100 million.

'We're groping in the dark. There's no one who will help us,' said Diane, referring to the US authorities. 'Oh, Daniel, we're so grateful – we know this is hard for you. You're a huge help – we want you to know that.'

When he put the phone down after an hour and a half, he sat out on the lawn with Arthur, smoking cigarettes.

'For Christ's sake, Arthur, this is so damn sad,' said Daniel. They just sat in silence a while.

'I'm afraid you're the last person that they'll talk to who has seen their son alive,' said Arthur.

Daniel went straight to bed and passed a restless night.

The barracks were intended to be a safe environment for four days, and there was a detailed plan in place that would help Daniel create a smooth transition to the life that awaited him outside the air base. He received the constant support of professionals who had experience of helping hostages return home.

One day he was taken to the hospital to be X-rayed and, in between appointments, he drove with his guardian to buy some more underwear. They went to H&M's underwear department, which turned out to be for women only.

Daniel stared at the lingerie, the posters of half-naked women and the female customers, feeling like an eleven year old. He hadn't seen an uncovered woman for more than a year and laughed at himself, telling his guardian that he could hardly remember what a pair of breasts looked like. He fled across the street to a hunting-and-fishing store, where he found a black balaclava and took a selfie with it on. He also bought an air rifle and got it wrapped up.

He often talked with Anita, who followed him closely in those early days. During their conversations, he asked frequently about Signe.

'Isn't Signe coming to Christina's graduation party?'

'Only if you two are still together, Daniel,' said Anita elusively.

A few days later, when she said goodbye to him in the barracks' car park, he was excited that Signe had said she would visit him.

Anita stared out of the window of the train from Aalborg to Odense. She finally had a moment to herself and the emotions overwhelmed her. In the middle of the train compartment, she burst into tears. Not so much over the suffering her brother had undergone in Syria, but over the pain he had to live through now. This time no one could make it easy for him. She could pick him up from kindergarten when he was little, raise money for his release and fill a toiletry bag with nice things, but she couldn't mend his relationship with his girlfriend after such an ordeal.

. * .

The wide pines encircled the lawn so that no one could see if Daniel ran around naked on the grass. The trees provided shade from the sun and a screen against the neighbours if you were sitting on the covered wooden terrace or on the sofa in the living room, which looked out over the garden through large, floor-to-ceiling windows.

Daniel loved being in the family's summer house, which served as his second safe house in the weeks after his release.

He had found a picture on the Internet of the Frenchman Mehdi Nemmouche, one of his guards, who had gone by the name of Abu Omar and who, by all accounts, was the perpetrator of an attack on the Jewish Museum in Belgium. Daniel had printed out a picture of Nemmouche's face, which he had hung up in the garden. Together with Kjeld, he drank beer and used it as a target for his air rifle.

After a few days at the summer house, he went to collect Signe at the train station. He spotted her immediately when she stepped out on to the platform. She stood there with a large suitcase, dressed in pure white trainers, shorts and a tight blouse. She hadn't changed a bit.

They embraced. Signe began to cry.

'Well, what's new?' asked Daniel when they had arrived at the summer house and were sitting together in the shade on the terrace.

Signe told him about the chaotic night when she had waited for him at the airport and that she'd had a difficult time while he had been away. She had tried to be optimistic and to help where she could, and she had talked a lot with Kjeld and Susanne. But around Christmas time, when Daniel had been away for more than six months, she had tried to move forwards with her life. She had stopped doing gymnastics and had found peace in her new apartment. She finally felt that she had moved on.

Daniel couldn't hold back the tears.

'I can really understand,' he said, 'but I've been thinking about you so much.'

Signe had been his light in the darkness. His thoughts about her had kept him going. Suddenly it felt as if something inside him had become constricted and his sobs overwhelmed him. He wept and wept until there was nothing left but relief; relief that he knew what he had to deal with – and that Signe no longer had to worry about him.

They put Queen on the stereo and danced until they collapsed, exhausted, on the sofa, where they lay watching a dreadful film until her parents came to pick her up.

Daniel waved goodbye as Signe left in the car.

A week after Daniel had returned from Syria, he and the rest of the family stood waiting impatiently in the corridor at Rosborg High School. He was holding one long red rose and his little sister's graduation cap.

She was behind the door, completing her very last exam in biology. In captivity Daniel had been so afraid that Christina would drop out of school.

The door finally opened and Christina came out to meet him in her sleeveless white dress, her curly hair hanging loose.

Daniel took his sister in his arms and cried on her shoulder as he hugged her so hard and for so long that his grip left marks on her arms.

Then he put the graduation cap on her head and toasted her with champagne for finishing high school, and for him being home to celebrate it with her.

Death in the Desert

Daniel dragged the bed from the small bedroom in the summer house into the living room, where the large windows let the sunlight flood in. Now and again, he went out on to the terrace and smoked a cigarette to soothe the restless quivering in his body. Otherwise, he spent most of his time in front of the computer, where he immersed himself in war documentaries such as *Al-Qaeda in Yemen*, *Taxi to the Dark Side* (about Afghan prisoners in US prisons) or *Dirty Wars*, about America's secret wars. He was constantly looking for stories and films about the region in which he had been held captive.

Every evening before going to bed he checked the latest news about ISIS, which was now also going by the name, the so called Islamic State or IS.

In early July 2014 Daniel stumbled on a video circulating on the Internet in which IS leader Abu Bakr al-Baghdadi appeared in public for the first time. Dressed in black robes and a turban, he went up the steps of the pulpit in the Great Mosque of al-Nuri in Mosul. The voluminous beard on his broad face had smatterings of grey. Young men in short-sleeved shirts stood facing Baghdadi and the black-and-white IS flag hanging on the mosque wall.

Before Friday prayers Baghdadi gave a speech about the Islamic caliphate, which now stretched across Syria from Aleppo to Raqqa, and from there eastwards into northern Iraq through Mosul and to the north-eastern province of Diyala. Al-Baghdadi had been appointed the 'Caliph', the supreme leader of the caliphate, and appearing in public in the middle of Mosul was a sign of defiance to the outside world. The driver in Syria who had shown Daniel a graphic of the IS areas was right: they had taken control.

When Daniel finally fell asleep, he dreamed the same dream over and over again, in which he had been kidnapped and thrown into a dark room. And when he opened his eyes in the morning, his first thought was about how James and the others were getting on in the Quarry in Raqqa.

At that time he didn't know that the hostages had been moved. It was only months later that it became public knowledge that, at around 2 a.m. on 4 July, US elite forces in Black Hawk helicopters had flown over the border to Raqqa to free the hostages. FBI agents had spoken to some of the released hostages to locate the site where they were being detained south-east of Raqqa.

According to an anonymous American Special Operations officer, who later spoke to *The New Yorker*, two armed drones had circled over the area in the middle of the desert while the operation was carried out. There was a gun battle and several IS fighters were killed, but there were no hostages in the building. The elite forces unit found traces of them, but it wasn't surprising that the hostages had been moved sixteen days after the release of Daniel and Toni. It was a tactic the Beatles used deliberately. They knew that those who had been released would be questioned by their countries' intelligence services. While Daniel had been in captivity the guards had twice faked moving the hostages, so that those freed would return home with incorrect information.

That failed mission was the first and only attempt to rescue James and his countrymen, Steven and Peter, together with their British fellow prisoners, John, David and Alan.

In the beginning Daniel was so restless that he took trips into town and began focusing on getting started with his photography again, but he soon had to admit that he couldn't cope with too many impressions or experiences. Being with a lot of people who didn't know his history made him feel drained. He felt that they were pointing at him and that he had to explain to them over and over again what he had been through.

'How terrible,' they said, looking at him as if he were sick.

For this reason, he usually stuck to smaller groups of people, where he didn't need to explain himself, like when he and his old friends from boarding school sailed to an island for a few days where they could just hang out and drink beer.

He flinched when someone knocked on the door or slapped a hand against a table to emphasize a point during a conversation. He recoiled if a well-meaning person happened to take hold of his wrist or touch his ribs, or when his parents embraced him as if he were a child. They obviously tried to hold back, as they had been told to, so as not to go overboard with love and affection, but at times Susanne and Kjeld felt an almost morbid concern for their son.

When Daniel needed to talk, he called his psychologist, the one who had met him in Turkey. It was going to take a while for him to return to a normal life.

In early August, in an attempt to get back into the routines of daily life, Daniel took the train out to Hillerød to visit his old college, where he had learned photography. They had offered him a room and the opportunity to teach a photography course. He needed to be somewhere where it was once more only about photography.

While he sat on the train he read a news item: President Barack Obama had announced that the Americans were going to bomb IS in Iraq. After the capture of Mosul and the declaration of a united caliphate across the Iraq–Syria border, IS had moved forwards in a significant offensive in several places in Iraq and for a moment had even threatened Baghdad.

Daniel looked around. There was a mother with a crying child and a young couple who were holding hands. For them it was just a matter-of-fact news update, as it would have been for him no more than a year and a half earlier. But he knew that the president's announcement about bombing Iraq could cost the lives of people he knew.

While he sat there on the train, somewhere between Copenhagen and Hillerød, he lost all hope for James and the other remaining hostages. Obama's political decision was a death sentence. He grabbed his mobile and called Pierre.

'Have you heard?' he asked.

'Yes,' replied Pierre.

They didn't need to say anything else.

. * .

The United States was drawn back to the war zone in Iraq less than three years after its forces had left the country at the end of 2011, following a lengthy campaign that began in 2003. The first bombings by American aircraft took place on 8 August 2014. Obama had prided himself on having ended the two wars in Iraq and Afghanistan, but now the Americans were back at the invitation of the Iraqi government and a failed army that needed help. The Kurds' otherwise effective defences in northern Iraq had also been overrun several times. Moreover, Mosul, which IS had captured, wasn't far from the Kurdish capital of Erbil.

The American military presence could also be interpreted as a tidying-up campaign following the recent war. The United States had itself played a role in creating the leader of the organization that they were now bombing, when Baghdadi had been held in their prison at Camp Bucca. Beyond that, the long-standing US policy failure regarding the Ba'ath Party and the Iraqi army had added fuel to the flames, which were fanned by the Shia Party's exclusionary policy towards the country's Sunni Muslims.

There were now several former Saddam supporters at the head of the IS leadership. At the same time the Sunni insurgency and the Shia rulers had both effectively marginalized anyone outside their own sect in the struggle for power that had pushed Iraq over the edge.

The Americans wanted to eliminate IS in Iraq, to which the Islamists responded promptly. IS was going to take revenge on President Obama and his policies in the Middle East.

. * .

Arthur walked around restlessly, thinking about the wording of the next message to be sent. After a long silence, James's family had finally received an email from the kidnappers. It was 12 August, just four days after US planes began bombing IS in Iraq.

On the basis of the email, Arthur judged that it had to have come from the same people who had previously written to the Foley family and to Daniel's parents. The email contained a message to the US government and the family that they would kill James as a consequence of the bombs raining down on Iraq. It didn't sound like either an attempt at extortion or an aggressive proposal for negotiations. It just sounded like a statement of fact, thought Arthur. Yet the family had to try to persuade the kidnappers to change their minds.

IS had succeeded in illustrating the difference between the European approach to hostage negotiations and the usual position of the United States and the United Kingdom, which was also why Arthur couldn't do anything. In Daniel's case, he had had a free hand to act without government interference.

In James's case, the US authorities had been trying to bulldoze the investigation and had wasted valuable time looking for James in Damascus; and when there had finally been an opportunity in December 2013, the family had nothing to negotiate with, because they weren't allowed to pay – or collect money for – a ransom.

Arthur feared the worst, in which case James would be the first hostage he had ever lost in his career.

. ∗ .

While in the United States they were battling for James's life, Daniel was settling into his seat on a plane to Paris. He was going to meet Pierre. They wanted to drive around England and Scotland together for a month. It was going to be just the two of them – along with the shared experience that only they could fully understand. Daniel was also looking forward to seeing Pierre in the surroundings he had talked so much about during his captivity, rather than as a hostage with a grey blindfold hanging around his neck, waiting for a cell door to be flung open.

At the airport Daniel came out into the arrival hall and immediately spotted Pierre, who was standing slightly back, behind the other people waiting. They gave each other a long hug.

He was the same as ever, in a thick black jacket, black jeans and leather shoes. His hair was shorter and he had shaved off his beard.

They drove to a house where some of Pierre's anarchist friends lived and spent the night in the garage. The next day, they took the train to his parents' house north-west of Paris, on the roaring river just outside the city of Rouen.

Pierre's mother picked them up in a car with their dog Olaf, who always came for the ride. She drove them along narrow roads until they turned down a dirt track at the end of which stood Pierre's childhood home. Olaf was jumping up around their legs as they made their way to Pierre's father, who was waiting in the living room. Daniel could speak neither French nor Spanish, so Pierre translated during a dinner of delicious French food that his mother had prepared.

Pierre's world was exactly as he had described it in prison. His father's sculptures towered above Daniel's head as he came into the workshop, where tools and gadgets were scattered between metal formations that looked like a mixture of animals and humans. There was an old boat and some rusty motorcycles that Pierre wanted to refurbish, and in the shed behind the house was Tonton the donkey.

'I felt bad about leaving you all,' Pierre told Daniel when the conversation turned to their captivity.

He still felt it was wrong to be bought out of the hands of the Islamists.

'The worst thing is that I accepted it,' said Pierre. 'I wasn't a human being any more, but an object that could be sold.' After his return Pierre had agreed to illustrate a children's book that he and their fellow former prisoner Nicolas Hénin were writing. It was about a daddy hedgehog who disappeared from his hedgehog family.

Pierre and Daniel spent a couple of days preparing for their trip. They furnished the silver car with mattresses and a nifty device that enabled them to fold down the seats and flip open a bed in the back.

Before they headed for the ferry to England, they first made a stop farther south at a French farm to attend Nicolas Hénin's wedding. Daniel drove, because Pierre had no driver's licence. When they finally reached the farm and the lawn where the wedding was to be held, they met a happy Nicolas dressed in jacket and tie.

'Hi Daniel, welcome! How good it is to see you,' he said, smiling, before quickly moving on to welcome the other guests, including correspondents and journalists from around the world.

Pierre and Daniel had been assigned a room in the farmhouse where they could spend the night, while other guests slept in tents. When the party and the music shut down at around 1 a.m. Daniel rushed up to the bartender, who was about to pack up, and asked him to leave them a few bottles of wine. He carried them up to the room, where he and Pierre sat on the floor and laughed, joked and drank. They consumed so much wine that Pierre got drunk for the first time in his life. When they woke the next morning, 17 August, with throbbing headaches, Daniel started laughing again.

'You just made it before you turned thirty. Happy birthday, my dear Pierre.'

. * .

Late in the evening on 19 August Arthur opened the door to his hotel room in London. He had been to a series of meetings and threw his computer bag on the bed and checked his phone. There was a message from one of his contacts in Syria.

It was a question: 'Have you seen the video with James?'

There were also several missed calls from his security colleagues in the United States. Arthur immediately called back.

'I'll send you the link,' his associate said. 'It's a video. I think they've killed him.'

'OK, I'll take a look and call you back in a minute,' replied Arthur. He fished his computer out of his bag and hurried to download the video from YouTube before it could be censored.

A picture appeared with someone who looked like James Foley in an orange prison uniform kneeling in a desert. Beside him stood a black-clad, masked man with a knife in his hand and a gun in a holster. The video was entitled 'A Message to America'.

James recited some clearly rehearsed phrases. It was a political message to his government: 'I call on my friends, family and loved ones to rise up against my real killers, the US government,' began James. 'For what will happen to me is only a result of their complacency and criminality. My message to my beloved parents: save me some dignity and don't accept any meagre compensation for my death from the same people who effectively put the last nail in my coffin with the recent aerial campaign in Iraq.'

He spoke to his brother John, who should think about whether those who had decided to go to war against IS had thought about him and his family.

'I guess, all in all, I wish I wasn't American,' he concluded.

Then the black executioner took over as he put a hand on James's shoulder.

'As a government you have been at the forefront of the aggression towards the Islamic State. You have plotted against us and gone far out of your way to find reasons to interfere in our affairs.'

The executioner proclaimed that an attack on IS was an attack on Muslims all over the world.

'So any attempt by you, Obama, to deny Muslims their rights to live in safety under the Islamic caliphate will result in the bloodshed of your people.'

The executioner brought the knife up against James's neck. At that moment, the video went black and the next thing Arthur saw was an orange-clad body laid out on its stomach, the head placed between the shoulder blades.

Arthur played the video three to four times and tried to focus on his task: to analyse what he was watching. He noted the way the film was edited. At the moment of execution, it went black. Could they have faked the killing? Was the decapitated head really James's? Why didn't IS want to show the actual moment of death? Was it out of respect? Was it because it would be too triumphant, or had they learned from the 2004 video of Kenneth Bigley, which frightened off al-Qaeda support?

Arthur played the video in slow motion, frame by frame, to interpret James's facial expressions and body language, as the knife met his neck, and compared it with other images he had of James. It didn't look like a fake. It looked like a murder.

For Arthur, it was the tragic culmination of nearly two years of searching. It was now clearly all over. A heaviness weighed on Arthur's mind. James's family had believed that he could do the same for James as he had done for Daniel.

He took a deep breath and called his colleague in the United States.

'I'm not in any doubt about it. It's James. He's dead.'

They talked about the strongly worded appeal addressed to James's brother, who was in the US Air Force, and to his family about not accepting a meagre compensation from the US government.

'If we're going to do anything to retrieve the body, we have to move fast. You must ask the family if they want us to try,' said Arthur. If that were the case, he would quickly get hold of his contacts in Syria. 'I have to run. There's someone I have to talk to as soon as possible, so that he doesn't get the news another way,' Arthur said and hung up.

Then he dialled Daniel's number.

. * .

It was dark and the English country road twisted in front of Daniel and Pierre as they sat shrouded in music inside the car. They had taken the ferry from Calais to Dover, where they had driven ashore and were now heading towards a small town that was lit up in the distance.

Daniel loved the tranquillity that oozed out of the nerdy marine biologist when he held long, enthusiastic monologues about fish and water fleas. Pierre was the sort of person who would never buy a smartphone and was completely satisfied with his little old flip phone.

Suddenly the ring tone from Daniel's iPhone interrupted Pierre's speech. He could see on the display that it was Arthur.

'Do you have time to talk? I have a message,' said Arthur.

'I'm driving,' said Daniel.

'Then pull over,' said Arthur.

Daniel could immediately tell that Arthur sounded different and that he hadn't said, 'What's up, you idiot?' or fired off a stream of jokes.

Daniel hung up while he found a place to pull in and turn off the engine. Pierre looked at him.

'Why are we stopping here?'

'It's Arthur. Something's happened,' said Daniel and rang Arthur back.

Arthur's voice sounded heavy.

'A video has just been made public. It shows James in an orange prison uniform in a desert, where he is being killed by a masked man.'

'No! How?'

'Yes, well, that's it – he was decapitated.'

Daniel stiffened.

'I have more bad news,' continued Arthur. 'They showed Steven afterwards. He's the next in line.' Daniel thought about his old prison companion, whom he had wrapped up in a blanket in December when he had been Steven's Secret Santa.

Daniel was beside himself. It was unbearable to think of James's brutal murder, and the fact that Steven had been forced to witness the killing, after which he would have to sit in a cell, knowing he would be next. His worst fears had become reality.

'I knew it could happen,' said Daniel quietly. 'That's the way things were going.'

'I need your help,' said Arthur.

He wanted to send Daniel the video.

'Could you listen and hear if it's James's voice?' asked Arthur. He wanted to get a clear confirmation or denial as to whether it was actually James.

'You just have to listen while he speaks. Stop the video after that,' warned Arthur.

Daniel hung up, his eyes empty. Pierre stared at him expectantly.

'They've beheaded James,' said Daniel. 'Steven is next.'

Pierre's eyes welled with tears and Daniel reminded him of the terrible last days in prison, when the Beatles had been agitated, violent and obnoxious. Everyone had sensed that it could end this way.

They got out of the car, unfolded a small camp table and sat around it. Daniel connected his computer to the mobile's network and downloaded the file Arthur had sent. In the darkness, they watched James in silence as he knelt in an orange suit in the middle of the desert, while he spouted what he had been told to say. It was James. Daniel and Pierre were in no doubt; the voice, the torso and his characteristic underbite.

'I think I recognize the landscape,' said Pierre. It looked like James was standing on a mound in the desert, where the Euphrates River, some green areas and the outlines of an urban environment were just visible behind him. It could be Raqqa.

They let the video play and watched the black figure standing with a knife in his hand beside James.

'It's John!' exclaimed Pierre, as the executioner began to speak.

He recognized his accent, his posture and his rhetoric – the way he put pressure on individual words: 'YOUR government.'

Daniel called Arthur back.

'There's no doubt. It's James,' he said. 'And the executioner is one of our British guards. Probably John.'

James's voice on the video was echoing inside his head. So was John's.

'Let's find a place to stay,' said Daniel.

They drove into a small rest area near some woodland. The air was damp as they arranged themselves on mattresses in the back of the car, where they also found a few cans of beer. Daniel called Arthur again and put the phone on speaker.

'Hello Pierre, hope you're OK,' said Arthur.

They agreed to hold a minute's silence for James. The rain drops were dribbling down the car windows. In that one minute the world shrank to just the two of them on a mattress as they sheltered from the rain, with a silent Arthur at the other end, somewhere in London. Daniel and Pierre stared into the distance and remembered the man they had shared a cell with for eight months; the man who so often sacrificed himself in order to be the best for others. Now he had finally found peace. The one minute became several, in which they stayed on the line without uttering a word. Arthur finally broke the silence.

'Since you both had to receive such bad news, it's good that you're together to share it with each other and vent your frustrations,' he said.

Arthur knew it would be natural for Daniel to feel shame that he had survived when James had not. Questions like 'Why him and not me?' were bound to come up. The typical response from an outsider would be: 'Well, you're lucky it wasn't you.' But for the survivor, that was exactly what they didn't need to hear.

'Just call if you need to talk,' said Arthur. 'Me or the psychologist.'

When the conversation was over, Daniel and Pierre went online to see how the story about James's death was being reported. There were items with judgmental reactions about the killing and photos from James's life and work in Syria, which were put up as a response to the execution. The newspapers were soon calling John 'Jihadi John', because they had found out that the hostages in the cell had named him John. The nightmare in the desert haunted Daniel's restless sleep that night.

The next morning they drove towards London. On the way they tried to figure out if their plan would still hold. The original idea was to visit Alan's and David's families to talk to them about the good times in captivity and give them encouragement, but both families cancelled the visit after James's murder. Pierre was relieved; there was nothing positive to say. Instead they drove north towards the wide open spaces of Scotland to be alone with themselves and each other.

· * ·

Since Daniel had returned home and was living in the summer house it had been a difficult time in Hedegård. Susanne and Kjeld walked around on tenterhooks, trying to gauge how Daniel was really feeling. At Christina's graduation party in the garage he was bouncing off the walls. Many of the guests had been nervous about meeting Daniel. 'What shall we say? How does he look?' they had asked Susanne.

He behaved like a helium balloon that would fly away if they didn't hold on to him. Beyond that, he was almost over-caring and kept asking everyone how they were, instead of looking after himself. At the same time, Daniel didn't feel up to the small, practical things, such as getting a new online security ID, a health card and driver's licence. Kjeld helped by driving him around to different government agencies. Daniel was granted two months' social security benefits before he began teaching photography at Grundtvig College.

Kjeld and Susanne thought he had changed, although he retained his upbeat attitude. Whenever they asked him how he was, the answer was always 'fine'. Nevertheless, they were concerned if they didn't hear from him, and Tina Enghoff, his teacher before he went to Syria, also sensed a darkness in her formerly enthusiastic student. The story of Daniel's suicide attempt was always at the back of Susanne's mind and it took some time before she could process her own emotional journey.

On top of everything, the family had a debt of just under a million kroner to deal with. The total expenses in connection with Daniel's kidnapping had amounted to more than 22 million kroner (almost €3 million or £2 million). The insurance had covered 5 million kroner (about £500,000) of it and other insurance policies had also kept the family's expenses to a minimum. But Susanne and Kjeld wouldn't be at peace until the entire debt was paid off.

Nevertheless, they had been released from the iron grip of terror that had held them for more than a year. They no longer needed to fear the next email or the next telephone call, and slowly everyday life returned to Hedegård.

. * .

In autumn 2014 Denmark became involved in the fight against Islamic State in Iraq, along with the United States. On 2 October 2014 seven Danish F-16s, in collaboration with a broad coalition of countries, flew from a base in Kuwait to bomb IS positions in Iraq. In coordination with the bombing from the air, Iraqi forces attacked IS on the ground.

The Danish government led by Helle Thorning-Schmidt also decided to send a team of soldiers to the Ayn al-Asad base in western Anbar province to train Iraqi forces. This was the very same base where former US President George W. Bush gave a speech in 2007 to the US military, who had fought the most tenacious insurgency of the Iraq War.

'Anbar is a huge province that was once written off as lost, but is now one of the safest places,' he proclaimed at the time.

When the Danish soldiers arrived at the base seven years later, that statement was no longer true, since it had now fallen under the control of Islamic State. The soldiers being trained were the dilapidated remnants of the Iraqi army, which had previously received training and equipment from the West. The army was now being helped mainly by Iranian-backed Shiite militias, whose goals were often just as sectarian as IS and who also committed atrocities against civilians. At the same time, then Iraqi Prime Minister Nuri al-Maliki mobilized the so-called People's Army, made up of thousands of young male volunteers who received only a few weeks of training before they were sent to the battlefield. The establishment of the People's Army and the influence of powerful Shiite militias meant that Iraq was being driven further in the direction of a divided, violent and sectarian society that could push even more Sunnis into the arms of IS.

It was in the midst of this chaos that Denmark and its allies were trying to exert their influence. It had always been impossible to intervene in Iraq without simultaneously exacerbating the underlying causes that made it possible for IS to thrive. The Iraq War in the 2000s had made one thing abundantly clear: the coalition would in all likelihood be flying over Iraq for a long time with no guarantee that it would stabilize the country or eradicate Islamic State.

. * .

The evening when the video of James was made public, Arthur had also sent a text message to Diane Foley. He wasn't at all sure whether it was the right thing to do. He didn't know what the authorities had told them and he hadn't wanted to be the first to commiserate on what was only circumstantial evidence, even though everything indicated that James was dead. Even so, he had written to Diane that his thoughts were with the family and the following day, after several attempts, he finally got through to her.

She had been receptive and happy that he had called.

THE ISIS HOSTAGE 329

'You helped give us hope to the last, and for that we will be eternally grateful to you,' she said.

She had invited Arthur to take part in James's memorial service and now he was sitting with Daniel on their way to New Hampshire. He wanted to pay his respects to James and to show the family he was thinking of them – and, along with Daniel, close a chapter of their lives that had lasted more than two years.

He was happy to have freed Daniel from captivity, but he was just as sad that he had 'lost' James, as it was called in his line of work. Not a day went by when he didn't think about whether he could have done things differently and if there had been openings along the way that he had overlooked. He wondered if it could have ended another way if he had had the same influence on James's case as he had had on Daniel's, and not just followed the decisions that the US authorities had mapped out. He didn't know the answer.

Arthur was nervous about how he would be received – if the family would direct their frustration and anger at him. The easiest thing for him to do would have been to stay away from the memorial service and remain as a negotiator, the role for which he had been hired. In his field it was considered neither professional nor beneficial to get emotional about the work. But as a human being, Arthur needed to look James's parents in the eyes and share their grief. So did Daniel, who hadn't yet allowed the murder of James to sink in completely. He and Pierre had relaxed and talked about it together in Scotland, but he hadn't wept. It still seemed unreal to him that his former fellow prisoner had been killed.

After James, the first to have his throat cut, it didn't take long before Daniel saw the next video. The Beatles had unfortunately kept the promise they made in the video of James: that Steven Sotloff would be the next, despite his mother in the United States making a public video appeal to spare her son's life.

Less than two weeks after Steven was executed, it was David Haines's turn. He left behind a wife and two children at home in Britain. And on 3 October Alan Henning was killed; he didn't make it home to his wife and their two children either. The only relief Daniel felt was that he knew they had found peace; the worst thing for him was the uncertainty about what would happen to the final two male hostages, John and Peter. It felt right to be on a plane beside Arthur on his way to say goodbye.

. * .

Arthur steered the car through the forests, while Daniel chose music to listen to on his iPhone that reminded him of James. They stopped at a Starbucks, where Daniel bought a pumpkin spice latte before they rolled up in front of the family's white house.

Daniel went in first and was received in the Foley family's kitchen, where the whole family was gathered. He got a long hug from Diane, who showed him round and introduced him to the family. When Arthur appeared in the doorway, he got the same reception.

'He's the one who tried to get Jim home,' said Diane.

In Our Lady of the Holy Rosary Church in Rochester, Arthur and Daniel sat next to each other in the pews. Arthur looked at Daniel, who was in tears. He placed a hand on his shoulder and passed him a handkerchief.

One of history's most notorious kidnapping cases ended here

for them. While Arthur sat next to Daniel, he tried to come to terms with the fact that he had managed to save one but not the other. More than anything else, he wished he could have reunited them somewhere other than at a memorial service.

. * .

Two days later in the predawn darkness, Daniel and Arthur drove off towards Boston. The sun was just rising above the horizon as they walked out on a headland near a coastal fort. The dark grey cliffs rose up from the Atlantic Ocean like jagged, inflexible monsters. They walked past signs saying 'DANGER' and 'NO SWIMMING', while they clambered over the rock formations. The fresh wind threw the cool ocean air against their faces and they shivered in their overcoats.

Daniel looked out over the water. He didn't hold a grudge against the people who had tortured him and killed his fellow prisoners. The hatred that governed their actions came from somewhere: either from the way their lives had turned out in the Middle East, where they had grown up in lawless states and under dictatorships that treated their citizens far worse than he had been treated; or in Europe, where the Beatles didn't accept what they saw as the hypocrisy of the western democracies, and instead used violence, terror and oppression to get their message across.

He had been one small pawn among many in a big political game in which the Islamic State was able to play a role because Iraq and Syria had collapsed, and because western countries had interfered, using methods that weren't perceived as a democratic alternative. He found it easier to forgive than to be angry and filled with hatred. Daniel jumped from one damp rock to another.

'I can just see the headline!' shouted Arthur. '"Former hostage killed on rocks in New Hampshire under supervision of security expert."'

They laughed at Arthur's bad joke.

'Let's take a dip,' suggested Daniel.

The waves were beating against the rocks and there was an undertow that threatened to sweep them out to sea and engulf them. They walked around the headland and found a place where the water was calmer.

Then they stripped off their clothes and dived in.

Postscript

Six of Daniel's male fellow prisoners died in captivity. The last person to be killed was the American Peter Kassig, who was executed by ISIS on 16 November 2014.

Nor have the female hostages been spared. On 6 February 2015 Islamic State published a photo of what the organization claimed was the bombed-out building where the American Kayla Mueller was being held, alone, when she was killed by a Jordanian air strike. In fact, IS probably killed the American woman itself when negotiations stalled.

In late 2015 new information appeared about Kayla Mueller's time in captivity. Apparently she had been kept in the residence of an IS leader best known by his nom de guerre Abu Sayyaf, who had a senior role in overseeing IS's gas and oil operations. His wife Nisreen Assad Ibrahim Bahar admitted to FBI agents that IS leader al-Baghdadi 'owned' Kayla Mueller while she was held in Abu Sayyaf's residence. According to US officials, Kayla was raped repeatedly by al-Baghdadi while in captivity.

The wife of Abu Sayyaf is now charged in federal court in Virginia with conspiracy in the death of Kayla Mueller.

Jihadi John, a Kuwaiti-born British citizen from London who was later identified as Mohammed Emwazi, was killed in a drone strike in November 2015. In January 2016 IS acknowledged his death in their online magazine *Dabiq*.

Two days after Emwazi was killed, the man who is believed to be George and another friend of Emwazi's from London were arrested in Turkey. Aine Davis, a former drug dealer aged thirty-one, was arrested on suspicion of planning attacks in Istanbul similar to the November 2015 attacks in Paris.

The *Washington Post* and *Buzzfeed* identified the third of the trio, Ringo, as Alexander Kotey, 32, a Londoner of Ghanaian and Greek-Cypriot background. His whereabouts are unknown.

On 24 September 2014 the United States placed ten new people on the so-called Specially Designated Global Terrorists list, which contains the names of the world's most wanted terrorists and terrorist organizations. One of the names added was Abu Athir, the Emir of Aleppo, who was responsible for the hostages. According to the US State Department, using another alias of his, 'As of mid-July 2014, Amru al-Absi was selected as ISIL's provincial leader for Homs, Syria, in the Aleppo region. As a principal leader of ISIL in Syria, he has been in charge of kidnappings.'

Syria is still one of the most dangerous places for journalists to travel to, and kidnappings of journalists and photographers continue as the media tries to report from the war zone.

. * .

Since the summer of 2015 Daniel Rye has been in the process of fixing up his new 150-square-foot allotment house in Odense. The house is where he is beginning his new life, in which he hopes to continue his photography.

Daniel's fellow prisoner John Cantlie, the British war correspondent who was captured with James Foley, is probably still in captivity. He has appeared in a number of ISIS videos, first in a six-episode series entitled *Lend Me Your Ears* and later, as an Islamic State 'reporter' who has filmed in Kobanî, Mosul, Al-Bab and Aleppo under the guard of his kidnappers. In one of the videos he interviews a man identified by some as Abu Mohammed, his former French prison guard from the children's hospital in Aleppo.

In November 2015 Cantlie appeared in a byline in the IS magazine *Dabiq*. The piece, entitled 'Shift: Paradigm Part II', which may or may not have been written by Cantlie, discusses the caliphate and its currency. And in March 2016 he appeared in a video posted online by ISIS in which he is shown presenting a news report from Mosul that derides US attempts to deal with the extremist organization.

In the summer of 2015 President Barack Obama announced that the White House would not prosecute families of American hostages who negotiated private ransoms with terrorist organizations. If that had been the situation while James Foley was alive, the family would have been able to try to collect the ransom money and potentially save his life without the risk of prosecution.

Otherwise, Denmark, the United States and the United Kingdom maintain their policy of not paying ransoms for citizens who are held by terrorist groups such as IS.

Foreigners Held Captive by ISIS

The following list refers to prisoners mentioned in this book. The stated profession indicates what the person in question was doing in Syria when the kidnapping took place. The dates are in some instances approximate and as accurate as can be, due to the nature of the hostage situation.

Daniel Rye, photographer, *Denmark*
    Kidnapped 17 May 2013; released 19 June 2014
Didier François, journalist, *France*
    Kidnapped 6 June 2013; released 19 April 2014
Edouard Elias, photographer, *France*
    Kidnapped 6 June 2013; released 19 April 2014
James Foley, journalist, *United States*
    Kidnapped 22 November 2012; killed 19 August 2014
John Cantlie, journalist, *United Kingdom*
    Kidnapped 22 November 2012; still in captivity
Nicolas Hénin, journalist, *France*
    Kidnapped 22 June 2013; released 19 April 2014
Pierre Torres, journalist, *France*
    Kidnapped 22 June 2013; released 19 April 2014

David Haines, aid worker, *United Kingdom*

  Kidnapped 12 March 2013; killed 13 September 2014

Federico Motka, aid worker, *Italy*

  Kidnapped 12 March 2013; released 26 May 2014

Steven Sotloff, journalist, *United States*

  Kidnapped 4 August 2013; killed 31 August 2014

Javier Espinosa, journalist, *Spain*

  Kidnapped 16 September 2013; released 30 March 2014

Marc Marginedas, journalist, *Spain*

  Kidnapped 4 September 2013; released 25 February 2014

Peter Kassig, aid worker, *United States*

  Kidnapped 1 October 2013; killed 16 November 2014

Ricardo Vilanova, photographer, *Spain*

  Kidnapped 16 September 2013; released 30 March 2014

Toni Neukirch, aid worker, *Germany*

  Kidnapping date unknown; released 19 June 2014

Alan Henning, aid worker, *United Kingdom*

  Kidnapped 26 December 2013; killed 3 October 2014

Sergey Gorbunov, unknown, *Russia*

  Kidnapping date unknown; killed March 2014

Kayla Mueller, aid worker, *United States*

  Kidnapped 4 August 2013; killed 6 February 2015

Dan, Médecins Sans Frontières, *Denmark*, and an unnamed
colleague, *Belgium*

  Kidnapped 2 January 2014; released 14 May 2014

Three unnamed women, Médecins Sans Frontières

  Kidnapped 2 January 2014; released 4 April 2014

An unnamed woman

  Name and nationality may not be published; her whereabouts
are unknown as of March 2016.

About the Book

I have attempted to write this story as accurately as possible from the recollections of the sources, keeping in mind that people perceive and remember events differently. Moreover, as much as possible I have verified information and experiences with other sources who were present.

In hostage cases it is well known that the Danish authorities remain extremely secretive. During the process of working on this book it has become clear how unusually reticent different authorities have been in terms of giving information or confirming or denying facts provided by other sources.

The authorities want as little information as possible to come out about Daniel Rye's kidnapping. One reason is to prevent damaging the chance of solving any future hostage cases. Another reason is so that nothing is revealed to potential kidnappers about what position the Danish government will take in hostage situations. They should only know that the state doesn't pay ransoms, in the hope of thereby avoiding further kidnappings of Danish nationals. That is why private security companies, paid by the families involved, take charge of the negotiations.

However, it is also a fact that groups like IS take hostages not only to get an economic benefit, but for ideological and political reasons as well. The security of Danish nationals has deteriorated in many countries, particularly since Denmark has joined the international coalition against IS in Iraq, regardless of Denmark's position on not negotiating with kidnappers.

In the final analysis, Daniel's ransom was only slightly cheaper than some of his fellow hostages, whose governments were responsible for the ransom sum and the negotiations. France, for example, paid €2.5 million (£1.9 million) per French hostage.

. * .

Signe, Daniel's former girlfriend, didn't want to participate in interviews or fact-checking. Therefore, in the few places where she is mentioned, the information is based solely on what Daniel and his family remember and have told me.

Dan, the Danish Médecins Sans Frontières worker, did not want his last name to be revealed.

Finally, I want to express my warmest thanks to my editors at Politikens Forlag, Tonie Yde Højrup and Kim Hundevadt, for their Herculean labour, their sharp eyes and their indispensable input along the way.